fruit flies like a banana

england by canal and classic car

STEVE HAYWOOD

summersdale

Summersdale Publishers Ltd
46 West Street
Chichester
West Sussex
PO19 1RP
UK

www.summersdale.com

Printed and bound in Great Britain

ISBN 1 84024 351 1

Cover illustration by Melanie Barnes

About the Author

As a child of the 1960s who never thought he'd make his thirtieth birthday, let alone his fiftieth, Steve Haywood is still reeling from the implications of his own longevity. Did he really study under Malcolm Bradbury at the University of East Anglia all those years ago? And was it really him who afterwards became a journalist and spent so many years pretending to be a TV producer that they eventually gave him a Royal Television Society award just to get him out of the industry? Thankfully, other parts of his life need fewer question marks. Nowadays, even after taking drink, he can be fairly certain that he lives in Blackheath in London. And that he has a partner called Moira. He also has a vague recollection of having written one or two detective novels.

Acknowledgements

IN WRITING those parts of this book concerned with the life of Tom Rolt I have relied extensively on the second part of his autobiography, *Landscape with Canals*. The concluding part of Robert Aickman's autobiography *The River Runs Uphill* which covers these events was unfortunately purged before publication, and so for details of his life and correspondence I am heavily indebted to David Bolton's *Race Against Time*, which is not just a good read, but an excellent work of scholarship.

I have also found Roger Squires' *Canals Revived* and Ian Mackersey's *Tom Rolt and the Cressy Years* extremely helpful, especially the latter which I have drawn on heavily in my final chapter, in particular his quotation about the fate of *Cressy*. Elspeth Huxley's biography of Peter Scott has also been invaluable.

Elizabeth Jane Howard's autobiography *Slipstream* was published after this book was written, and although it told me very little I did not already know about her affair with Aickman – indeed, it is disappointingly sparse on the topic – I have nevertheless incorporated occasional facts and quotations where it has seemed appropriate to clarify events.

Finally, I'd like to express my gratitude to Graham Robson whose *Triumph Herald and Vitesse: The Complete Story* is as comprehensive as it claims and a mine of information for any enthusiast.

Time and tide wait for no man.
– Old English proverb

Time flies like an arrow; fruit flies like a banana.
– Old English joke

One

CHRIST, BUT LONDON'S tiny when you've lived in it for thirty years and fifteen of them have been under Margaret Thatcher and most of the rest under Ken Livingstone. Frankly, I was looking for any excuse to get away from the place – totally away from it. And I can tell you, I wasn't just thinking about a couple of weeks' holiday either.

It was a birthday that finally galvanised me into action.

Well, not so much *a* birthday in the general sense, as *one* birthday specifically, one of mine as it happens. It was a particularly unfortunate one, the sort that I've noticed come along with alarming regularity every ten years or so, and which have a zero on the end. OK – it's no use being sheepish about it – it was my fiftieth birthday. It happened in November, the same as it's been doing for as long as I can remember, so I can't say it came as a surprise. Actually, my forty-ninth birthday the year before was a bit of a pointer to the way things were going.

So one evening over dinner, halfway through a bottle of Cabernet Sauvignon, I began talking to Em about the essential nature of the English soul. It was an idea that had been banging around in my head for a while.

She listened to me blankly. Some of these cheap wines can be high in alcohol; you need to treat them carefully.

'The essential nature of the English what?' she said eventually, a tone of bemused incredulity in her voice.

'The English soul,' I explained again. 'The basis of our being, the core of our identity… I thought before we got too far into the new millennium I might take a trip around the waterways of England… to sortta look for it…' My voice trailed off to nothing.

The truth was that although I'd been thinking about making this journey for some time, I wasn't really much persuaded by my own justification for it. This must have been all too obvious to Em since the more she challenged me on what was in my head and the more I attempted to rationalise what I was planning, the less of a good idea it seemed. Even to me.

A search for the soul of England? What planet was I living on? I might just as well have gone on a search for a new design of wheelie bin. Or the perfect pork pie. Even I could see that getting away from London was the main thing. All this stuff about the English soul was important, yes. But not *that* important.

Even so, Em was surprisingly amenable to the idea, given that it was likely to involve me spending protracted periods of the summer on a boat cruising through some of the most picturesque parts of England while she'd be battling daily on the 7.43 a.m. to Charing Cross on mortgage duty. If you ask me, the real clincher for her was the promise of finally getting shot of me moping about the house grumbling about the sad state of contemporary British television.

OK, so I'd been moaning about this on and off for as long as I'd been working in the business, but I think that even Em began to recognise I might have a point after my hard-hitting investigative documentary on the Lockerbie bombing had been beaten for a top industry award by *Who Wants to Be a Millionaire?*.

And I'll tell you one other thing: it wasn't a neck-and-neck race to the wire either.

But I suppose there were other incentives for her as well. We've owned a canal narrowboat for years, and as any owner will tell you, the idyll of getting away for weekends on the water is nowhere near as… well, as idyllic as it sounds. Once you've fought your way out of town through the Friday-night traffic and actually got to your boat; and once you've unlocked it in what's probably by now the dark; and turned on the electricity and the water and the gas; and got the heating going to warm the place through; and made up the bed and unloaded the shopping (assuming you've had time to do any shopping); and run the engine to charge up the battery and set about those thousand and one other tasks which invariably face you – from clearing out that packet of chicken legs you inadvertently left in the (switched off) fridge, to getting rid of the spiders that have colonised in your absence – well, once you've done all this, it's pretty well time to start packing up to leave for home again.

Perhaps it was the prospect of weekends when she could arrive painlessly at the water's edge and just enjoy cruising without all the hassle that led Em to be so laid-back about my proposal. Or maybe it was because she never believed it would actually amount to much, given my tendency after a few drinks to come up with big ideas that never did amount to much in the sober light of dawn. I'm not sure I even believed it myself at that stage.

The fact was, I was totally immersed in London life. I might toy with the prospect of escaping from it, but it was more fantasy than reality. Apart from Em, there was the family, friends, the job... And then there was the house which we'd bought a few years before, but was still in such a sad state of disrepair that had there been such a thing we'd have been targeted by the Royal Society for the Protection of Cruelty to London Victorian End-of-Terraces (This-Room-Hasn't-Even-Been-Touched-Since-You-Moved-In Department).

Under normal circumstances the house was a constant niggling worry in the back of my mind, a sort of agonising mental checklist of things I'd promised myself to do. Now, though, as I seriously considered the prospect of being away from the place for a protracted period, all its infuriating defects and failures that defied me to rectify them became no more than irritating idiosyncrasies that made me nostalgic just to contemplate. The top-floor landing I'd been considering painting for more than two years made me dewy-eyed just to behold, and I'd go schmaltzy reflecting on the idea of redecorating the spare room (and maybe even replacing the carpet which had become so threadbare that recently even the cat disdained to use it for sharpening its claws).

And the garden! Aaaah, the garden. What wasn't I going to do to the garden? The mere thought of the garden was enough to reduce me to a simpering, tearful jelly.

I thank the washing machine going on the blink for putting paid to all this mawkish claptrap. One day it took it into its head to overflow – not a very desirable state of affairs at the best of times, but a pretty catastrophic one when (as in our house) it's located in a bathroom at first-floor level so that the water went straight through the floor and brought down the living-room ceiling below. I was fond of that ceiling. But then again, I was fond of the books and CDs which we kept directly underneath it, and their condition wasn't exactly enhanced by what happened either.

'I suppose we're covered?' Em said anxiously as we surveyed the damage after getting back late from a night out with friends.

'Covered in the sense that at least we have a roof over our heads, if that's what you mean,' I replied grimly.

'I was talking about insurance.'

'And so was I,' I said. 'But I don't know if we have enough of it to put this lot right.'

The collapsed ceiling re-excited my desire to get out of London and put the whole day-to-day grind of ordinary life behind me, but it actually delayed my departure, for I couldn't just dump everything on Em, could I? I couldn't just walk off without getting things cleared up. So I went back to work again, and totally unexpectedly my plans for a cruise on a boat underwent a significant evolution. It came about, paradoxically, as a result of a car.

It was all Debs' fault. And I hope after reading this she's sorry for the hurt and distress she caused me.

It started when I looked up from my computer one particularly tedious afternoon to find her gazing at the screen of her own machine, the beginnings of a tear glistening almost imperceptibly in the corner of an eye. Now, I'm not a New Man for nothing; I realise that contemporary women carry burdens beyond the perception of most of my gender. Not ours to question this, or the intense depth of feeling it engenders; ours merely to lend what little kind support we can in a world characterised in the main by harsh, unthinking cruelty.

Debs was scheduled to be married soon. For months the office talk had been of little else but dresses and receptions, and rings and honeymoons. Had her intended left her in the lurch? Dumped her? Had he posted her a short and bitter e-mail, a twenty-first-century 'Dear Debs' letter, sacrificing her on the altar of new technology?

Actually, when I went over to comfort her I found her gazing at a picture of a car.

'Beautiful, isn't she?' she said.

The image had evidently been downloaded from the Internet. I surveyed it critically. I am no car fanatic, and certainly no expert. As far as I could see it was a red car, a convertible, a sportyish number with lots of chrome and rakish American fins. Pretty enough, I thought, but nothing worth crying about.

I assumed it was to be her wedding present to her intended. I assumed she'd realised that she couldn't afford it.

'Too expensive?' I asked.

'Well, I'm not dropping the bloody price, if that's what you mean!' she snapped back at me with a look I recognised all too well. I have worked with Debs for years, you see; I can read her like a book. The look said: Are you a lunatic or something to think I could afford to buy *anyone* a car for a present? But maybe not. Maybe with the benefit of hindsight this is the look she gives to every sucker she sees coming her way when she's selling a car.

One way or another, a week or so later I found myself on a train with her to the nether regions of Surrey, beyond the unexplored badlands of the M25, where in some out-of-the-way barn I took my first look at the 30-year-old Triumph Herald convertible which, although I didn't know it, was already mine.

There was no denying it: it *was* a pretty car.

For those who, like me, know as much about car design as the theories of thermonuclear physics, let me say that the Triumph Herald is not just a rare example of British motor engineering, but an even rarer example of *successful* British motor engineering. Long before 'swinging London' and 'flower power' made the Mini the design icon of the age, British engineers had scored a commercial bull's-eye by the simple expedient of recognising the deep and disheartening desire of every man on the planet to own a racy sports car.

And realising too that most of them didn't have the money for it.

The answer was the Herald, a low-slung, chassis-built saloon that boasted four seats, the back two so tiny that they weren't much use for anything except kids or those with severe growth problems. This, of course, was actually the sort of inspirational design for which we were once world-famous since it allowed single men to pretend they were buying a sporty two-seater, while a family man looking for a car could persuade himself of exactly the opposite.

The Herald was actually designed by an Italian, Giovanni Michelotti, who took some of the worst excesses of gas-guzzling American cars of the 1950s and imported them into a Britain not long escaped from post-war austerity. It was all very understated in a way that played well to the puritanical British market. Triumph Heralds, for instance, have rear fins which were made popular on American classics like the Corvette; but whereas on the Corvette they're loud and brash and say 'Look at me, I'm one big f**k-off motor', on the Herald they're smaller and more discreet, and if they say anything at all they say it with a naughty giggle and the promise of illicit fun, a bit like a Donald McGill seaside postcard.

Actually, for its time, the Herald was really rather a nippy little machine. The later models had 1300cc engines and generated 60 brake horsepower, which is laughable today, but which in its time was an achievement the designers were proud to flaunt by putting the logo 13-60 on the car's boot. Between 1959 and 1971 more than half a million Heralds were sold, which as motor success stories go is OK, but on its own isn't really enough to explain the extraordinarily affectionate place the car seems to occupy in the British psyche.

Part of it, I suppose, is that the Herald was an accessible car. Even if people couldn't afford one, it wasn't so outrageously expensive that they couldn't believe that one day they *might*. And it was a fun car too, the sort of car which people enjoyed driving, so pretty well everyone you meet of a certain age, men and women alike, seem at one time or another to have owned one, or been associated with one, or had the use of one. And they feel differently somehow about the Herald to other cars they've driven.

With other cars, people remember them as, well… as cars. Cars in which they've done the sort of mundane things people do in cars like shopping and ferrying around the kids. But the Herald's the sort of classic driving machine in which a large percentage of the population seem to have undergone some crucial rite of passage or another: they have taken their driving test in a Herald, for instance, or lost their virginity in one, or had some other life-changing experience.

Like the rather staid man I met in a pub once in Daventry who persisted in telling me at great length one afternoon when I'd got better things to do how he and a friend had been picked up as 17-year-olds by some sixth-form totty from a local posh girls' school who'd borrowed the car off Daddy and used it to give them a fantasy weekend out of the Letters Page of a top-shelf magazine.

He was typical. People who've had anything to do with Triumph Heralds are the sort of people who are prone to engage you in conversation in pubs, and the sort of people who tell you more than they really ought to when they have.

Most of them, I guess, are a little older than me, and brought up at a time when you were expected to display a certain reticence with regard to your personal life. Not that this seems to stop them much where the Triumph Herald is concerned, and the mere appearance of one in a suburban street or a multi-storey car park is the signal for a horde of sentimentalists to emerge from the woodwork, determined to unburden themselves in a sort of mass therapy.

My brother, for instance. OK, so there are one or two dark areas of his schoolboy past which you're best not probing too deeply; but even so, the mere suggestion that I was thinking of buying a Herald was a signal for him to confess how years ago he'd written one off against a tree joy-riding in the grounds of his school. The revelation shocked me, I can tell you. That's the sort of thing you do with beat-up old Cortinas, not cars like the Triumph Herald.

'Let me think about it,' I said to Debs that day in the barn, affecting a certain detached insouciance which I thought might somehow help me in negotiating a price with her. Some hope! Nothing would have helped me that day. Way before the penny had dropped with me, Debs knew that my name was on that car. More significantly, she knew it would soon be on an enormously large cheque she'd be getting from me for it.

So a couple of days later the deal was done, and I found myself wondering for the first time whether it might be possible to take the car on my canal trip. Perhaps by using a bike, and shuttling between the two, I could somehow work it to travel with the Herald and the boat in tandem, which would give me a much greater range for sightseeing as I travelled about.

First, however, I had to test the Herald on a real road in real driving conditions. This was not easy. You see, the thing about a classic car – and everyone should drive a classic car at least once in their life – is that among other things it makes you realise that motor engineers have hardly been on a long tea break for the last half century. Not being a car expert, I really didn't know what to expect of the Herald. Probably much as I expect living in a Victorian house, I suppose: all period design with full mod cons.

Forget it. An old car isn't a style icon, it's a piece of machinery, and by today's standards not a particularly sophisticated one either. A Herald, for instance, hasn't got what's called 'syncromesh' on its first gear – a term that meant absolutely nothing to me until I attempted to engage first gear just as the car was about to stop at a set of traffic lights. The tumultuous grinding and crashing sound that emanated from the gearbox ensured that though I'd never learn what syncromesh actually *was*, I'd never forget what not having it could actually *do*.

It was the same with the acceleration on the car. It actually wasn't too bad once you got moving, but from a standing start it felt a bit like I imagine it must be coaxing a traction engine into life. Of course, I exaggerate; but how can you avoid feeling like a lumbering archaeological relic of the road when every other car around you is so new-century and so damned sophisticated? Your mere presence obviously gets up the nose of half the driving population. That is to say it gets up the nose of male drivers, generally young male drivers, and generally young male drivers in cars so powerful they'd take off if they could only get clearance from flight control at Heathrow.

These sort of people tuck in behind you at traffic lights for the mere pleasure of terrorising you if you don't move on green like a Formula One Ferrari off the starting grid. And, should it be your misfortune to be in front of one on a minor road where there's no apparent and easy overtaking opportunities, you'll be treated to a bizarre 'love you and leave you' ritual in which at first they'll drive up your exhaust pipe and then, without so much as a post-coital pleasantry, they'll be off into the great unknown, passing you with only inches to spare and generally on the brow of a hill with a phalanx of articulated lorries bearing down on you just to add a final frisson to the liaison.

Driving back home from Surrey, it must have been apparent to every predator on the road that I was a virgin in these matters, for with the car heralding my innocence, the maiden bit of my drive lasted no more than minutes, and within the hour I felt like a raddled old courtesan who'd been on the game too long for her own good.

My first plan had been to get home by way of the M25, but I'd soon abandoned it. I mean, let's get real here! I may be foolhardy, but I'm not totally suicidal. The M25's bad enough in a modern vehicle unless it's equipped with the sort of gadgets you see in James Bond films. The fact is that if you really want to kill yourself, a bullet through the temple is a far cleaner, if less reliable method than driving a Triumph Herald around a motorway that sometimes seems as if it's being used as a warm-up circuit for Silverstone.

A quick glance at the map had revealed that there was an alternative open to me in the form of a road called the A25 which ran almost parallel to the motorway. On my Michelin it was marked in a soft cuddly yellow, the colour of an Easter chick, as opposed to the lurid red, like a flesh wound, which was the colour of its big brother. All in all it seemed a far more attractive proposition for someone in his middle years who was determined to reach his late ones.

It turned out to be a charming byway, which passed through such delightfully picturesque places as Bletchingly, Oxted and Brasted. I couldn't believe how relentlessly rural it was. At one point I was held up by a set of traffic lights positioned so close to a village cricket pitch that I actually watched a wicket fall before they changed to green. Even drivers on this road seemed different. OK, not exactly courteous, for that would have been asking too much – but at least they didn't seem totally determined to rip off my testicles through the undercarriage.

This was a real eye-opener, and not what I expected of an A-road, so when I got home and retraced the route I'd travelled, it was with a totally different eye that I surveyed the map. It was – if not exactly a life-changing experience – then at least the sort of episode that makes you see the world in a different way.

Extraordinary! I'd travelled on a yellow-chick road, but there were other roads, a whole rainbow spectrum of them, each as potentially promising as the one I'd evacuated to in order to escape the M25. What about these green fronds – B roads – which seemed to be all over the place? The A25 through suburban Surrey was rural enough; but these green routes were the very colour of the countryside. What would they be like? What would the alarmingly insubstantial uncoloured ones be like – the ones which seemed to stretch across every inch of the map like hollow spindly fingers? Or – the ones that intrigued me most of all – the completely uncategorised roads, represented by single black lines, each one as thin as a child's hair. They were all over the place, yet, being the sceptic I am, I couldn't help doubting that they existed at all; I couldn't help suspecting they were just the impalpable figment of some cartographer's memory, his last tribute to an England that had long since gone.

Surely it'd be impossible to use these roads to actually go anywhere? I decided to test it out, and with no real intention of actually doing the journey, I mischievously rang the RAC and requested a suggestion from them for a route which would take me from where I was based in south-east London to Leicester, where my family lived, the first two places to come into my head.

The young woman dealing with my request was extraordinarily helpful and if she was nonplussed by my request that the route should avoid motorways and A-roads, then she certainly didn't show it. I heard her hit a few characters on the keyboard of a computer before she rattled off a route that started in the East End and took me to the Midlands by way of a wide swinging arc through Cambridgeshire. It was a journey that involved an intricate series of twists and turns through villages with improbable names like Steeple Morden and Gamlingay, a journey that apparently involved never travelling on the same road for more than a mile at a time.

I was intrigued, and, since the young woman was so polite and accommodating, I spent more than half an hour transcribing the route in meticulous detail. It only then struck me that perhaps part of the reason I was being treated with such indulgence was that I was on a premium-rate line. By the time I was finished I could probably have bought a gold-embossed set of leather-bound Ordnance Survey maps of the same route for the same price. Now I felt that I had to actually *do* the trip to justify the expense.

Well, maybe some things are decided for us in heaven. The fact was, I hadn't visited my mum for a long while…

The following Saturday I filled up the Herald with a tank of environmentally unfriendly lead-enhanced fuel and, with Em as passenger, I headed for the Blackwall Tunnel at a time early enough to avoid the stoppages which, as every Londoner knows, begin at the weekend so as to be safely in place for the Monday rush hour when they're most needed in order to cause maximum disruption to the life of the city.

It was one of those rare English summer days when the sky is a consistently clear blue for as far as the eye can see and when what clouds exist are so insubstantial it seems their only purpose is to give a depth to the horizon. By 9 a.m. it must have been in the eighties and with every mile we travelled our decision to put down the roof of the Herald and use it for the first time as a convertible seemed less the act of fun that it first had, and more a necessary part of the survival technique we'd need to get us through the day.

We followed the suggested route to the letter and headed for Epping Forest. Soon the busy, blistering roads of London turned into Arcadian country lanes which tunnelled through cool stretches of woodland or wound over tracts of gently undulating farmland which, when we were lucky, caught the slight cooling breath of a breeze. Out of town it was a different world, one where the sun was equally hot and the temperatures equally high, but where it somehow seemed altogether fresher and sharper and brighter and cleaner.

The absence of traffic was almost eerie. Surely England is a country of traffic jams and gridlock? Not in deepest Cambridgeshire it isn't, or the middle of Huntingdonshire for that matter either. In each of these counties it sometimes seemed as if we were the only car on the road. Even the villages we passed through seemed deserted.

I remember that near a place called Much Hadham our route took us onto an unclassified road that was so narrow it was as if we'd strayed onto a farm track. There wasn't even a hedge to separate us from the field through which we were driving, and I was convinced we'd end up in someone's barn. Later, on another similar road, we parked under the damp penumbra of an irrigator, waiting for the jets which were watering crops to complete their long revolution so that we could enjoy an impromptu shower to cool us in the heat of the scorching sun.

We had lunch in a pub that appeared abruptly and almost miraculously only moments after we'd realised we were hungry. It had a low thatched roof, a long bar with a low-beamed ceiling, and a flagstone floor which made it so cool it could have been a cellar. The place was totally unspoiled, and so far away from everything and everyone that it didn't seem part of the present. Even the chicken we ordered tasted like chicken used to do; and a bowl of potatoes and a salad we ordered with it were so fresh and flavoursome you felt they'd probably been growing an hour before.

But that was the way of things that extraordinary afternoon when everything seemed so perfect that we no sooner had to think that it was time for tea than there was a Georgian tea shop around the next bend, with chairs and tables laid out for us on a lawn and freshly baked home-made carrot cake all but cut and waiting for us on the plate.

'Do you think this is for real?' I said to Em at one point during the day. 'Do you think we'll wake up soon?'

Yes, it all did seem like a dream, and so entranced was I by it that my mind was made up: I had decided to take the car with me on the cruise.

Towards late afternoon the route took us into Northamptonshire where we passed so close to the village of Fotheringay that it would have been a crime not to have made a detour and looked around. The village is most famous as the place Mary, Queen of Scots was tried and executed after her long imprisonment at the hands of Elizabeth I; but it has other associations too, especially for someone my age, since in the 1960s the singer Sandy Denny recorded a haunting song of the same name with Fairport Convention; and she later went on to use the name for her own band. Her pure, unsullied voice was one of the sounds of its time, immortal in its own way – which is a bit of a paradox really, since she died at the tragically young age of 30 after falling down a set of stairs drunk, the way rock stars did in the days before they started working out every morning and getting off on Evian.

I can't believe that Sandy ever actually visited Fotheringay, though, or surely she wouldn't have tempted fate in the way she did; since even in the height of summer, and on a perfect day, there's a fearful hint of strangeness about the place that reeks of tragedy. The actual castle where Mary died survives today only as a featureless mound of earth overlooking the plain of the River Nene which curls around it like a natural moat. It isn't much, but believe me – it's enough to stimulate the imagination.

We parked the Herald in the main street, and it wasn't long before the sun began to drop, casting long shadows across the countryside. By the time we'd climbed to the summit of the castle mound, dew was forming over the fields, and evening mists had begun to rise off the river. We stood gazing across the landscape as faint wisps of vapour lapped the base of the old castle and began slowly creeping upwards to where clumps of wild thistles grew, their iridescent purple crowns in full flower. I have to admit, it was creepy. The place can get to you; a lot of other of people have said the same.

It must be something to do with Mary's story, which seems to touch a deep chord in the subconscious psyche, being a sort of allegory of innocence pitched against corruption, with Mary cast as the innocent young queen and Elizabeth, the wicked witch of the south. Twaddle, of course. Mary was a contender for the

English throne, and the story was marshalled in the service of power, not truth. It's like a lot of stories generated out of the politics of the English past: it falls apart in your hands at the first rational analysis.

Mary? Innocent? Can anyone seriously claim she knew *nothing* about the plot to murder her husband Darnley? Knowing what I do of Strathclyde plod, I'd like to have seen her try that one on in an interview with the CID: 'Well, Mrs Darnley, you've been estranged from your husband for some time in circumstances which have caused you considerable embarrassment. Then for some reason you decide to play the loving wife and invite him back to Edinburgh where you claim you wanted to keep an eye on him while he was ill. Curious that he just happens to get blown up a few hours after you visited him. And strangled afterwards when that didn't kill him. Convenient for you, some might think.'

The woman's a myth: she's construction from start to finish. Does anyone really believe those wild thistles on the castle mound are actually wild? Of course not. Someone planted them, for heaven's sake. They're *part* of the myth. Even this long afterwards it's in someone's interest to keep it going – even if it is just the Northamptonshire Tourist Board.

Even so, Fotheringay isn't exactly a major magnet for trippers, and the milling crowds we'd anticipated on the castle mound amounted to precisely one young family – and even they left very soon after our arrival so that we virtually had the whole village to ourselves. We walked to the church, which actually is what remains of what was once a massive religious college, built in what in any other place in the country you'd describe as a Tudor style.

Not here, though. In Fotheringay that would be like ordering a Greek coffee in Istanbul. Fotheringay, you see, was the birthplace of the hunchback Richard III whose defeat and death at the Battle of Bosworth at the hands of the 21-year-old Henry Tudor, later Henry VII, gave rise not just to a design of architecture, but a dynasty, an historical era and a royal succession that still survives at the heart of government today 600 years later.

And if you're talking myth in the service of power, it doesn't get better than this; though to listen to the apologists nowadays, you'd think royal succession was handed down incontrovertibly from generation to generation, ordained by God. In fact, the truth is that for the Windsors today as much as the Tudors then, it comes from nothing more than the point of a sword.

The connection between Fotheringay and Bosworth is more than just an historical one. The River Nene, which flows past the castle mound, connects beyond Northampton to the Grand Union Canal, which leads by degrees to the Ashby Canal. This cuts through the very centre of Bosworth battlefield. In fact, the canal is so close to where the action was that one year when I was on a boat and found myself with a full lavatory, I woke early one morning and discreetly buried a bucketful of shit close to where it's thought the hapless Richard had been hacked down hollering to exchange his kingdom for a horse.

I wasn't being disrespectful. The way I feel about royalty, I'd happily bury a bucket of shit near the place Henry Tudor died too if it was a question of maintaining basic boat hygiene.

Besides, I did Dick more of a favour than some of his so-called friends, for when I went back three or four years later, the hole I'd dug was marked by one of the most vigorous dog roses I've ever seen. It stretched from the bottom of the embankment that carries the canal over the battlefield to the small stone monument that commemorates the event.

It was in flower when I saw it. And covered in roses.

White, of course. It goes without saying.

Two

IT WAS A CRAZY IDEA, this journey; and if I'd really been serious about getting to grips with my mid-life crisis, then I'd have been better opting for a course of therapy than going off travelling. Or if I had to travel, I'd have been better opting for somewhere warm with a beach rather than condemning myself to schlepping around England in what was shaping up to be a typical English summer; that is, one that was wet and cold and not summery at all.

I was still in two minds about the whole thing. OK, I'd set myself to search for the soul of England, but apart from the fact that I wasn't sure I knew what that actually meant, I had this gnawing sense of unease that even if I was able to identify it and discover something of it on my trip, I wouldn't actually like what I found.

The signs certainly weren't auspicious, and around this time there was a lot happening that was tending to show us, as a nation, in a very poor light. One morning, for instance, on my way to work, I'd watched a young City-executive type who couldn't have been worth less than a hundred grand a year berate a young woman who was begging on the pavement with a child at her breast. The woman was from somewhere in the Balkans, probably an asylum seeker. What I noticed most about her was that she kept smiling through his whole performance. She must have thought he was expressing angry solidarity with her in the struggle against Serbian imperialism.

But it didn't say much for the tradition of tolerance that as a nation we'd once been so proud of.

My imagination began to run riot. Where would it all end?

Canal boats are traditionally decorated with paintings of roses and castles derived, it's generally thought, from Romany styles. Since a significant proportion of those applying for asylum at this time were said to be Gypsies fleeing persecution in central Europe, I wondered just how wise a journey of this sort was at this particular time. It struck me that on a Richter scale of moral wrath, the attitude of some of the English middle classes was just about to hit 6.3, and I feared for my life should the fault lines slip while I was quietly and unsuspectingly moored near to some fomenting suburb or another during barbecue season.

You think I'm exaggerating?

Believe me, for a country that extols eccentrics the way it does, you don't have to spend much time on a boat before you realise that by being different in this country you touch a deep vein of mistrust in the English that can easily turn to antagonism. Why else does it seem that whenever you steer a boat under a bridge, half the population feels the need to stand on the parapet and gob on your head as you go by?

Besides, if I was going to do a trip in the way I was thinking I would do it, then the boat wasn't really in the right location to start. It should have been in Banbury in Oxfordshire; that would have been the obvious place to begin something like this because Banbury is associated with Tom Rolt, one of the great characters of contemporary waterways history, and the man who more than any other single person is responsible for the survival of canals today.

Rolt was the author of the book *Narrow Boat*, an account of the honeymoon cruise he and his wife Angela took through the Midlands in the summer of 1939 on their wooden ex-working boat *Cressy*. It was a time when the country's 3,000-mile network of canals and rivers was virtually unknown to the general population – a time when it was falling into disrepair too, and when the boat people who had worked it for centuries were close to extinction. The book alerted people to the impending destruction of what Rolt recognised as one of our greatest national assets, and it led directly to the birth of the canals restoration movement which today has grown to such an extent that now we're not just restoring old canals, but building totally new ones.

I've always been fascinated by Tom Rolt who, incidentally, was a classic car enthusiast himself. Pictures of him always make him seem like an army man, with his lean frame, his straight back and pencil moustache. But this aura of old-fashioned respectability is deceptive, and you don't need to learn much about him to realise that though he may have been conservative in his outlook, at heart – paradoxically – his traditionalism was of a radical bent which strikes a familiar note in terms of the Zeitgeist of our own age.

Rolt took *Cressy* to Banbury after he'd bought her, and Banbury was where he and Angela adapted her for living, building a roof over her cargo hold and fitting out the space underneath as a houseboat. Banbury was *Cressy*'s home port, and Banbury was where Rolt returned whenever *Cressy* needed maintenance. Banbury too was where most of *Narrow Boat* was written and – to add promising potential to all this – Banbury is our home port as well; the place Em and I fitted out our boat *Justice* after she was launched, and the place that we've moored different boats on and off for almost twenty years now.

The trouble was, for all its importance as a natural starting point for a trip of the sort I was planning, the boat wasn't actually in Banbury.

True, I grant you, it wasn't a million miles away. It was in Oxford where we'd left it one weekend, moored on the canal, but trapped between the Thames and the River Cherwell by floods that had come up suddenly after nearly a month of almost incessant rain. So I couldn't have got to Banbury to start the trip even if I'd wanted to, and at that stage I didn't want to, for I'd got some notion of travelling to Bristol, which is in entirely the opposite direction.

You see the problem.

I'd even considered driving to Banbury in the Herald and

giving myself a ceremonial send-off at the famous Banbury Cross, though this hardly seemed in the spirit of the project, especially so early on. Call me a traditionalist too, like Rolt, but you can hardly start a boat journey from Banbury in a car from Oxford, can you? It somehow doesn't feel right.

But then I thought, Sod it, Steve, you're being too literal about this. The fact is (I told myself) the starting gun's already been fired on this one; and if that means you're condemned by vile weather to start a journey you're still not certain you want to make from a place you never wanted to be, then just get on with it and be comforted by how much of an analogy for life that is.

And at least there are worse places to be stuck than Oxford. Or maybe not, for Oxford's the sort of place that excites such passion in people that if they don't love it to death, they can just as easily loathe it with vehement intensity. I've found that many Americans fall into this latter category, since along with London and Stratford-upon-Avon, it's one of the very few places they come to England specifically to see. They arrive expecting it to be an unspoiled theme park straight out of some costume drama they once watched on PBS, and they become inconsolable when they find out there's been a bit of building work since the 1500s.

Actually, I think there's another reason a lot of Americans don't like Oxford: I think the place subliminally affronts their egalitarian principles. They may not know much about the British class system, and they may not care much about it either; but what they do know they don't care for; and they certainly don't care for big beefy authority figures with silly names like 'Bulldog' telling them that the college precincts are closed to tourists when they've travelled 3,000 miles on vacation to see them. I have to say that I'm with my transatlantic brothers every inch of the way here. OK, so there's no denying that Oxford is a very beautiful city – sometimes breathtakingly so. But it's an exclusive city too, as much for the English as for visitors from overseas.

I never totally realised quite *how* exclusive until I once went to a wedding of a friend of mine who, because her father was something big in one of the colleges, was able to command not just the personal use of the fourteenth-century chapel in which to take her vows, but the full college choir to eulogise them, as well as the college dining room to celebrate them afterwards. Tourists were excluded from the place for the whole day. Mind you, it was a magnificent occasion, and one I wouldn't have missed for the world since it was the first and only time in my life when – with morning suit and champagne glass as passport – I was legitimately allowed to set foot on one of the meticulously manicured bowling greens that pass for lawns in these parts.

There's a pompous story they tell in Oxford about these lawns. It's said that many years ago when a curious Texan once enquired how the gardeners managed to get them so perfect, he was told that, actually, there was really nothing much to it. It was just a matter of choosing the right site and the right grass seed, and putting the one on top of the other.

And then rolling and mowing it for 400 years.

I know if I'd been that Texan, the patronising punch line of this story might have turned into something more literal. At the very least it would have been the cue for me to go in search of a powerful weed killer which – special relationship notwithstanding – a posse of your polite English bobbies wouldn't have stopped me dumping on the grass.

But that's Oxford for you. Personally, I've never had a problem with it. I realised long ago that the university's the sort of place you can only get to by being very intelligent or very stupid, and since one requires brains and the other an aristocratic lineage, my best chance of getting there was always going to be on a train out of Paddington like most people. So I don't hold Oxford's elitism against the place. Indeed, I have come to admire the effrontery with which it gets away with it.

Just look at how many prime ministers and other world leaders have studied at the place. Just look at how many top lawyers, doctors, churchmen and scientists. Just look at how many eminent academics and philosophers, musicians and writers. Surely no one believes that *any* university's *that* good? Surely it's obvious that it's just creaming off the sort of talent which would be just as successful at any other seat of learning anywhere else in the world?

As far as I know Tom Rolt never aspired to even a university education, let alone an Oxford one – which is probably just as well since from an early age his bent had been towards practical engineering, a subject which has hardly been Oxford's forte (or at least not at its university, that sort of oily-rag stuff being left to the motor-wallahs out in the car factories at Cowley). Surprising this, when you think about it, because anyone of my generation – born in the years when the sun was setting on the British Empire – was brought up to believe that it had been built on the achievements of people from the top universities, the administrators through which the blessings of Englishness flowed to an uncivilised world.

And yet it stands to reason that that this can't have been true: administrators don't actually *build* anything. The people who do – or at least the people who build mechanical things – are engineers: men like Tom Rolt who function not in the realm of the intellect, and certainly not in the attractive medieval colleges of the old universities, but in the ugly physical world of labour where things have to be assembled and repaired and men have to roll up their sleeves and get a bit of dirt on their hands to do it.

Rolt did an old-style apprenticeship, five years long, which used to be the norm in British industry when we had industry in Britain. Afterwards, a young lad with a brain and a practical bent was able to build an engine from scratch, including being able to cast, turn and mill the main component parts for it. In return he was led to believe he had a job for life if he wanted one.

Not that Tom Rolt could have ever been happy spending his life working in a factory. He was suspicious of too many contemporary values, and he questioned whether industrial progress was always for the best. Besides, those jobs he'd been promised didn't materialise in the Depression years. After his training he spent some time running a garage which didn't suit him much either, though it gave him time to devise the practical and philosophical strategy which eventually took him to the canals. He called this his 'design for living' – essentially it was a template for how he could earn enough money to live on a boat without the support of an independent income.

This is where Rolt's book *Narrow Boat* fitted in. Though on one level it's just the simple account of the honeymoon cruise with Angela, on another it was Rolt's (ultimately highly successful) attempt to give physical purpose to his ambition by starting to earn his living as a writer.

If any confirmation were needed that he'd made the correct decision, then it came in the autumn of 1939 when war was declared and he had to put the writing on hold and go back to engineering as part of the war effort. He and Angela were living on *Cressy* by then, and they based themselves in Cheshire where Tom worked for Rolls-Royce in Crewe, making the Merlin engines that powered Spitfire aeroplanes.

The experience nearly destroyed him.

By then it had been almost eight years since he'd worked for a large engineering firm, and he'd fondly imagined that with his skills he'd be assembling engines from start to finish as he had during his apprenticeship. Instead he found himself mindlessly tapping an endless series of holes in cylinder blocks, even this soulless task reduced to nothing by the use of a jig which, as he observed bitterly, removed 'the last vestige of human skill from the work'.

Tom Rolt was no political fanatic, and if you plough through even a few of the 30 books and numerous articles he was eventually to write in his career, you can't help but be struck by the uncomfortable right-wing vein of some of his thinking. Perhaps it's unjust to blame him too much for this, for though he's an idealist, he's a sentimentalist too – and very much a product of his time. *Narrow Boat*, written before the war and published after it, harks back to a mythical sylvan age where honest ruddy-faced rustics toiled in the fields and village workshops before repairing to thatched country inns to quaff foaming pints of ale from pewter tankards.

Something not a million miles from *The Archers*, in fact.

But frankly, who's to say we wouldn't all have been up for a dose of nostalgia after six years of having the crap bombed out of us by the Nazis?

Towards the end of his life even Rolt himself recognised the book's failings, admitting that he found it 'too self-consciously Arcadian and picaresque' and its escapism 'slightly embarrassing'. But this sort of revisionism, where people yearned for a world which had never really existed, helped to create the conditions in which fascism could foster in this period; and it's difficult to divorce the ideas of a book written in 1939 from the full implications of the war that started that year.

Tom Rolt only worked at Rolls-Royce for six weeks, but the experience scarred him for the rest of his life. It represented such a nadir that in his despair he even used to look forward to using the lavatory – less as a relief to his bladder than as a respite from the unmitigated tedium of the job. The experience led him to an odd conclusion, or a conclusion odd for a man who I can never visualise without his having a copy of the *Daily Telegraph* tucked under his arm. He wrote: 'After such an experience, the strikes that have plagued the engineering industry since the war are no surprise to me. No amount of money can make such durance any less vile.'

I was reminded of this during my time stranded in Oxford, when, after a further two weeks of incessant rain, I caught such a bad case of cabin fever I just couldn't endure the place a day longer. I was moored on a stretch of canal a little way short of Isis Lock which is separated from the river by just the width of the towpath. It's only a ten-minute walk from the city centre, and, with the overhanging trees giving the place the air of woodland grove, and the regular chatty stream of cyclists and pedestrians who use the towpath as a cut through, it's normally as delightful and companionable a spot as you'll find in the middle of any major city anywhere.

But I felt I'd done Oxford after a week, and after ten days I was screaming to get on the move again. I'd visited the Sheldonian and the Bodleian and the Asmolean; I'd poked about in as many colleges as they'd let me into; and I'd taken sodden evening walks along Christ Church meadow, and even bought a bicycle so I could make even wetter and longer excursions to explore some of the university parks and outlying suburbs. One day I even rode across Portmeadow to Godstow Lock on the River Thames – which I might have enjoyed except that it was totally flooded and the path I was riding along was the only thing above water level, so I got the weirdest sensation of cycling across the surface of a lake.

The pitiless rain I could have taken, but the mud that it created on the towpath got to me in the end. After a couple of days this got churned up so much it was like whipped cream; and after a week it was such a comprehensively infused mixture of old leaf mould, sludge and dog shit, I swear I could have bottled it and marketed it in Body Shop as a traditional face pack. What made it worse was that the weather didn't stop the pooches taking walkies, it just stopped their owners coming with them, so for the duration a sort of towpath anarchy prevailed with the canines taking over the world and crapping all over it with uncontained glee.

However much you wiped your feet or meticulously changed into slippers whenever you entered the boat, it always seemed to somehow permeate by one means or another; for the sordid and unsanitary fact of the matter is that in its colour, mud looks much like dog shit when smeared across a cabin carpet.

My friend Captain Beeky has done some research on this around his home mooring of Stourport, and he's become convinced that the local mutts have actually evolved the capability of dropping their load in a way consistent with the surrounding terrain. He believes the dogs' backsides have developed the ability to detect the nature of the drop zone and, using special glands, apply a thin layer of camouflage to the ploppies which tumble from the dispatch bay so they lie chameleon-like and unnoticed, awaiting only the inattention of the unwary pedestrian. This, he believes, accounts for Stourport's unenviable position at the top of the Shitty Streets League (Premier Division) as well as for the otherwise unaccountable popularity of browns and russets in the catalogues of local carpet shops.

Eventually I'd had enough of it – a bellyful you might say in different circumstances – except that the mess had got into the galley too, and using that turn of phrase might be getting altogether too close to the truth to be comfortable. So one morning after I'd woken to find the rain hammering on the roof yet again, I turned the boat without a moment's hesitation and headed north, determined that if I was going to get constantly rained on, then at least it would happen nearer the Cotswolds where the onset of the lambing season would ensure that unaccompanied dogs met a hygienic, if brutal, end.

Of course – sod's law! – it stopped raining the moment I started the engine, and once I'd got beyond the colonies of New Age travellers that live on boats out towards Wolvercote, the sun had forced its way through the clouds and the sky had become the soft colour of pale blue lint, bringing in its wake a host of fishermen. This was unusual because I'd never before seen fishermen out in such force this early in the year, this being the first season that they'd abandoned a closed season on the sport. But it was unusual as well to see so many fishermen anyhow on a weekday, especially when so many of them seemed young blokes, and obviously not unemployed or short of a bob or two either, judging from the quality of the tackle some of them were using, which looked as if it must have cost the equivalent of a small terraced house.

The reason became apparent after I got into a chat with a couple of them. It turned out they were car workers at Cowley, which had once been owned by Leyland until it had been sold a year or two before to the Germans, who'd then subsequently become so sick and tired of the British motor industry that they were at that very moment looking to offload the company to anyone who showed the slightest interest in making cars in Britain. Or making *anything* in Britain, for that matter. Or not even *making* anything, actually – as long as someone would just take the company off their hands quick, no questions asked...

You may remember that they finally sold the whole shooting match for a fiver to some consortium headed by a former manager. He'd been partly responsible for getting the company in the mess in the first place, so presumably he had a pretty shrewd idea of what it was worth. But even at that price it wasn't as if people were falling over themselves to buy it. In fact, the situation was so desperate that I'm sure that if I'd stayed in Oxford much longer, someone would have eventually approached me to see if I was interested in it.

The fishermen, it transpired, had been sent off home for an enforced holiday under an arrangement for flexible working which the unions had negotiated with the management some time before. Of course, I use the word 'negotiated' here in its loosest sense – the sense that if you gave someone your wallet after they'd held a gun to your head, you might be said to have negotiated a price for your life.

What this meant in practice was that in return for not demanding wages from the company which had contracted to employ them but hadn't got anything for them to do, the men would nevertheless get paid on the basis that at some stage in the future they would agree to work every last hour that God sent without the bothersome inconvenience of claiming overtime for it. I somehow guessed that this idea hadn't come about as a result of a spontaneous groundswell of rank and file opinion. What it seemed to mean was that when the blokes eventually got back to work – if they ever did – they wouldn't be taking another day off until about 2015. But this I suppose is the way of British industry today – or at least the bit of it that's still left.

The whole affair seemed to me yet another example of the protracted death of trade skills in this country and the humiliation of its once-respected workforce. Of course, anyone who's shown any sort of interest in the decline of the British car industry over the years knows how it happened; how the British workforce proved itself inflexible in adapting to new technology, and how British management proved itself reluctant to invest; and how this led to uncertainty, and to the incessant strikes of the 1970s, which spawned the mindless militancy of extremist shop stewards like Red Robbo at Longbridge in the West Midlands, etc., etc.

But reading Tom Rolt's account of working briefly for Rolls-Royce all those years ago, it all seems such a depressingly predictable result of taking away people's pride and self-respect in their work.

Three

My first experience of canals was one grim windswept day in the early 1970s at an old mill building outside a small village in the East Midlands. For some reason I can't remember now I hadn't used my full holiday entitlement that year, and so after scouring a series of brochures offering everything from an extravagant two weeks in Spain to an exorbitant fortnight in the Seychelles, Em had finally suggested that I might care to set my sights a little lower and consider somewhere a bit closer to home.

Like how about renting a canal boat? She'd taken a canal boat holiday with some university friends one summer a year or two before and she'd had a great time. What was more, holidays on canal boats were cheap, she assured me, so cheap in fact that if I were able to convince my best friend Dave to split the costs with me on the first week, she might be able to afford to join me for the second.

And so it was that some time afterwards, Dave and I found ourselves trudging through mud in a rainstorm, attempting to negotiate our way along a footpath across a field where someone had directed us as a short cut to a boatyard we'd been struggling to find for the previous hour. From this boatyard we were scheduled that very morning to take command of a 30-foot narrowboat nautically resplendent with the name *Nelson*.

Neither of us, it has to be said, were in the best of humours that morning. The truth was we were both suffering monumental hangovers as a result of a binge the previous night – one for which I have to confess I was entirely responsible. You see, when I'd casually suggested to Dave that we might go for 'a drink', I was aware not only that it was unlikely we'd stop at just one drink, but also that actually we weren't likely to stop drinking until we were totally rat-arsed.

In fact, this had been what I'd intended from the outset. It was a very carefully engineered strategy.

You see, I've known Dave for a very long time. We were at school together, and over the years I've come to respect him as someone who has his feet very firmly planted on the ground. He's a realist, you understand, a pragmatist. He recognises things for what they are, not what he hopes they might be.

OK, he'd been enthusiastic enough about the project at the outset when we'd talked vaguely about lunches at thatched waterside pubs and long languid afternoons cruising. But what seemed like a good idea in mid-August, when the sun was shining and there was still some life left in summer, seemed not quite so attractive a proposition a few weeks later after our booking had been confirmed, and the weather had broken, and the isobars were in place for what was to become one of the vilest autumns for a decade.

As we'd got closer to our start date, Dave's enthusiasm had waned as every successive day brought another cheerless weather forecast delivered by a lugubrious forecaster who seemed to be taking personal delight in what lay ahead for us.

But that's the sort of person Dave is. We all listen to weather forecasts. It's just that he's the sort of guy who takes notice of them. 'It's not as if we'll lose a lot of money,' he tentatively suggested on the eve of our departure. 'If we just don't turn up, I mean…'

'You could be right,' I agreed carefully. 'Let's talk about it. Over a drink, maybe?'

We'd finished the night in predictable fashion with one of those caustic vindaloos made from horsemeat marinated in Nitromors which we were so fond of then. By this time the alcohol had well and truly kicked in, and not only had Dave regained his former enthusiasm, but he'd become veritably swashbuckling about the whole venture.

'Do you think a man like me's gonna be put off by a drop of rain?' he announced contemptuously to the bemused waiter in the Star of India. 'Do you think I care a monkey's toss about a bit of bad weather?' he'd asked the Marks and Spencer mannequins in the High Street as we'd stumbled home. 'I mean, Steve…' he'd appealed to me as I attempted to get him into bed, 'I mean, do you think I'm a soft-centred wuss or something?'

I took some pleasure in reminding him of all this as we were traipsing across the field looking for the boatyard. By this stage the rain was hammering down with the force of a power shower, and I think it had dawned on both of us that starting a holiday with the remnants of two and a half gallons of lager slopping around our insides wasn't exactly guaranteed to launch proceedings on a particularly positive note.

Dave had got his own problems. His curry had begun to repeat on him. He'd already eaten it four times. I'd eaten it three times with him.

'You're making me feel sick,' I said.

'I already feel sick,' he countered. 'I feel like puking, and I want a crap too. Do you think the boat will have a toilet?'

'No,' I replied. 'I think we'll be expected to stand on the roof and evacuate downwind.'

Nelson actually turned out to be a well-appointed, tidy boat; and, for its time, modern enough. It had a steel hull with a fibreglass superstructure, and inside there was a small living area with seats built around a small table set in the floor. It had a serviceable galley with a cooker that had a couple of gas rings; and up the front of the boat – the pointed end we learnt we'd now have to call 'the bow' – there were two single berths.

To Dave's relief there was even a lavatory of sorts, though his delight at discovering this was somewhat mitigated by learning that the system on the boat was a basic 'bucket-and-chuck it' set-up in which, rather than wave your waste products goodbye, you bid them a sort of brief *au revoir.*

'You empty the toilet when it gets full. There are special sanitary points,' said Mr Boatyard Man. 'You'll soon get used to it. Not a problem.'

This seemed to be his friendly and all-embracing response to everything to do with boating. Steering this 30-foot monster by way of a tiller which you had to point in the opposite direction to the way you wanted to go?

Not a problem; we'd get used to it.

Taking the lid off the box in the back and fishing around in the slimy water if anything got wound or trapped around the propeller?

Not a problem; we'd get used to it.

And locks! That extraordinary system whereby water travels up and downhill taking boats with it? That mystery of beams and ratchets and paddles and gates which you had to open and close in exactly the right order at exactly the right time in order to prevent emptying the canal of water and thus avoid causing such floods and mayhem and disaster that it could threaten the safety of the State and the future of mankind?

'Not a problem,' said Mr Boatyard Man, sheltering under his umbrella as he waved us off from the quay. There wasn't the vaguest notion in his head that he ought to initiate us into some of these mysteries, if only for the welfare of his boat, let alone our safety.

'Not a problem,' he said again. 'You'll get used to it all.'

The extent to which we knew absolutely nothing about anything to do with canals or boats struck us with a vengeance very soon afterwards. One thing I've learnt subsequently about canal people is that on the whole they are some of the friendliest and most laid-back you'll meet anywhere in the world. Perhaps it's something to do with the pace of life on a canal, for at three miles an hour, life's boy racers hardly gravitate towards narrowboats for their kicks. Or maybe it's something to do with the ambience which surrounds these quiet byways threading through the countryside, for there's something about water –

any water – which seems to act like a sedative, making people calmer and quieter, and on the whole more considerate and forgiving than totally land-centred people.

Imagine our surprise then, as we left the very first lock we negotiated, when we were suddenly confronted by someone screaming at us with such anguish I was inclined to believe he'd been recently involved in some contretemps involving his testicles and a wild dog.

Now, we thought we'd done very well at the lock. Dave had steered *Nelson* through and out the other end without any evidence of major damage to either the brickwork or the boat; and by a combination of pure luck and the application of O-level physics, I'd managed to roughly work out the principles of the mechanism and had just dropped the metal ratchets that close the paddles that control the water flow.

This, it turned out, was the problem. These paddles were made of cast iron and dropping them in the way I had so that they crashed shut could easily break them. Paddles, I learned, had to be treated with care and lowered gently. Like so much else on the canals in that era, they were virtually worn out, and there just wasn't the money available to repair them.

It was a steep learning curve all round that day, but we persevered and got better as we went on, so that we were able to get a few miles under our belt without further mishap. Then, as a result of some minor inattentiveness, one or the other of us managed to run *Nelson* onto a mud bank where no amount of heaving or pushing or straining on ropes or bargepoles could elicit even a hint of movement from her.

All this was frustrating enough – humiliating even, for while she was floating the boat had been so elegant and graceful, so apparently insubstantial that we'd been able to move her with our fingertips. Now, like a beached whale, she'd suddenly become ungainly and unyielding, and downright cussed in her awkwardness. We sat back, breathless at our exertions.

'That'll learn you,' said an old bloke who at that moment

happened to be walking by with his rodent-like Jack Russell terrier. 'You were going too fast.'

Dave was exhausted and in no mood to take this sort of flak. 'We were within the speed limit,' he snapped back in an irritated tone of voice that sounded belligerent enough even to me, but which must have sounded even more confrontational to the pet rat for it began yapping so viscously I got the impression that if there hadn't have been a couple of feet of water separating them, it would have leapt at Dave and ripped out his throat.

'Bugger the speed limit! You were going too fast,' the old man said again. 'Bloody wave behind you that you could surf on, washing away the banks! No wonder the canal's so bloody shallow hereabouts.'

Well, there was no denying the truth of that observation, for even to beginners like us it had become apparent very quickly that the idea of canal depth was more of a conceptual notion than a physical reality. In fact, looking back at that trip, it was a wonder we ever got anywhere given that for most of our route there was so little water that we weren't, strictly speaking, floating at all, but wallowing in mud. What we laughingly called 'cruising' could be more accurately described as 'ploughing'. I swear it was so bad that in places you could have walked along the canal with no need for a boat at all. But that was the way of things in those days when the waterways had virtually been abandoned to their own devices, and no one ever seemed to dredge them.

Today it's very different. Today everything is so infuriatingly, exasperatingly chocolate-box twee.

In the early 1970s you were part of a secret, undiscovered world which was of the present, yet separate from it. The canals then were winding, overgrown ribbons of water which took you across aqueducts and embankments, and through cuttings and bat-filled tunnels to a world that seemed unchanged for centuries. Or they were black inaccessible ditches tucked away behind factories and leading to the dark, oily recesses of cities unfamiliar even to the people who lived in them.

Where contemporary life touched at all in those days it seemed to turn its back on the canal system. Houses faced away from the water, and great rusty tracts of corrugated-iron fencing separated people from it. On a boat you could be like a fugitive in your own land, ignored and spurned, with voles your only company, their tiny noses forming a V-shaped wash in the water as they cut across your course on their way from one bank to another.

Now, in the main, the voles have gone, eradicated partly as a result of mile upon mile of new metal piling, which has secured the crumbling canal banks, but also prevents the voles getting access to their traditional breeding sites. The corrugated-iron fences have been pulled down too, the waste ground behind laid with turf and planted out as public gardens or recreation grounds. The canals themselves are seen as 'linear parks', and this has had a remarkable effect on the value of adjoining properties – the sort of places that people would have turned their noses up at twenty years ago. In this day and age estate agents will make a feature of any house that's close to a canal, and any which is actually alongside the water – with its own frontage – will command a premium price.

And don't the owners know it. Some canalside houses are such a welter of jetties, piers, lawns and barbecues that you sometimes think the property itself has become an irrelevancy.

Better than it used to be, yes; who could deny it? But at the same time something has been lost, and lost irretrievably.

It's just that you can't change an environment so totally in the way that canals have been this last quarter century without fundamentally altering the sort of people who are attracted to them. In the past the only rule for getting involved in canals was that you were interested in them for their own sake – for the sport they afforded, for the wildlife they harboured, or for their history. If you had a boat at all, all you had to do was license it, a process that involved nothing more complicated than sending the authorities a modest sum of money. Nowadays, although hundreds of thousands use the waterways annually for fishing, walking or study, it sometimes erroneously seems that you can't really feel a part of the canal community *unless* you have a boat.

And even this isn't the simple process it once used to be since it's governed by a plethora of bureaucratic regulation. In the past you just bought a boat and cast off. Today, though, boats cost a fortune, way beyond the aspirations of most families; and even if you can afford one, your biggest problem will be working out whether your door handles comply with regulation 137a, subsection vii (d) of the 1996 Anorak Act, or if your sink taps breach the 1998 European (Tear Your Hair Out Amendment) Directive.

In the past the waterways were the preserve of hippies who couldn't quite accept that the 1960s had finished, and enthusiasts who were certain that the 1760s hadn't.

The hippies saw canals as offering an alternative lifestyle where they could be left alone to indulge in various solitary pursuits involving illegal substances and loud psychedelic music. The enthusiasts – 'rivet counters' they were called, after their tendency to argue passionately about the details of boat construction – all had old working craft, the equivalent of Victorian lorries where most of the hold was for cargo and they were jammed for living space into a tiny tea chest of a cabin at the back.

But your average rivet counter welcomed the privation this entailed. He regarded it as part of the enduring pleasure of the canals.

And then there were the cruisers: plastic boats, not unlike Tupperware boxes, powered by whining outboard engines which may have been only the size of food mixers but which were capable of generating a sound like Concorde at take off. Cruisers always seemed to be kept a gleaming, polished white, despite the amount of mud and grease that was a feature of the waterways then. And they always seemed to be under the control of middle-aged men wearing captain's caps – the sort of blokes who thought wearing pressed slacks and a cashmere sweater was dressing casually.

In that period, though, what you cruised in mattered less than that you'd cruised at all, for everyone in their own way was a pioneer of the new leisure age. Come the end of the day when the mooring stakes had been driven in for the night, the hippies, and rivet counters, and the Tupperware crowd alike would all repair to the nearest pub where they would chat harmlessly for hours on end about engine specifications, routes through Birmingham, or propeller sizes.

But wherever two or three like-minded people gather together in the same room, you can always trust the English to devise a class system. Gradually – insidiously, almost – a different sort of boat began to arrive on the canals. Some of them even had showers. And some of them – can you believe this? – pump-out lavatories!

Not an unreasonable development you might think. But think a little more, for there's a paradox which lies at the heart of this.

You see, given that we're one of the richest countries in the world, and that we live at an unprecedented level of comfort surrounded by material possessions undreamt of by previous generations; given that we now take as normal things like central heating, running water, and waste and rubbish disposal that are still considered the height of luxury in many parts of the world; given all this, what earthly reason can there be for living like an itinerant eighteenth-century working-class labourer?

Unless, of course, you reject a little of modern life and everything it stands for.

A pump-out toilet may seem a perfectly modest aspiration, but that was just the beginning of it. Most modern boats don't just have showers, they have baths too – and some of them jacuzzis and bidets too for all I know. They have hot water and central heating as standard, not to mention a huge range of consumer durables that would put your average Currys to shame: fridges, TVs, videos, hi-fis, microwaves, computers with e-mail capacity from mobile phones. Is it any surprise that thieves have begun to target narrowboats, and that owners are responding by installing increasingly more sophisticated security devices?

Some rejection of modern life!

These higher specification boats have attracted owners with higher incomes – people who have come to expect a certain standard of living at home and who aren't going to compromise on it in their leisure hours. Sadly, many of them aren't people who are particularly interested in canals, but who treat boats as floating country cottages, homes from home.

And so, much in the way a yeast which is nurtured to produce alcohol eventually produces so much that it destroys itself, so the early canal pioneers created the conditions in which they themselves were virtually wiped out and everything they held dear devalued.

Dave and I moored up earlier than we'd planned that first night. This wasn't out of choice so much as a result of an unfortunate incident with a rope which one of us had left trailing in the water so that it had got itself caught around the propeller, making it impossible to go on. Whichever of us was responsible, neither of us was admitting it, and we were both feeling testy – a mood not helped by the weather. It hadn't stopped raining all day, and we'd got to the stage where we were just too wet to care. We spent an hour with our arms contorted in the icy water cutting the rope free with a blunt kitchen knife. Afterwards, united in conquered adversity and at least talking again, we dried off as best we could and cracked open a couple of cans of beer we'd brought with us.

By now the rain had finally begun to ease off, and soon afterwards it stopped completely. The wind which had been blowing with it suddenly dropped too, and the dark clouds fell away, allowing us to bask in the surprisingly warm glow of a vivid sunset. I have many times since noticed how after an appalling day, the English weather can suddenly change for the better in the hour before dark; and I feel sure there must be some meteorological explanation for it somehow associated with the cooling of the earth.

But that day we could only gaze in wonder at the metamorphosis. We sat on the deck as a pale mist began to form across the water, watching the fish rise to the surface to feed, while on the bank a couple of nervous coots scratched about scavenging for titbits, their preposterously thin legs scarcely able to bear their weight. Above us the swallows dipped in the air and then dived to the water, skimming the very surface until it seemed it must have turned to ice and they must have been skidding along its top. All around us the world seemed bathed in a sort of magical half light which, curiously, didn't seem of this world at all.

Before night had fallen I was hooked.

In seven days, Dave and I cruised from Leicestershire into the centre of Nottingham, back up the river towards Burton upon Trent, and from there to Nuneaton and on to Tamworth. Afterwards, when he'd gone, Em joined me for my second week, and we cruised to Coventry and Rugby, into Northamptonshire and back to Leicester to complete a circle of some eighty miles or so.

These are the mundane geographical facts of the trip; but actually, the more essential truth of that journey was that I cruised to Shangri-La. Somehow, by dint of just hiring a boat, I'd gained access to this new and strange world I'd never known existed before. It was a world which – strangely – seemed familiar to me, though it was so unfamiliar, like one of those places you've visited in your dreams. It was my world but it was not my world: it was a world which seemed to exist parallel to the one I knew; an older and quieter and more constant world than mine which was brash and angry and so tiresomely, constantly capricious. It was a world rooted in the soil of the countryside and the changing patterns of the seasons, a world where work was integral to people's lives rather than just imposed upon them to the point of exploitation – which is how it so often seemed to me, observing that great swathe of humanity that dragged itself reluctantly through the rush hour madness at home.

And people were different on the canals – I recognised that

immediately. For a start they were less conventional than those who lived entirely on the land, more reluctant to conform to accepted behaviour and more questioning of it. They were more helpful too; less exclusive about their knowledge, and more willing to share it. But the breadth of that knowledge was staggering, derived from a whole network of shared experiences that linked them together into a community. All around me were men and women who were as comfortable talking about protective anodes as they were about wildlife; people who could tie a rope with a couple of twists of their wrist, or be rolling a cigarette as they steered a 20-ton boat into a lock with just an inch to spare on either side; people as familiar with the Northern towns as they were with the isolated Fenlands; people who were altogether so much larger and louder and brighter and more alive than the overwhelming majority of people I met as a journalist in my normal life.

I suppose I'd fallen in love, though I didn't know it at the time, naively believing then that it was only people who could touch your heart and make you ache with yearning, longing for them. I suddenly felt this gnawing, persistent need to be close to the water, and after the holiday was over and Em and I had returned to London, nothing was more certain in my mind than that canals would play an important part in my life.

I think I've hardly been far away from them for more than a month or so at a time since.

Four

THRUPP IS NOT WHAT you'd call a big place – not unless you're one of those people who live on an isolated farm in rural Norfolk twenty miles from your nearest neighbour. Even then, I don't think you'd find it all bright lights and big-city bustle. It lies six or seven miles north of Oxford, just beyond Kidlington, which is hardly one of the world's major cities either, but which people have at least heard about because it's the headquarters of Thames Valley Police where Colin Dexter's Inspector Morse was supposed to have been based.

But Thrupp is about as different from Kidlington as the fictional detective is from the real thing. Kidlington at least has shops and offices and places where ordinary people live; whereas all Thrupp has is a cruising club with a lot of moorings for boats, and a row of about a dozen tiny houses – 'artisans' cottages', as they're now known – prettied up with white paint and red geraniums. Oh, and it has a pub too. Strictly speaking – officially – Thrupp has two pubs, but the other one is round the bend of the canal and to a purist like me not really in Thrupp at all and just another regrettable example of a small place getting ideas above its station.

I washed up in the place the way you do a lot of locations on the waterways, entirely by chance and completely without planning. Travelling north from Oxford the conditions ensured that there weren't many other boats on the move, and I didn't meet one until Wolvercote Junction, where the canal branches off to join the River Thames. Single-handed boating is exhausting enough at the best of times with locks, but on this stretch of canal you also have to deal with lift bridges. With their distinctive upright balance beams, they're a feature of the Oxford Canal, and they may look twee and pretty enough on postcards, but believe me, they're a swine to get through on your own. You either rope them down or jam them up. Either way, as you go underneath, you find yourself praying that a ton and a half of Grade Two listed Georgian doesn't come crashing down on your head.

I haven't been properly fit for years, so by the time I got to Thrupp it was as much as I could do to collapse into the Boat Inn and crawl to the bar for sustenance. And after a session of sustenance, it was as much as I could do to drag myself back to the boat for an afternoon nap. After that? Well, after that it was opening time again, and I didn't see the need to move at all that day and so – as is the inexorable nature of things on waterways – I finished up staying at Thrupp for more than a month and a half.

You can perhaps understand now why it's such a long time since I've been fit.

Thrupp suited me perfectly as a place to wait for the floods to subside. It was filled with canal people, a lot of them, like me, holed up by the weather, and most of them – like me too – happy enough to keep themselves to themselves during the day, but at night content to assemble companionably around the bar of the Boat. By degrees I soon found myself drawn into a surprisingly lively social scene. On some nights there'd be an impromptu folk club where we were all expected to do a turn, or at least join in with the general chorus; other evenings we'd play Aunt Sally, the idiosyncratic Oxfordshire version of skittles that's survived in these parts.

One Saturday the boat club even had an open day to introduce disadvantaged kids to the waterways, and I somehow found myself roped in to help, sitting around a campfire by candlelight cradling a burnt sausage and yelling out the incomprehensible words to some song about cranky poohs and goolley goolleys. The kids were great, full of drive, energy and curiosity – though

I must confess there were some of them I was happier to have sitting around singing with me than following me up a deserted street. But no doubt I do them an injustice. I'm nothing if not typical of my countrymen, and we English aren't terribly keen on young people, being somewhat fastidious about the procedures necessary to beget them and somewhat uncertain of what to do with them once we have.

In the old days when we had an Empire we used to ship them off to school so we could get on with more important things. However, with our current involvement in world affairs reduced to a part-time role, and with school fees rising steeply, we're more inclined to keep our children at home; though I have noticed over recent years a propensity to try and introduce a system of nationalised boarding education by the back door as we successively reduce the age of juvenile criminal responsibility, and at the same time legislate to make most of the things kids do short of stamp collecting an indictable offence.

In contrast to the nights, my days at Thrupp were spent in congenial solitude when I had the first opportunity for ages to spend some time mulling over my life. Most of the things I found myself thinking about at that period were totally trivial and irrelevant. I spent hours just staring at the fruit bowl, for instance: watching swarms of tiny flies congregate sociably on my browning bananas. Funny things fruit flies – simple creatures, but infinitely complicated too, as the American biologist Thomas Hunt Morgan found when he used them for the research which in 1910 led to him becoming the first scientist to pin down the location of a gene to a specific chromosome. So it's not going too far to say that in fruit flies lies the very meaning of life.

In the same vein I also spent a lot of time thinking about eggs.

I am quite fond of eggs, and one day I frittered away an entire morning working out how many of them I'd eaten over my lifetime. It came out at more than five thousand. Five thousand! Can you imagine it? Even allowing for periods when I didn't eat any at all, and other periods where I glutted on them (pickled eggs in pubs, for instance – I had a mania for them in my mid-twenties) I've probably consumed eggs at an average of three a week since the age of eighteen. That's 156 a year for 32 years – 4,992 of them, not counting the ones I ate as a kid. That is one bloody big omelette by anyone's standards.

And then I began to think about everything else I'd eaten: the tons of potatoes, the fields of vegetables, the herds of cows, the broods of chickens, the shoals of fish… And what about my other consumption? What about all the raw materials I'd used, all the wood, metal and plastic expended on my behalf? All the energy I'd exhausted, all the gas, all the electricity… And this is only me, remember, just one insignificant soul among millions in this country, one of hundreds of millions in the world at large – just one man who admittedly might be tending to plump around the midriff in his middle years, but who hasn't exactly led a life of constant hedonistic excess.

What got me started on this train of thought – what was totally responsible for it, in fact – was a sociable moorhen that pitched up outside *Justice* one morning as I was standing in the sunshine, sipping at the day's first cup of Ceylon and tossing crusts of toast into the water. Now, when I use the word 'sociable' here, understand it's only in the context of a bird which in normal circumstances takes one look at anything that isn't of its own species and flees in frenzied, uncoordinated panic.

Moorhens have long spindly legs the thickness of drinking straws. They do not run gracefully, especially when they try to do it on water. In fact, they don't walk particularly elegantly either, even on land. Come to think of it, their swimming action, which involves much redundant bobbing of the head, leaves much to be desired too. In short, this is not a bird endowed with much in the way of natural poise and assurance, and certainly not one you should seriously be considering as a household pet.

It swam around aimlessly for a while, and pecked haphazardly at the surface of the water before taking up a precarious position on a thin branch that trailed from a bush on the opposite bank; and here over the following days it based itself, disappearing at various times and returning with such predictable regularity that eventually it began to dawn on me what I was dismissing insensitively as just a branch of a bush was actually... well, this creature's home.

This was a bit of an eye-opener, I can tell you. OK, I realise there's a danger of becoming too anthropomorphic here; but even so, the reduction of a concept so inexorably bound up with bricks and mortar to something no grander than a twig took a bit of getting my head around. How many twigs had I inadvertently bulldozed in my boating life by wantonly inattentive steering? How many forests of them had I demolished on towpath walks by mindlessly snapping them off to hack at stinging nettles?

This was all a salutatory reminder of how lightly some living things tread on the world, and how heavily does humanity. And it touched a deep chord in me when one day the moorhen swam nearer than it had ever done before and delivered one of those shrill cries which I'd always thought agonisingly mournful, like the shriek of the existential soul railing against the nihilism of the universe.

Or something like that.

Actually, the damn thing began screeching at me regularly from then on, four or five times a day, until the penny finally dropped and I realised that his was less a cry of metaphysical angst than a demand for more of the toast that I'd stopped feeding it after switching to muesli for breakfast, which, as everyone knows, is a much better source of fibre to assist bowel movement.

Ah well! In the midst of a life crisis there's a tendency to search too hard for deeper meaning in everything. It served me right for being too sentimental, I suppose.

Thrupp lies very close to the village of Woodstock in which lies Blenheim Palace, stately home to successive Dukes of Marlborough; and one weekend towards the end of my stay when

Em was up for the weekend we decided to drive there in the Debsmobile for an afternoon of heritage. The village is a Cotswold picture postcardy-type of place, filled with tourist buses, listed buildings and fancy restaurants selling food at London prices. There's an expensive 'heritage hotel', and a lot of extraordinary shops as well. One sells just knitting patterns and precious little else. Another sells shoes with genuine gold-plated soles – well, I took it that they *must* have genuine gold-plated soles at the prices they were charging for them. Another only sells goods from the Third World. With a facetiousness verging on the tasteless it's called One Village.

Blenheim Palace was built in the early eighteenth century after Queen Anne had granted John Churchill, the first Duke of Marlborough, the manor of Woodstock and £240,000 for defending Holland and Austria from invasion by the French, so saving us – at least for a generation or two – from acidic and overpriced wine, sloppy kissing and Golden Delicious apples. It's as good a use for quarter of a million quid as I can think of – never mind that we got one of the most beautiful baroque houses in the world out of the deal too.

But it's probably as Winston Churchill's birthplace that Blenheim is best known. The tourists are told that he came into the world prematurely in the cloakroom after his mother had been taken in labour following a bout of dancing, though I've always suspected a more prosaic truth, and think he was probably born in the lavatory after she got caught short, desperate for a pee. Churchill had heard this said himself. He used to joke that he couldn't confirm it one way or another. Although he was present at the event, he said, unfortunately he had no personal recollection of it.

The curious cocktail of the military, the royal and the political which characterises Blenheim was summed up for me neatly in the menu of one of Woodstock's many tearooms where we were eventually forced to seek sanctuary from the rain which, in this most appalling of summers, had begun bucketing down yet again.

There, for a light morning snack, you could have Colonial Rarebit (cheese on toast with a pinch of curry powder), Churchill Rarebit (cheese on toast with parsley) or – what I took to be a concession to modernity – a Rarebit Diane, which I supposed misspelt, but named after the late princess. Actually it turned out to be named after Diane the owner of the tearoom who – the waitress informed us with the deference the ordinary show to those in whom they instinctively recognise greatness – had actually invented the dish.

'And is it secret?' I asked.

'Secret?'

'The recipe. It's cheese on toast, I suppose. But do I get to know what makes it so special?'

The waitress leaned over to me conspiratorially, as if imparting some nugget of information bearing on national security. 'It has a tomato on top,' she said.

Now call me old-fashioned, but I do find it difficult to reconcile myself to the fact that the country that devised the concept of parliamentary democracy, invented the jet engine, and dreamed up the format for *Changing Rooms* can have fallen so low in its own estimation that it feels the need to celebrate the originality of adding a tomato to a toasted cheese sandwich. Still, apart from this unsettling burst of innovation, the tearoom was reassuringly predictable, for when our beverages eventually arrived they were cold in the way that has become as much the endearing hallmark of the contemporary English tea shop as the grubby packets of sugar and pots of UHT milk which arrived with them and which similarly have come to represent a benchmark for everything that is tacky about us in the new century.

It was still raining when we left, and by now we'd given up any idea of visiting the palace itself, having discovered how much it would cost us to get in. We were also put off by the banks of luxury tourist coaches parked all over the place which gave us more than a hint of what it would be like inside. A much more pleasant proposition even in the rain, we decided, would be to turn up our collars and walk around the grounds where we could avoid the crowds and enjoy one of Capability Brown's loveliest creations in relative solitude. Even this cost us an arm and a leg, though, since I didn't discover until later that there's a public footpath running through the place to which you have right of access if only you approach the gatehouse without waving five-pound notes around like I did. Once inside, we hardly had the place to ourselves either, for considering it was such a miserable day, the grounds were surprisingly busy – a fact I put down to a characteristic of the English which I have often noticed: our ability to persist with whatever it is we have planned for our leisure hours totally regardless of what the weather may be on the day.

You see it on seaside beaches where families in swimming gear sit huddled behind gaily coloured windbreaks as Force 9 gales sweep in from the Atlantic. You see it in parks where young dads doggedly continue kickabouts with their kids way beyond the point where even a hardened Premiership pro would be looking to the referee to abandon the game. And we saw it in the grounds of Blenheim that day in early April where we found ourselves stepping over families wrapped up like Atlantic trawlermen but still battling gamely to have picnics though they'd long ago given up any pretence to pleasure in what they were doing.

Mind you, I suppose we were doing much the same ourselves, walking around in what by now had become a serious storm.

Eventually we gave up the struggle and visited the palace after all. Well, we visited the gift shop – which apart from the café is the only place in the dry they'll let you in for free. But it was a good gift shop, classy: the sort of thing you'd expect in a stately home like Blenheim. It was filled with posh presents like cut-glass whisky glasses and expensively woven tartan – both of which must confuse the Americans something wicked since they associate both with Scotland and don't realise that all the best bits of that country, including the whole of the Highlands, are owned by the English aristocracy.

The 'traditional' limited-edition teddy bears that adorn Blenheim – and indeed every other country house gift shop you visit – must fox them too. But then, they baffle me as well; for I've never been able to work out this connection between furry toys and the aristocracy, over and above suspecting that at its root is some illicit sexual practice I've never been initiated into, being too much of a proletarian. But I have to admit, I suspect the same thing about wearing riding boots and having a nanny, so as far as these things go I'm not to be totally relied on.

Nowadays, though, everything English seems to be 'traditional' in one way or another. God knows, you can't even walk into a common or garden supermarket these last few years without being regaled by shelves of 'traditional' goods, whether it be packets of ginger biscuits or bars of soap. And everything you buy besides, from a table lamp to a digital clock seems to be modelled on 'traditional' lines – which generally means it's been given a wood-look plastic fascia and brass-effect finish. Actually, I've finally worked out what 'traditional' means in this context: it's a word you attach to anything that's been around for so long no one can remember who designed it, or where the design's so crap it's obvious it was put together by a committee.

All this is not helpful for us as a nation. It's bound to affect the way we see the modern world, for it reinforces old patterns of doing things and acts as a check on new thinking. So someone drops a cheese on his way home from a market in Derbyshire and for the next 300 years there's a cheese-rolling contest at the same spot. Or some creepy-crawly falls into a mixing bowl in Burslem, and the traditional Potteries Spider Cake is born. If anything, it's got worse because we seem so hell-bent on establishing new 'tradition' that all it takes is for a couple of blokes to get together for a drink in a pub for a few weeks running and before you know where you are people are weaving tapestries of the scene and sticking their fingers in their ear and singing folk songs about it.

The concept of 'heritage' is just as bad. The idea's become so debased as to be virtually meaningless; or if it has any meaning at all it's not in the general sense of being what we've inherited from history, but in the very specific sense of what we've selected from history to define what we think of ourselves. So all this Black Rod bollocks thumping about in the cellars of the House of Commons pretending to look for explosives at the start of every new parliamentary session – now that's defined as 'heritage' because it's all bound up with the Gunpowder Plot and thought to be important because of what it says about our attitude to parliamentary government.

But what about other aspects of our past where England has an unparalleled track record of exploitation, whether it be sending kids up chimneys at home or getting coolies hooked on opium in China? You don't see many Wedgwood plates commemorating that, do you?

Heritage! Tradition! Don't you just love them both? In the gift shop in Blenheim they were selling boxed sets of coins from 1966 with pictures of the then England football captain Bobby Moore emblazoned all over them.

1966, for God's sake! The year we won the World Cup! The *only* year we won the World Cup!

Part of our heritage maybe, but sadly far from being traditional.

Back on the boat Em was the first to notice that the moorhen wasn't in its customary place on its twig and that the bread we'd left for it that morning remained untouched, even by any of the flocks of scavenging ducks that can usually be relied upon to patrol any patch of English water on the off-chance of finding floating carbohydrate.

I took this as a bad omen, and so now that the floods had finally abated and the river was open once more, I determined to move back to the Thames and head for Bristol at the first opportunity. I'd anyhow stopped on a mooring restricted to a 14-day maximum and I was overstaying my welcome. As I made preparations to go the next morning – as sad to leave Thrupp as I've ever been to leave anywhere – I noticed a moorhen a little further up the canal hovering about another trailing branch. Now don't get me wrong. I'm not saying it was the *same* moorhen, but this one did seem inordinately interested in my departure and – was I imagining this? – did it seem a little sad to see me go?

'No, of course it isn't sad,' said Em, when I pointed it out to her. 'And yes, you *are* imagining it. It's just a bird – and a particularly dumb species of bird at that. It wouldn't even recognise you if you were its mother, let alone an anthropoid in the equivalent of an ocean liner.'

Later I drove her to the station, and as she left me, she kissed me lightly on the cheek. 'Get a grip, Steve,' she said. 'Or at least make an effort to get a grip.'

I cast off as soon as I could, feeling a new lease of life now I was on the move once more.

It was two hours before I realised I was travelling in the wrong direction.

Five

READING *NARROW BOAT* you'd think that May to September 1939 had been the perfect English summer.

Except that statistically, it wasn't actually that good. During three of those five months, temperatures at Kew were below the average for the time of year; and in one – August – it was half as wet again as it normally is, with rain falling pretty much every third day.

My stay at Thrupp had given me the opportunity of reading the book again, and I'm not embarrassed to admit that I found it as emotionally compelling as I had when I first read it. There was still a sort of strange and haunting atmosphere about it which I found compulsive; and I was attracted by its style too: its curiously stilted language that was sometimes lyrically beautiful, sometimes almost archaic. I was surprised that after so long the book was still capable of encapsulating for me that mystical sense of the English canal landscape I'd first felt on holiday with Dave all those years ago when the waterways had touched such a deep chord in me.

Yet even as my heart warmed to the book once more, my head was warning me there was something inherently dangerous about its sentimentalisation of the whole canal environment and its appeal to a lost and better England. It was like Rolt's version of the weather – it wasn't objective, external truth, more of a reflection of what he was *feeling* at the time. War was declared in September; so that summer was the last period of peace for six years. And he was on his honeymoon. He was in love and ecstatically happy. Of course it was sunny.

Not that you'd know very much of this from the book itself.

It's only in a concluding chapter that you learn that the events around which it was based took place when they did, and the fact of the honeymoon isn't mentioned directly at all. Indeed, Angela herself only warrants a couple of mentions in the text, one of them when she brings up curtain fabrics from London while they are fitting out the boat – a role that hardly does justice to her importance to the whole project, let alone her independent spirit.

The truth is that the love affair that most inspires *Narrow Boat* isn't the one with Angela, but Tom's romance with England, the English landscape and English tradition. It jumps out at you from every page of *Narrow Boat*. Which is curious really, because his obsession with these things stands so starkly at odds with his job as an engineer where he was involved in the cutting edge of the contemporary world.

It was a paradox Tom Rolt recognised in himself, and as he got older he finally came to realise that he despised much of what modern life had come to stand for. His England was an England in which people's self-worth grew organically out of the work they did and the pride they felt in that labour – which is something he felt had been lost by modern industrial processes, and which is why the boat people so captivated him, even though their way of life carrying freight was all but dead even then. For Tom Rolt, the life of the boat people *was* their work, and he saw that their work engendered its own culture in the songs they sang, the stories they told each other, and the pubs they drank in.

Never mind that what they did was mostly grinding and repetitive labour carried out in filthy weather at all times of the year. Never mind that even then most of them were reduced to virtually begging for work, and that to get what little they could, they – or the companies which employed them – had to cut margins so low that what could be earned from the job was only just enough to keep a family above the breadline. Never mind either that given the opportunity, most canal people would (and did) abandon this relentless treadmill as soon as there was so much as a hint of a viable alternative open to them.

Despite its lack of documentary realism, it's not difficult to understand how a book of the tenor of *Narrow Boat* – written as the curtain came down on an age of colonial certainty – should have such a hold on the imagination of those facing the insecurities of a new age in which the very nature of work itself would change. No, what's more difficult to comprehend is that it *still* has that allure today. Really! What sort of saddos are we to believe that this has the slightest relevance to our modern lives? What sort of saddo am I?

For a start, even the events the book describes didn't happen in any real sense, any more than the journey itself did. Yes, of course, Tom and Angela actually travelled the route, and it would be silly to claim that there isn't at least a loose relationship between things that happened and the description of events in the book. But what appears in the book is embellished and selective: it's artefact; fiction not fact. For the most part it's just a confection constructed out of nothing more tangible than Tom's mawkish romanticism.

The world of *Narrow Boat* isn't a real world any more than those fantastical castles of traditional narrowboat painting are real places. It's just one of those idealised summers with long sweltering days that we can all drag from the deceptive recesses of childhood memory, but which we all know are pure nostalgia, since a sky like that could surely never have been such a perfect azure blue, and the shape of a cloud surely never so unblemished and faultless.

I got to the stage eventually where I couldn't stomach any more of it. The relentless whimsy was bad enough, but I realised for some reason that I was trying to find Tom Rolt in the book, and Tom Rolt wasn't there. Instead there was just a vague shadow, evocative enough of the real man for me to recognise it as him, but without enough definition for me to get anywhere close to him. It was like that cloying start to Pink Floyd's 'Grantchester

Meadows' when the bees seem to be swarming around your head and there's that irritating skylark singing on the wing, so that even in the depths of winter you're aware of the sunshine burning into your neck, and you can smell the heavy, slightly sickening odour of new-mown grass about you.

And you feel summer though it isn't summer.

It's the same in *Narrow Boat* where you can see the figure of Tom Rolt sitting writing at the desk he'd built specially on *Cressy* for the purpose, his shoulders stooped and his head slightly hunched over the keyboard of his typewriter. Sometimes in the book it's as if you can hear the very intonation of his voice across half a century. Yet somehow you can never get to him or his world, which seems another age away, as far removed as if he'd been a Victorian, or maybe from an even more distant past than that.

Thankfully for my purposes, *Narrow Boat* wasn't the only thing Tom Rolt was writing that summer. As he and Angela travelled slowly northwards, winding through the Midlands counties and into Derbyshire and Staffordshire, he was also keeping a log of the journey which he'd begun the day he left Banbury, and which would become a major reference some years later when he came to write his autobiography. He kept this log for the whole of *Cressy*'s cruising life, writing it every evening in his neat handwriting in an unremarkable red hard-backed notebook; and it's an altogether more mundane piece of writing than *Narrow Boat*, factual and unadorned. It's mainly filled with details of distances covered and locks passed, though there are occasional mentions of the weather he and Angela experienced, and even – sometimes – the meals they ate.

But it's no less powerful for that, for in the artless way of these things, the small details of personal narrative it records become part of the great tide of history itself. They were approaching Stoke-on-Trent, for instance, when they heard that Hitler had invaded Poland; and they were close to Middlewich in Cheshire on 3 September when, confirming the worst they'd feared, they heard the 'solemn' voice of Neville Chamberlain on the radio announcing that Britain had declared war on Germany.

You won't find it recorded in *Narrow Boat*, but Angela broke down at this news, convinced not just that her and Tom's immediate plans had collapsed, but that their whole life together would suddenly break down too. Angela had reason to worry about being left high and dry by the war, since she had a good deal more invested in the relationship than Tom. It's said she was from royal stock and could trace her ancestry back to William IV, and however true or not this was, one thing was beyond dispute: in marrying she'd been compelled to confront the hostility of her father who'd harboured ambitions she might marry into a title, and who had turned his back on her when it became clear this wouldn't happen.

He'd acted like a Victorian paterfamilias, summoning the Rolts to a meeting at the Café Royal in Piccadilly in London and demanding a settlement on his daughter.

It's hard not to believe this whole question of Angela's estrangement from her family and the potential isolation to which the war could condemn her wasn't discussed between them the night war was declared, since immediately afterwards – and with an evident new purpose to their cruising – they moved to a mooring in the small Cheshire village of Church Minshull. It was from here for two months that Tom travelled to the job as a fitter that so nearly destroyed him at Rolls-Royce – but which, as a reserved occupation, at least kept him out of the army.

Again, there's none of this in *Narrow Boat*, where the most we're told as readers is that they made a 'prolonged stay' in the village. Because nothing, absolutely nothing – even a conflict on this scale – could be allowed to destroy the book's carefully nurtured alchemy of an idyllic English summer...

There was a change in my own plans too after leaving Thrupp. Well, there couldn't help but be a change in my plans seeing that I was travelling in an entirely different direction to the one I'd intended. But what the hell? Who ever *really* makes decisions in this world? Decisions are things that just happen to you while you're working out what to do next. So I decided to keep pressing on the way I was going.

Not that it mattered a lot. Em telephoned me as soon as she got back to the Crumbling Pile; there was an unmistakable note of concern in her voice. Some drainpipe had started leaking while she'd been away, and the living room walls were soaked and mould had started growing across the paintwork. Or maybe I'm thinking of some other time she rang? Maybe this call was when she'd discovered that the roof had been leaking and that there was a wet patch in the bedroom and fungus sprouting across the ceiling. One way or another, you get the idea: the house was dripping from every orifice and the natural world was treating it like a Petri dish. There was nothing for it: I'd have to go back to London.

I made my way to the small village of Lower Heyford where a boatyard lies adjacent to a station, and where I could leave *Justice* and the Debsmobile safely. Frankly, at this point I wasn't too unhappy to get away from canals, for all this obsessing about the good weather of 1939 had only served to accentuate the fact that the weather I was experiencing was relentlessly wretched. April had been the wettest on record; May the rainiest for 17 years. Altogether the world seemed so waterlogged that it was a wonder *I* wasn't covered in growth, let alone the house. The fact was that even though it was already June, it was difficult to believe it was summer.

Thankfully the journey from Oxfordshire was a painless one for which I was grateful. People who don't use trains around London just haven't any idea of how agonising rail travel can be. If it's not drivers passing through red signals, then it's the overcrowding you get from jamming twelve carriages of passengers into a four-carriage train as a result of some dumbo with gold braid on his cap not having enough fingers left to count into double figures.

Of course, sod's law dictated that the minute I'd arrived at Marylebone and had the chance to adjust to the pace of the traffic, and the smell, and the noise; and realise just how unpleasant a city London can sometimes be, the weather changed totally. The thermometer hit 80, making London even more abhorrent than usual, and making me wish I'd never left the canals at all…

I live in Blackheath, which is south of the river and one of London's famed 'villages' – only unlike most of the others, which are the contrivance of estate agents, this one's actually genuine. It has genuine village pubs, and genuine narrow village streets, and genuine village shops – which in the spirit of genuine village commerce charge top-whack premium prices for absolutely everything. Not that you can blame them, I suppose, since with skyrocketing rents and rates in this part of the world, it's been a struggle for any of them that sell anything useful to keep going at all. So over recent years there's been a tendency for utility shops to close, to be replaced by restaurants which have spawned in such concentration that at the rate of one a night it would take you the better part of a month to eat your way round the place.

All told, Blackheath's a pleasant enough area to live considering you're in one of the biggest cities in the world. The air's hardly alpine but it's cleanish all the same, and it's green, and there's an overwhelming sense of history about the place which when you live in it seems to guarantee you a role, however insignificant, in the great tapestry of events which have shaped England's past.

The 100,000 followers of Watt Tyler protesting against the poll tax in 1381 assembled on the heath, for instance; and Henry V was welcomed back from France here after his victory at Agincourt. Neighbouring Greenwich Park is one of the few places we know for certain that Shakespeare performed as an actor; and Henry VIII was born there, in the royal palace of Placentia which once stood on the site of what used to be the Royal Naval college and is now Greenwich University. Elizabeth I was also born in Greenwich, which she came to love as her favourite palace. In fact, it was at Greenwich that Elizabeth signed the death warrant for Mary, Queen of Scots; and at Greenwich that news was brought to her of Mary's execution.

Greenwich, with its National Maritime Museum and its Royal Observatory, is one of Britain's World Heritage sites, and there's so much heritage in evidence as you walk around that when you get to my age you sometimes fret about spending too long in any one spot for fear of suddenly finding yourself classed as a listed building. But Greenwich is that sort of place, and spending any amount of time in it, it's hard not to find yourself in sympathy with those who say we've just got too much junk from the past in this country, and that the stuff's bringing us down, and that we'd be just as well to sweep away the whole caboodle if we're to stand any chance whatsoever in the new century.

Walking around the 'antiques' markets in Greenwich on a Sunday – and on a Sunday the *whole* of Greenwich becomes an 'antiques' market – is an object lesson in how to make a fetish of the past. There's stuff on sale here fetching a fortune that you couldn't have given away at a church jumble sale when I was a kid. Utility war furniture in genuine plywood, flouncy 1950s standard lampshades in ruched pink nylon, pairs of patched and faded 1970 denim loon pants. Can someone please tell me who actually buys this crap? Who actually wants it in their house?

And all this 'craft' stuff on sale – what exactly is it except modern tat in a heritage cloak? Hand-made wooden children's toys, hand-made stained-glass lampshades, hand-made soap, hand-made earrings. My God! Sometimes you'd think the industrial revolution never happened for all these fresh-faced youngsters with their dyed and plaited hair, dextrously creating new Utopias on their kitchen tables. On and on it goes, stall after stall of it: wrought-iron candlesticks, candles to put in them, oil lamps for when the candles fade, oils to put in the lamps, dyes to colour the oils... Frankly, you could be forgiven for thinking there was a power-supply problem in this part of the world, judging by Greenwich market on a Sunday.

What I always thought would benefit Greenwich – what I

thought would benefit Britain as we moved into the millennium – was something to counteract all these dusty reminders of our bygones: something uncompromisingly modern which could stand as a radical symbol of national growth and rebirth; some great project that would bind us all together in common purpose and proudly emphasise to the rest of the world the essential qualities of our national character.

Then they built the Dome.

The place has been the bane of my life ever since. At least in the past, if there was ever any uncertainty about where Blackheath actually was, I'd say it was 'close to Greenwich' which more often than not people seemed to have heard of. They've heard of it now, all right. In fact today – years after the Dome has closed – the mere mention of Greenwich anywhere in the English-speaking world is the cue for elephants to start blanching and for normally level-headed, law-abiding citizens to pin you against the wall, the better to be able to stuff your radical modernism down your throat.

Sad this, because I feel for the Dome as I feel for kids that you've watched grow up. From the top of Greenwich Hill, close to the Observatory, there's one of the best views of London that you'll find anywhere, and from here I watched over months as it was being built. One afternoon, spellbound, I gazed in disbelief as groups of men played out a sort of aerial ballet on the struts, swarming around the structure like flies and trailing behind them the massive cables which would support the roof but which in the distance looked as delicate and insubstantial as the threads of spiders' webs.

So after all this I couldn't get away without visiting the place, could I? Though given the debate that was raging in millennium year, even this trifling and inconsequential resolution was ascribed the weight of ideological political statement. 'What! You're thinking about going to the Dome? Actually *going* there?' friends would gasp, a note of distaste in their voice as if I'd just announced I was inviting Osama Bin Laden to a nativity play.

If I was told once that the cost of building the Dome would have built six hospitals, then I was told it a thousand times; though precisely what I was to do with this information and why it was imparted to me, I never properly discovered. Perhaps the idea was that once I got inside the place, I should surreptitiously establish a bridgehead for some massed SAS-type attack by the white-coated forces of the NHS determined to improve the quality of the country's primary healthcare. More likely it was mentioned in some dog-in-the-manger way so as to ensure that if by any accident I happened to actually enjoy anything I saw, I should immediately be plunged into despair, knowing that on my shoulders rested the fate of at least a dozen cancer patients.

Cussed as I am, all this made me more determined than ever to visit; and so one morning, with a sort of jaunty V-sign to political correctness, I hopped on a 108 bus from the top of the road and sat somewhat self-consciously surrounded by groups of pensioners with heavy shopping bags who eyed me suspiciously, each and every one of them no doubt scheduled for a hip-replacement operation and holding me personally responsible for their place on the waiting list. Fortunately I'd brought a paper with me, and so I was able to lose myself in the sports pages. In fact, I became so engrossed in the sport reports that the next thing I knew everything had become dark as if night had fallen. The only light now came from the glare of car headlights which were dazzling me through the bus window.

What had happened, it seems, was that despite it being the biggest thing in these parts, twice the size of Trafalgar Square and an icon of international repute, I'd only gone and missed the Dome completely. I was now speeding through the Blackwall Tunnel towards the East End.

I got off the bus with the intention of crossing the road and simply hopping on another one going in the opposite direction. It seemed a straightforward enough thing to do; how was I to know it would all go wrong? How was I to know that the 'road' at this point is the A102 (M) – the critical designation (M) signifying a clamorous six-lane highway, solid in each direction with queues of commercial traffic belching thick exhaust fumes and kicking up the sort of racket that threatens to shred your ear drums? Take it from me, you don't negotiate roads like this with the sort of quick right-left-right they teach you in the Green Cross Code.

What you have to do instead is navigate yourself up and down a series of staircases decorated with some X-rated graffiti until you emerge at a complex of traffic lights and roundabouts with roads splaying off in all directions. From here you constantly keep catching brief and tantalising glimpses of your destination as you follow a pedestrian one-way system which takes you round on yourself by such a spiralling route you eventually come to think that the only way you'll make further progress is by crawling up your own colon.

The place is extraordinary – they really should market it as the East End's answer to Hampton Court maze.

Eventually when you've reached the point of despair and you're just about to give up, sink to your knees and die, you come across a series of ramps which lead you to the opposite side of the motorway through a tiny opening in a 20-foot-high concrete wall.

This – believe it or not – is the bus stop for the 108, Greenwich direction, and it is without doubt the ugliest and most unpleasant bus stop I've ever encountered in my entire life. It's just a lay-by in an underpass with the traffic spewing crap all over you while you're forced to stand terrified, only a kerbstone from a hideous, mangled death. I can't believe that in the whole world there is any other bus stop as unpleasant as this one. It shows real signs of the sort of creative sadism which you find only very rarely anywhere nowadays, even in this country, where it sometimes seems we teach the subject as a course option in architectural schools.

Did any of the people who conceived this set-up ever spend one moment of their precious design time considering how human beings would feel using it? Did any of them ever wait for a bus there? Did they feel proud at what they'd built?

It was a freezing cold day, and with me were an elderly woman well into her seventies, and a young black guy who was late for work, judging by the way he kept looking anxiously at his watch every few moments. The buses were officially scheduled to arrive at ten-minute intervals that time of day, but it was nearer half an hour before one finally turned up – only to go flying by with its 'Not in Service' sign proudly displayed to us in the manner of a talisman intended to protect the driver from evil spirits. I must have made some involuntary cry of frustration, for the old lady smiled supportively as if to reassure me that this couldn't go on forever. The black guy pursed his lips and looked to the sky for deliverance.

It made me very angry. Angry, at the pitiful state of public transport in this city, yes; but even angrier at the stoical, uncomplaining forbearance with which people accept the situation when what they should do is riot, cause mayhem, spread civil dissent and foment revolution.

Or at least get cross and complain to someone.

But perhaps people these days are just cowed? Perhaps they don't expect better? When a bus did finally arrive, the old lady was so full of amiable chat to the driver as she climbed on that I wouldn't have been surprised if she'd invited him back to her place later for a cup of tea. Even the black guy risked a smile as he flashed his season ticket. At this stage he was no doubt so relieved that he was actually going to get to work that inside he was probably doing an ecstatic song-and-dance routine.

I just said: 'Why have we been waiting so long? Is there a problem?' And frankly, if I'd caught the Queen farting at a royal garden party I couldn't have been made to feel more embarrassed for admitting I'd noticed anything amiss. The driver looked me up and down as if I was something that he'd just picked up on the sole of his shoe. He said, 'Traffic,' as if this were some calming mantra which explained everything from the meaning of life, to Jonathan Ross's sense of humour.

I just thought, 'Sod the twenty-first century,' and I stayed on the bus and went back home.

So I never saw the Dome.

Six

SORTING OUT THE problems at home took me a week; afterwards I returned to the boat at Lower Heyford. But I'd hardly been back an hour, and had scarcely settled in, when I was beset by new trouble in the form of the Debsmobile. I was using it to drive to the supermarket to stock up with provisions when, for some unknown reason, it suddenly lost power and began to coast to a halt. Without thinking I automatically started pumping the accelerator, and it was as if something that had become disengaged became suddenly connected again, for the car surged forward with such an alarming burst of speed I thought the most sensible thing was to put my plans for shopping on hold and get to a garage as soon as possible.

Unfortunately, with the car in this state, I could see that even a journey of a mile or two might be an ambitious target, and so I turned tail and just about managed to splutter back into the boatyard before it gave up the ghost. For a moment or two I sat deflated behind the wheel, pondering my next move. Nothing was clearer to me than that the Debsmobile, now it had stopped, was not going to start again without serious professional attention. This just about took the biscuit, coming on top of the difficulties I'd had at home with the Crumbling Pile – difficulties I'd managed to address only by the application of great wads of currency to the greasy palm of some dodgy builder. I felt the world was against me, and that the car had joined the Provisional Wing of the Army of Inanimate Objects in what seemed to be a war of attrition being waged by Fate.

I lifted up the bonnet and prodded around a bit – which might have been more impressive if I'd had so much as the first idea of what I was doing. It gave an impression of expertise, though, and pretending to a know-how you don't possess is always a good strategy with a broken-down Triumph Herald since it was once such a common car that sooner or later someone who has taken the thing apart a dozen or more times is bound to appear out of the woodwork and diagnose exactly what's wrong with it.

Sure enough, after a few moments one of the engineers at the boatyard emerged from a workshop, rubbing his hands on an oily rag, which is always an infallible sign of someone who knows what they're doing. 'The main cylinder on the clutch, I should say,' he announced after a cursory glance.

'Fucked,' he added, in case I hadn't quite grasped that technical point.

'Just what I was thinking,' I nodded – a statement that, admittedly, may not have been the epitome of truthfulness, seeing as how I hadn't got the first idea of what was wrong with the car. But at least it was an opinion voiced with the right degree of professional panache, because I don't know whether you've noticed, but people who deal a lot with machinery always do nod a lot. They do a lot of spitting on the floor too. And they smoke those rancid roll-ups with wet ends which gives them an air of proficiency even if it makes you want to throw up looking at them.

Unfortunately I then blew it totally, for instead of taking off my jacket and proceeding to fix the said problem by recourse to a new main cylinder which I should have been able to produce routinely from my back pocket, I said somewhat timidly, 'I think I'll just call… er… the RAC.'

When he arrived the RAC man was absolutely delighted to see the Herald, and you can understand it really since how would you feel if you'd spent a lifetime learning how to repair cars only to wake up one morning and find they'd turned them into computers so that fixing even a jammed window needed programming skills? At least with a Triumph Herald, if something goes wrong you've a fair chance of being able to patch it up with a pipe cleaner and a blob of chewing gum.

Not this time, though. This time it was more serious. This time the car would have to go off to a garage, I was told.

'Main cylinder on the clutch,' the RAC man explained.

'Fucked,' I interjected confidently.

He nodded, spat and reached into his inside pocket for a packet of Old Holborn.

He'd got me down as a pro by then, you see.

Without a car to get me to the supermarket I was in some trouble in Lower Heyford since like most of the villages up this length of the Oxford Canal, it isn't exactly a teeming metropolis. In fact, it's not even a proper village really. Most people who live in the place either work in London and commute by rail; or they don't work at all since Lower Heyford is one of those pretty Cotswold hamlets which people retire to when they've made their pile. And so – though it has a delightful church, a quaint village green and a hundred picturesque cottages trailing honeysuckle around the door – it's only got a couple of shops. OK, this may be two more than you find in most villages, but it doesn't exactly make for massive choice or wide opportunity for culinary creativity. Especially for someone like me who fancies himself as a bit of a chef.

Even so, I managed to hunt down a chicken joint and a couple of onions so that along with some garlic and ginger left over from my last stay, and some other basic ingredients which are always kept on the boat, I was able to knock together one of my favourite meals: a sort of soul food that makes you so as you couldn't care less that your car's just been towed off to a garage where you just know you'll get a bill so steep it'll make your eyes water.

Make them water instead with the food. Try it; it's a version of a Madhur Jaffrey recipe, one of those one-pot curries which is perfect for cooking in cramped spaces and which tastes just as good in June as it does midwinter.

The Recipe
(for two people)

Skin and cut up a couple of chicken joints, and put them in a pot with a small teacup of red lentils, a roughly chopped onion and an inch-long chunk of fresh ginger, grated finely. Add a teaspoon of ground cumin and a half teaspoon of turmeric if you've got it handy (but don't worry otherwise, since its function is mainly cosmetic, making the dish look a fabulous yellow as opposed to a murky grey). Chuck a couple of sliced green chillies in there too if you have them – and if you like spicy food they're the sort of thing you should have since you can buy them fresh, and dry the ones left over.

Cover all this with about three-quarters of a pint of water into which you've crumbled a chicken stock cube. Or use genuine chicken stock if you want to be posh.

Bring to the boil and simmer for 20 to 30 minutes, ensuring that 1) the chicken cooks through so you don't kill yourself with botulism; 2) the lentil sauce in which it's cooking attains the consistency of a purée (add more water if you think it needs it, or boil some off if it's too liquidy); and 3) the sauce doesn't burn on the bottom of the pan as it's prone to do.

Stirring occasionally helps all round.

When the dish is getting near to completion, thinly slice a couple of garlic cloves and fry them in a little vegetable oil until they brown lightly. Stir them into the pot along with the oil in which they've been cooked. Sprinkle in some chilli powder according to taste, and add a handful of chopped fresh coriander leaves if you can get hold of it because it really does add to the flavour. Don't fret if you haven't, though – a bit of chopped greenery of any sort will make the dish look pretty on the plate. Serve with plain boiled rice.

Puzzling, isn't it, this love affair we English have with Indian food. It's now reached the stage where the statisticians tell us it's more popular as a takeaway meal than our own fish and chips. Sometimes I have to pinch myself to believe that I'm not dreaming, so much have the English changed in this respect over my lifetime. The word 'revolution' hardly describes it! When I was a kid, food was watery mashed potatoes and overcooked cabbage; it was bland slabs of meat fried to the consistency of leather, or stewed to a mush. The idea of eating anything spicy was an abomination, and anything with garlic would have debarred you from polite society, unless it was the reunion of some now disbanded regiment of the Raj.

In that era garlic was like olive oil: it was one of those ingredients categorised under the disparaging heading of 'foreign food' and spoken of with an instinctive repugnance, as if the term were an oxymoron. But these were the days when recipes for a 'Continental Salad' advised you to rub the bowl you were going to use with half a clove of garlic – a practice which, in Elizabeth David's immortal words, was fine if you were going to eat the salad bowl.

My parents were very much of their time, and suspicious of anything unfamiliar – which was probably why, being the cussed sort, I first got interested in cooking. An added incentive was when I woke up to the attractions of the opposite sex, for it dawned on me pretty quickly that though as a man my stomach was the quickest way to *my* heart, as far as women went, a good meal was the easiest way into *their* knickers. My mother and father probably suspected as much, since they'd always be sniffing around me apprehensively whenever I took a girlfriend out to a restaurant.

'You've not been eating any of that *smelly stuff*, have you?' my dad would always ask, reluctant even to name the offending ingredient. And then, before I could answer, my mum would add: 'You've not been forcing Liz/Susan/Judy to eat it too, have you?', as if my idea of a wild night out at this stage in my life was pinning young women to the floor and forcing garlic into their mouths. Believe me, with their prejudices I reckon my parents would have preferred me to give my girlfriends babies rather than the sort of foreign muck flavoured with an ingredient they associated less with cooking and more for its faculty to deter vampires.

My father, sadly, is dead now; but these days my mother shovels the stuff down as if it's going out of fashion. And not just in curries. Or in foreign food, either. She's addicted to the stuff and puts it in traditional English dishes like Hot Pot, and Liver and Bacon, and I swear that it's even finding its way into her breakfast cereal recently since she constantly walks around, even first thing in the morning, reeking vaporously of the Paris Metro.

It's the same with chilli. In the past the mere proximity of food to a jar of chilli powder was the signal for my mother to go pogo-ing around the table, waving at her mouth as if her sincerest desire was to wish it a speedy departure from her face. Now the most traditional of her recipes can come in what she calls 'Delhi-style', which is another way of saying it's got so much chilli in it you'll be suffering third-degree burns as part of the eating experience.

It really makes you wonder what English food actually *is*. There's a sixteenth-century village pub in Lower Heyford, a picturesque thatched building with a flagstone floor and windows which look out across the village green to the old village church and the River Cherwell. Actually, it's now more of a restaurant than a pub, and not a bad restaurant at that, except that though it would be impossible to avoid garlic in any of the food on offer, you'd be hard pressed in this most English of villages to find a genuinely English dish on the menu.

It's almost as if, having embraced food from other countries, we've devalued our native cuisine to the state where we lack any confidence that we've actually got one. And this leads to the crazy situation where supermarkets stock produce from the four corners of the earth, yet can't find shelf space for locally made pies or cheese. In France supermarkets are forced by law to stock regional cuisine, and it occurs to me that in this country the village shops which are generally at such a disadvantage against the multinationals could actually get ahead of the game for once by ensuring they offer customers the sort of choice which the big stores currently won't.

With all the angst we suffer about our fall from major world power to US bag carrier, I think we actually undervalue food as part of our national identity. Understandable, perhaps, since for us English this concept has always been confused due to our tendency to swarm all over the world without much regard for who owned it. Even so, the vaulting colonial ambition of our past doesn't dull the pride we feel when we stand on the heights of Lakeland, the Malvern Hills or the Long Mynd in Shropshire.

Why should we curl up in embarrassment at the mention of faggots, chitterlings or brawn; the Bath chap or the Bedfordshire clanger?

Maybe if we were more confident about this basic aspect of our culture then we wouldn't find it so necessary to overcompensate as we tend to do so much nowadays, whether it be throwing our weight about in meetings of the European Union out of some spurious idea that we're somehow innately better than other countries, or dismissing everything England has ever achieved from an equally bogus conclusion that we're worse.

While I waited for the car to be repaired, I moved from the boatyard around the corner to a peaceful mooring adjacent to Lower Heyford church where I found myself thinking a lot about these sorts of things. This was mainly because the weather had finally changed and it was actually pleasant enough now for me to spend the odd afternoon lying on the roof sunbathing, letting my mind wander aimlessly the way it does when you're dozing in the warmth, half asleep. I couldn't help recalling a year or two before when I'd moored at this same spot during the European football championship when England were playing in the old

Belgian city of Charleroi and thousands of young fans went on the rampage, storming drunkenly through the old medieval streets. It was hot that summer too.

Now as far as national pride goes, I lost the plot years ago; and I confess I haven't the first idea why the desire to support your national side in a football tournament should be associated with a need to pour so much lager down your throat that you finish up comatose, rolling about in your own spew.

It's the overcompensation thing again: the feeling we have as English people that we're so much the best, we've got to be the worst.

And so every morning during that most idyllic of periods, I'd be woken by the fierce sun piercing the gloom of the cabin where I slept, or by the soft rhythm of a boat gently slipping by in the early morning mists; and I'd cycle to the shop for milk and a paper, only to find, staring out at me from the tabloids, galleries of ugly, repulsive men, their faces contorted in vile rage and their bloated bellies draped obscenely with the flag of St George.

On the night before England played the 'old enemy' Germany (even that innocuous phrase pointing to the sort of coarse mentality that can't distinguish between a sporting contest and a world war), the Belgian authorities put 3,000 riot police on standby after a day which had seen tension in the town rise to the point at which everyone knew that eventually the pressure cooker would blow. And sure enough, blow it did in the old Charles II Square where so-called fans spent the build-up to the match randomly hurling beer bottles and chairs about until the long-suffering gendarmes had enough and brought out the water cannon.

I stood in the boat galley that night cooking, my own bottle of cold beer to hand, listening to events on the radio as they unfolded. Even now I don't know what I thought was most repulsive: the raw, purposeless violence that these thugs provoked, or their incoherent belly-aching about it afterwards, as if the police response to their behaviour had somehow been an infringement of their basic human rights. Really! You had to laugh.

It was the same story after English hooligans had virtually demolished the Sardinian town of Cagliari during the World Cup in 1990 when they justified their behaviour to the writer Pete Davies by saying that the Italians had provoked them.

'How did they provoke you?' Davies asked.

'Well, they was speaking Italian, wasn't they?' one explained.

The result in Charleroi was a laugh too, for the 1–0 win over Germany was really no more than a third-rate footballing nation scrabbling a nervous and scrappy victory against one of the few other sides in the tournament that was actually less talented than it was. But the victory was heralded at home as the beginning of a new renaissance of the English game, with so many references to 1966 that I wouldn't have been surprised to have heard that a re-issue of 'Yellow Submarine' had made number one in the charts.

And that photograph of the thug being led away by Belgian police, that was a laugh too.

You may remember that the papers enlarged the image of his arm on which he must have spent considerable cash and endured much pain, for in the space between his right elbow and his shoulder, he'd tattooed a large if somewhat artless map of the country with its name emblazoned underneath.

You couldn't doubt his patriotism, though you might have questioned how he defined it. All the same, you had to wonder at his ignorance.

He'd spelt it 'Great Britian'.

Just down the towpath from Heyford church, beyond Heyford Bridge where the main village road crosses the River Cherwell, is Rousham Park House, a splendid country house built for Sir Charles Dormer in the early part of the seventeenth century and amazingly still in the same family today.

It's built in the Tudor style, and the main wing has three bays, the centre one proudly crowned with a leaded cupola, and the whole thing topped with a battlemented parapet which gives the building a gracious, solid feel. Apart from the replacement of some of the original glazing by sash windows in the nineteenth century, it remains pretty much unspoiled; and since subsequent extensions have been built in the same style, there's a pleasing unity about the place which is immediately captivating.

Rousham Park House is open to the public a couple of afternoons a week throughout the summer, though the garden – which is far-and-away its best feature – is open every day. Don't expect to be pandered to, though, for when somewhere has been in the same hands for as long as this has, you can't expect many concessions to modernity. You visit the house on its own terms, not yours; and this means that Rousham is never going to be the sort of place to attract the coach parties like Blenheim, since it doesn't encourage rowdy kids chasing about disturbing its calm. In fact, it doesn't encourage kids at all, so if you're a theme park sort of family on a search for a fun experience, I'd give this one a miss since there's not so much as a café or gift shop here, let alone the hint of a white-knuckle water ride.

Instead you're invited to bring a picnic and treat the place as your own. Fortunately, not a great many people do this, so that as you wander around in isolated tranquillity, you virtually have it to yourself and can almost imagine that it *is* yours. I visited on one of those dog-day afternoons you sometimes get in June when there's hardly a breath of air to disturb the exquisite stillness of the day, and when the sun is so high in the sky it throws shadows as sharp as knives across the green, luxuriant countryside. It's only a short distance from the canal, but I cycled there, which turned out to be a good way of approaching since the extra height of a bike allows you to see over hedges and walls, and you catch tantalising glimpses of the house through the trees and across the open parkland which surrounds it.

My route took me down a narrow private lane which leads to the tiny village that is part of the Rousham estate. There's a delightful church there, with a row of bulbous close-cropped yew bushes, and there's what was once a small school, as well as a clutch of cottages which were built as homes for estate workers, and which probably still are since today Rousham is a substantial working farm around which – a final charming touch, this – wanders an impressive herd of rare-breed long horn cattle.

Such was the extent of my poor preparation for this trip that although I knew of the existence of the place, I wasn't sure that it was actually open to the public. So as I drew close to it, my approach was less as a tourist and more in the clandestine style of an intruder, with me trying to make myself as inconspicuous as possible in the hope that if I got stopped, it wouldn't be before I'd got close enough to the house to be able to say I'd seen it.

But it isn't easy to be inconspicuous riding a bike down a country lane. Especially a bike like the one I'd bought in Oxford which has so many chips and scratches on it, repaired with so many daubs of different coloured paint that Joseph's dreamcoat would be a bit on the dowdy side compared to it. Even so, imagine my surprise as I was discreetly making my way around the side of the house to be confronted by someone I couldn't even see at that point.

'Two pounds! Two pounds!' whoever it was screamed.

The voice turned out to belong to a woman who stood at the top of a small flight of steps leading up to the main door of the house. She had wild flyaway hair the colour and texture of a starched sheet, and she was wearing a shapeless Indian skirt of a 1970s vintage, with a torn grey cardigan draped across her shoulders. The most extraordinary thing, though, was that she was batting balls across the lawn with a warped wooden tennis racket for a couple of mangy Collies to retrieve. I could only imagine this was an unconventional way of exercising them. Either that or she was stark raving mad.

'Two pounds! Two pounds!' she shrieked again. And then, as if anticipating what was in my mind, she said, 'Saw you coming down the drive. Thought you looked a bit shifty. Thought you might be trying to avoid paying.'

She seemed to find this prospect intensely amusing for she broke out into a long, throaty laugh. Another tennis ball went skidding across the lawn and the dogs raced off in hot pursuit, snapping at each other as they ran and scattering in their wake two or three of the miniature chickens which I'd noticed for the first time were scratching about the grounds in great numbers.

They were very peculiar creatures. They all seemed to be wearing little pairs of flared trousers made of feathers.

'Belgian Booted Bantams,' the woman barked, making much of the explosive alliteration of the words. 'Supposed to have come over a couple of hundred years ago in a crate of furniture,' she explained. 'Been here ever since.'

Handing over my entrance fee, I wandered into the recesses of the garden, which straggles the steep bank of the River Cherwell. It isn't actually a very extensive place at all, except that it gives you the illusion that it is because it's planned to twist and turn on itself so that new and startling vistas are constantly opening up as you walk around the glades and groves. The design is the work of William Kent, who may be a household name to anyone interested in this sort of thing, but who isn't exactly up there with the Capability Browns of this world for an ordinary Joe like myself whose horticultural knowledge doesn't extend much beyond knowing the route to the local garden centre.

It's all very classical with Italianate porticoed temples and meaningful statuary of dying gladiators and the like, but it's arranged so that you keep seeing things from different angles. This is OK if you're just looking at statues, since these on the whole tend to be predictably located and not much given to ambulation. But trust me, this type of layout can be most confusing if there's anything around that *is* actually moving.

So I thought there'd been a job-lot of flowery blue skirts and cavalry twill trousers on sale locally until finally it began to occur to me that the retired couple who were sauntering around the pond must have been the same couple I'd seen on the terrace, and the self-same pair that moments before I'd glimpsed close to the Cold Bath.

Since in the confusion of the garden's twisting paths these three places seemed too far away from each other for this to have happened in the same time frame, the whole manifestation verged so much on the miraculous that a man of more mystical bent than me might have confided in others about what he'd seen and ended up a guru as a result.

But the Cold Bath, I hear you saying? The Cold Bath?

OK. Imagine a small pond. But deep. Fed by a tiny stream in a gully a few inches wide, and so deliciously cool and clear that on a day like this with the temperature in the eighties you feel drawn to throw off your clothing and plunge into it. But in winter? Covered in ice? Brrrrr! Gaze upon it with foreboding, and recognise how much hardier than you were your forebears.

Or recognise how much of a soft-centred namby-pamby you've become.

Because along with the increasing use of garlic in cooking and the inexorable rise and rise of curry as a national dish, the propensity of the English to act like cosseted infants whenever the temperature falls sufficiently to require them to wear a sweater is one of those contemporary social developments that makes me realise that at 50 years of age I wasn't just brought up in a different world, but on a totally different planet. Where I came from the idea of central heating was so totally alien that in the mornings as a kid I had to scratch the ice off the inside of my bedroom window in order to see just how bad the weather was going to be that day.

Can you imagine that happening on Planet Millennium where the mere act of opening an outside door is more often that not the signal for the young of the species to fall over themselves to get to the nearest radiator? This isn't just an age thing either, for friends in my own peer group have now got so sensitive to any slight temperature variation that they rip their houses about to install vast quantities of insulation, double glazing and draughtproofing in an attempt to exclude every last vestige of fresh air from their lives, the presence of which they seem to treat as a personal violation of their space.

I can't understand what on earth has happened to us as a nation recently that we feel the need to mollycoddle ourselves like this. Time was when England had a reputation that was the envy of the world for its cold and draughty houses, its appalling plumbing and its doughty disregard for the benefits of hot water. And did it do us any harm apart from the odd bout of pneumonia and a poor international reputation for personal hygiene?

The trouble is that we just don't realise how high our present standard of living is, and how much it's improved. If we did, maybe we'd value it more.

Years ago, when I was working as a journalist in Manchester, they dug up the remnants of what had once been an abbey crypt where they found the tomb of someone they believed had died in the twelfth or thirteenth century. Inside – probably a result of the unusual nature of the soil, though I don't think they knew for sure – they were astonished to find the body of a man who was perfectly preserved except for a small amount of decomposition around one foot. He was maybe 35 to 40 years old, probably a man of some substance, judging by his burial place. Perhaps even a knight. But what particularly excited curiosity about him was a flap of skin, three or four inches wide, resting on the top of his inside leg. This was so puzzling they carted him off and had the coroner do a post-mortem on him before he fell to bits.

Funny how sometimes in this country history leaps out at you from beyond the grave, and strange too that when it does you discover more that links you to the past than separates you from it. They cut open Sir Rotfoot's stomach, from which they could conclude with some confidence that the morning of his death he'd breakfasted on oats and dried grapes – a sort of medieval muesli. This confirmed my prejudice that it's the health food freaks who always die first, though to be fair, this man's demise was less to do with his diet than it was with his neck, which he seemed to have broken after taking a fall travelling at high speed.

This was hardly a case for Hercule Poirot since at this period in history there weren't many ways of travelling faster than walking pace. Sir Rotfoot had obviously had a riding accident.

Yet the strange flap of skin on the top of his leg, they concluded, was the remains of a badly swollen testicle. A swollen testicle? A badly swollen one?

And he was riding a horse…?

As a bloke this is the sort of thing that makes you want to cross your legs in company. But even unsympathetic women might see the point I'm trying to make, because during the post-mortem they also discovered a hole in the side of his face, the result of a tooth abscess that had eaten its way to the surface.

Probably no more than an infected cavity, I was told. The sort of thing you could deal with by a routine trip to the dentist today.

I had a far more comfortable journey cycling back to the boat from Rousham Park House on what was a perfect summer's evening, still and balmy with the failing light gentle and luminous above the fields, and choruses of wood pigeons softly serenading me as I passed. I took an indirect, meandering route, and, in one of the villages I passed, I stopped for a couple of pints of Hook Norton bitter, which I drank gazing through the bar window as a perfectly spherical, shimmering gold sun sank behind the horizon.

Mind you, it had turned a bit chilly by the time I got back so I had to give the central heating a bit of a blast before going off to bed…

Seven

A FEW YEARS AGO you'd have moved heaven and earth to avoid staying on a boat a moment longer than you had to in Lower Heyford or its sister village Upper Heyford, a mile or so north up the canal. The waterways guidebooks literally warned against it, and there were signs posted along the towpath for those rash enough not to take them seriously. Nevertheless, every so often you used to hear of people who'd stopped there for an afternoon nap, or worse, attempted to moor there overnight.

Their lives were never the same again.

Never mind that beforehand a person might have been one of those impassive, steely-nerved types who become Olympic marksmen or bomb disposal experts: afterwards they'd mutate into excitable hysterics – the sort who go for a high jump record whenever anyone inadvertently startles them. The kind that look at you as if you're Hannibal Lecter when you approach them on the street to ask directions.

You can blame the Americans for this. Until just a few years ago Upper Heyford was home to a massive United States airforce base and its fleet of F1-11 supersonic fighters. In fact, it was one of the bases that in 1986 was used to launch the attack on Tripoli from which the Libyan leader Colonel Qaddafi only just escaped with his life. Which is a strange thing to contemplate, and as good a demonstration as I can cite of how small a world it is we live in; for as you quietly slip past the village and navigate Allen's Lock, which is really the only thing that identifies the place from the canal, it's difficult to believe there could be anything conceivably linking this sleepy, secluded Oxfordshire hamlet with the hot and dusty North African capital.

Yet it's the reason you never stayed around this area. It stands to reason really, since the skills an airman needs to reduce Tripoli to rubble inside a couple of hours aren't ones you get sitting in bars drinking Bud and popping pretzels; so when the base was operational, pilots would be out most days honing up their technique with an enthusiasm that took the Anglo-American relationship to a new level.

Such a close level, in fact, that they'd fly over this part of the world taking the heads off the daisies. It was bad enough if they buzzed you during the daytime while you were cruising, since you sort of half expected it. And anyhow, they travelled at such speed that they'd be gone before you knew it – even if they did leave your ears resonating in their wake for hours afterwards. But the worse thing was if you *weren't* expecting it, and much worse by far was if you'd been incautious enough to moor for the night and were maybe asleep, so that the shock of the experience could leave your nerves very badly affected.

Not to mention your bed linen in need of laundering.

I often used to wonder whether the pilots were actually aware of the boats and whether they were playing games with us. After all, it must get pretty boring skimming across the top of the world so fast your face distorts. Much more entertaining surely is to pass the time with amusing diversions – *Enemy narrowboat armed and proceeding at 7 o'clock. Request permission to attack* – that sort of thing? But then I met a man who knew about these things, and he told me that those babies (by which I take it he meant the F1-11s) travelled so fast that even if they were looking out for a boat and spotted one, they'd be over Belgium before they could react to it. Which struck me as logical enough, but still didn't go any way to explaining how the Americans ever thought they could take out Colonel Qaddafi by the pinpoint bombing of downtown Tripoli, which is pretty much what they were claiming they could do in 1986.

Ah well, I'm no military man; and America, like the God it often plays, sometimes moves in mysterious ways.

For all I know the decision to stop regular flying from Heyford could have undermined the very security of the western world, but I was still delighted when it happened, for it re-established this section of the canal as one of the quietest and most rural stretches of its whole route; and in particular it made it possible once more to tie up overnight peacefully at Somerton Deep Lock, which to my mind is the epitome of a perfect waterways mooring, and a place I've stayed so often I've probably got squatters' rights if I was ever to assert them.

The lock, four miles or so north of Upper Heyford, takes its name from nearby Somerton village, and it lies in the shallow valley where the River Cherwell and the canal are so close together they're only separated by a narrow water meadow. It's a beautiful spot with a view that in any other country in the world would be called spectacular, except that in England a vista only ever merits that description if it's associated with gradient and mountains and tracts of high forest. Yet in its own way the gentle 360-degree patchwork panorama of undulating pastureland that you see from Somerton Deep Lock is just as breathtaking.

A simple cottage adjacent to the lock is the only sign of civilisation – but far from detracting in any way from the attractiveness of the spot, it adds to it, dovetailing into the landscape naturally as if it's always been there and was always meant to be. It's an example of what has recently been given the grand name 'vernacular architecture' – which is just another way of saying that it's the sort of unconsciously elegant design that was created by people whose first concern was to build houses people could live in, and who just happened to formulate their style as a by-product.

This is very different to contemporary architects who set out to devise a style first. And finish up building places no one in their right minds would want to live in.

This should be given a grand name too: it should be called 'crap architecture', which is what it is.

The cottage at Somerton is a very simple two-storey structure, but built higher than you might expect, and with eaves at a steeper angle to make it seem deceptively bigger and more dominant than it otherwise would. A lot of canal architecture is attractively functional like this. The old warehouses, for instance, which are almost classical in form; the maintenance yards, which sometimes take your breath away with their overall harmony; or even the charming but commonplace humpback bridges which crop up all over the country.

As far as I know the lock cottage at Somerton, being so remote, still has no mains electricity, and is still lit as it has been for years by a 12-volt system powered by a wind vane. There used to be no mains running water either, and what fell onto the roof was collected in large butts. In those days the place was totally self-sufficient, since like a lot of houses in the country it wasn't attached to the sewers either, and all its waste 'grey' water went straight into the canal and everything else into a cesspit.

For many years, despite its remoteness and lack of mod cons, it was occupied by a couple in their fifties who used to work in London. Since there's no road anywhere close, they used to moor a skiff with an outboard motor below the lock, and they used this to cruise to the nearest bridge where they kept their car. If ever you moored at Somerton – and there was a period I could never travel up the Oxford Canal without spending a night or two there – you'd see them when they got back, for on fine evenings they'd invariably take a walk along the towpath to unwind from their day in the city. What was remarkable about them was that they'd always be accompanied by three or four enormous cats, which would follow at their heels like spaniels, and which would even answer to their names the way dogs do.

They were fearsome brutes, these creatures: not your normal sort of domestic moggie. They were the size of small Rottweilers, and they apparently had the same sort of temperament as well, since I was told once that whereas your normal cat might occasionally aspire to the odd mouse as a reminder of its feral past, these three would be satisfied with nothing less than the ferocious mink that populate these parts and which they'd hunt down in a pack. One of them was said to have chased and killed a fox totally on its own – which I can actually believe. Trust me, if you stood around for too long exchanging pleasantries with its owner, you could sense it sizing up your leg with the sort of rapt attention that cats normally reserve for cans of Whiskas.

Unfortunately for the character of the canals, if not for the continuing survival of Oxfordshire wildlife, both cats and owners left Somerton a few years back, probably forced out by the floods that regularly swamp the countryside here and which can't exactly make commuting a reliable business. The area was still in flood from the spring rains when I passed, and I didn't feel comfortable stopping, so I pressed on a few more miles to Aynho Weir Lock where the canal and the river, after having carried on a flirtatious on-off affair for so long, now consummate their relationship in a brief and passionate union as they cross at right angles.

It's another delightful spot, and an unusual one too. Eighteenth-century canal engineers were building arterial highways for haulage transportation, and they didn't trust the unpredictability of rivers which they kept away from as far as they could, so that this sort of coming together only happens at one or two places on the system. The lock here is odd as well: it's a lozenge shape, designed to feed a greater volume of water from the river into the canal in order to aid water supply, which was always one of the constant problems facing the early canal architects. Nowadays the lock itself is the problem, or at least it is to boaters – especially single-handed ones in craft more than 50-foot long which for some reason always seem either to get slewed across the chamber and jammed against the odd angle of the walls, or trapped approaching or leaving the lock against an inconveniently high wooden rubbing-strake that's there to stop you getting swept into the river. Either way, getting through Aynho Weir is a bitch and requires a rare combination of intellectual acumen and brute force.

So my tip if you ever get stuck there is not to panic. Don't automatically rev the engine up as high as you can in the hope you can somehow force your way against the natural elements. Instead, take stock of the angle at which you're jammed and the relevant counter forces which the boat engine will create against the rudder. Consider whether the propeller might be fouled. Examine whether you're caught in the cross current, or held by wind, or somehow impeded by floating detritus under the water. See if the brass on the boat is clean. Water the plants. Floss your teeth.

Then rev the engine up as much as you can. More often than not you'll find the problem has solved itself.

Otherwise you could try screaming at the boat: 'Come on, you bastard, move… MOVE!' is a favourite of mine. Or alternatively: 'Shift, you useless heap of moribund pig iron! SHIFT!' – something of that sort. It may not help you get away from the lock any quicker – certainly not as quickly as a more powerful engine would. But it'll certainly make you look butch, and who knows but that that itself might make you happier, depending on how you're feeling about yourself at the time.

We single-handed boaters have to develop specialist techniques like this to make up in shrewdness what we lack in… well, what we lack by being stupid enough to cruise single-handed and not have anyone with us to help us when we get stuck in places like Aynho Weir Lock. On your own even the most mundane of tasks – things you'd hardly think about with someone else on board – can become major logistical operations.

Take tea-making, for instance. Normally as a bloke this is an easy one. You just bark out a demand to the nearest female in the sort of confident manner you use when you're a pig who rules the world. But even as a woman, getting a cup of tea on a boat is not difficult since you just fix a bloke in your gaze, lower your voice an octave or two and start to whine through your nose, adding the word 'luv' to everything you say.

That's 'luv' as in 'Make us a cup of tea, luv,' or 'I could murder a cuppa, luv.'

Cruising on your own, though, there's nothing for it but to stop the boat, moor up and put the kettle on. Except that if you're under way and making good time, or if you can't moor because it's too shallow – well, then there's no alternative but to brew up on the move, which is a tricky little operation requiring the right knack.

We used to have a boat where the cooker was just a step or two under the steering position so you could leave the boat to its own devices for as long as it took to rush downstairs, fill a kettle and strike a match. The worst you risked was a bad bout of embarrassment if you crashed into the bank while a fisherman was watching you. With *Justice*, though – being altogether a grander and larger vessel – the kettle and teapot are in the front cabin nearly 50 feet away, so the technique you have to use is to gradually slow the boat down, bringing it to a halt in mid-stream. Then you have to run up the narrow side gunnels as fast as you can before the wind, or the current, or what's left of your momentum, drives you off course; or worse, before some other vessel appears from around the bend to find this inland *Marie Celeste* blocking the way ahead.

Take it from me, this is not an easy manoeuvre – and sometimes it hardly seems worth it just for a cup of tea. I mean, you can live without a cup of tea, can't you?

But what do you do when you're desperate for the toilet?

Of course, for a woman travelling alone – and under some circumstances, for men – there's no alternative except to stop the boat, moor up and do the whole business properly. But if you're a bloke and just need a pee, then there's too much of a temptation to cut corners. Certainly, I don't know many men cruising on their own through the middle of the countryside who won't try it on the move, regardless of the fact that they're attempting to control a urine flow and 20 tons of solid steel at the same time.

It's hubris; and it's a recipe for disaster.

Even in the middle of nowhere, miles from civilisation, you can count on the fact that at the very moment you're relieving your bursting bladder, you'll be disturbed by some farmer's daughter out riding, or by a gaggle of ramblers on a country walk. Tell me, why is it that ramblers always seem to be inexorably cheerful people? And why is it that they always seem to come down to the towpath on the blind side of a bridge? You may think that because canal boats move gracefully and slowly, so do those navigating them; but let me tell you that there is nothing in the world that moves faster and with less elegance than a single-handed helmsman caught short at the tiller with his privates on parade.

It was getting on a bit by now – gone eight o'clock in fact, and way beyond the point where I should have found a mooring for the night. By now I was close to Kings Sutton, which is a devil of a place to get to from the canal, but which is a remarkably picturesque village scattered with clusters of thatched cottages fringing a wide green. At one end there's a pub, and at the other a handsome church which has a main spire buttressed by four smaller ones that give it the appearance of a space rocket. It used to be a favourite overnight mooring spot of mine, but sadly not any more. Picturesque or not, tying up at Kings Sutton you now face the same sort of discomforts you once did at Lower Heyford – except that the problem here isn't the noise from American planes but the din from our home-grown M40 which at this point skirts so close to the canal that it's like cruising up the central reservation.

It's heartbreaking really because as you approach Kings Sutton from the south, there's what used to be an ideal mooring spot on a bend opposite a lush meadow where an old oak tree spreads lazily across the towpath. Many's the afternoon I've spent there stretched out on the roof of one boat or another, shielding my eyes against the hot summer sunshine listening to the cricket or the tennis on the radio. Many's the evening I've spent with friends sipping chilled wine while the smells of the barbecue fused with the heavy scents of the evening air.

Gone. All gone now in the name of progress. Like the peace of the Birmingham and Fazely Canal as it edges towards Staffordshire, shattered by the roaring M42. Like the calm of the Trent and Mersey Canal, fractured by the A38 thundering towards Burton upon Trent. Like the aching serenity that was once the River Soar in Leicestershire until they upgraded the A6 and destroyed the whole valley. Gone. All gone for the sake of ten minutes or so off a journey between some ugly conurbation and another, from one no-hope suburb to the next.

Cruising the canals – which is surely the slowest way of travelling anywhere – I've often found myself musing about what happens to all these saved minutes of motorway time. There'd be hope for the future, wouldn't there, if all these movers and shakers of the modern world were to spring from their BMWs to devise new and better systems of justice or more equitable financial structures to rid us of poverty and obliterate hunger and disease? But don't you just know in your heart of hearts that they'll be flopping in front of the box like the rest of us once they've got home, so exhausted at the stress of their journey they'll need twice the time they've saved just to recover from it?

I did think about mooring in the old spot, but I knew I wouldn't be able to sleep through the incessant growling of traffic, and so I pressed on for a mile or so further on to Twyford Bridge. But even there the wind was in the wrong direction, carrying the sound my way, so that there was this annoying low burr in the air which was even worse, since it was as if some demented insect was flying around inside my head.

It was the same at Grants Lock another couple of miles further on where there once used to be the prettiest of cottages in the middle of nowhere. It was leased for a long time to the wife of a London MP, but it now stands empty, boarded up and vandalised – so dominated by the motorway and so polluted by noise that it was all but abandoned years ago. In fact, the sad situation at the moment is that a stretch of canal which the guidebooks once described as amongst the prettiest and most rural of the whole

British canal system has been so sacrificed to the motorcar that there isn't a decent rural mooring to be had in the 11 miles between Aynho and Cropredy.

Oh well, you might think cynically, not much of a world crisis there, then.

But surely you don't have to feel particularly concerned about boats, or canals, or even Oxfordshire, to see that something fundamental and irreplaceable is being gradually lost here? Take it from me, for I've seen it pottering around the waterways year after year at 3mph: this destruction has been duplicated in a thousand different places in a thousand different ways over the last twenty years. An ugly new estate here, a by-pass there; a formless concrete bridge in one place, a vile new supermarket somewhere else.

Surely if we're concerned to any degree about the landscape of England as we take our first few faltering steps in the new millennium, then it must be apparent that we're not so well endowed with beauty spots in this overcrowded island of ours that we can afford to lose what few we have in the surreptitious and dispassionate way that has happened? And surely it must be apparent that the gentrification of the countryside that so often passes for conservation in this day and age is really no substitute while so much of the day-to-day fabric of our nation disintegrates under stress from the modern commercial world?

I've seen too much of this sort of thing on the canals – the creation of a sort of national theme park, a *Reader's Digest* England where certain segments are designated as 'areas of outstanding beauty' or 'sites of special interest'; parks that lie across the land like so many sterilised, lifeless laboratory specimens – while the rest of the country's left so much to its own devices that even when our most common species of flowers and birds are threatened by pollution and overdevelopment no one seems to give a damn.

Eventually I finished up mooring in Banbury town centre, just above Banbury lock. It was dark when I arrived, and I was somewhat startled as I was tying up to catch sight of a shadowy figure standing against a wall watching me. It was a man in his twenties, perhaps a little older. Once my eyes had adjusted I could make out a dog at his feet which I concluded he must have been taking for a walk before I'd arrived to distract him.

'Bit late to be boating,' he said.

I smiled and nodded noncommittally in the sort of way designed not to encourage conversation. I didn't want to be rude, but the fact was, I was tired. I'd much rather have been inside with my feet up. I'd much rather have been halfway through a bottle of beer.

'Come far?' he asked.

Still fiddling with my ropes, I grunted something which at first I didn't think he could have heard for he launched himself into a nostalgic eulogy on the beauty of the route I'd just travelled. It took me a while before the penny dropped. When it did, I realised with a shock that he knew that section of the canal very well, very well indeed. Not because he'd ever cruised it himself, or even walked it; but because he'd seen bits of it a hundred times as he'd thundered towards Oxford in his car.

'Surprised you've decided to stop here,' he said at length.

'Here?'

'Well, you know, in a town. After passing through all that country, I mean. It's... well, it's a bit of a noisy place to stop, isn't it?'

And at that moment, as if to give force to what he was saying, a massive bread lorry turned at a nearby set of traffic lights, making the boat vibrate as it changed gear.

Yes, there was no denying it: Banbury *was* noisy.

But at least you *expect* a town to be that way.

Eight

So AFTER ALL THAT SOUL searching about where this trip should start, I'd finally washed up in Banbury, where it should have begun in the first place. Mind you, when I woke up the next day it didn't *seem* like Banbury. It had been at least a year – longer – since I'd been back, and as I gingerly prised open the front doors of the boat and poked my nose into the morning sunshine, I was regaled with the somewhat startling sight of a massive new shopping centre which in the interim they'd built opposite the lock. It was so close to where I was moored I could read the bargain offers on the price tags in Woollies.

Well, that's Cherwell Council for you.

Cherwell Council has a complex relationship with the Oxford Canal. Firstly, as the local authority that covers Banbury, it's responsible for a town that owes a massive debt to this waterway which once brought it untold prosperity. Secondly, for years now it's given every impression of hating the canal and everything to do with it.

Well, I call that a complex relationship. I certainly don't understand it anyway.

In the late 1700s when they were building the canal as a route through to the River Thames and London, the promoters underestimated their costs and ran out of money when they reached the town; and so for 12 years it ended at a basin near the centre. This was the municipal equivalent of winning the lottery. In no time at all the place became a busy inland port which prospered beyond anyone's wildest imagination; and the town soon had to expand to accommodate it, so that there was a great deal of construction of mill buildings, warehouses, and labourers' cottages. Canal basins like this aren't uncommon in towns, and they can often provide the focus for urban renewal, as they have in Wigan, or on a larger scale in Birmingham and Manchester where whole new districts of cafés and restaurants have been fashioned out of what was until recently just derelict land.

Not in Banbury, though. In Banbury they filled in the basin years ago. To build a bus station.

This imaginative spark of town planning didn't exactly bode well for the canal when the idea for a shopping centre was first mooted, especially since some of the early proposals for the development would have threatened the small dock which for more than two centuries had been located in the town. It was known as Tooley's, this dock, after the Tooley family who'd bought it in 1900 from a man called Chard who'd got it from a family called Neal who'd bought it in 1864 from Benjamin Roberts who'd acquired it from someone called Evans who'd been running it since the 1790s when it was first built.

History notwithstanding, you got the sense that Cherwell Council would have preferred to have bulldozed the place along with the basin, except that it was listed as an historic monument and protected.

When I first went to Banbury, Herbert Tooley – Bert, as he was known; the son of George Tooley who'd bought the dock at the turn of the century – was still living on the site in a small, shabby caravan. You'd see him sometimes pottering about, an old man stooped with age and not in the best of health; though he always seemed contented, and determined to die where he'd lived and worked for most of his life. The place then was still a focus for anyone in the area with an interest in boats or inland waterways. It wasn't just that it was a working dock – one of the precious few where there was still the surviving equipment and expertise to repair old wooden boats – but it was also something of a shrine to the survival of the waterways, for it was at Tooley's that Tom and Angela Rolt fitted out *Cressy* before the honeymoon cruise of *Narrow Boat*, and it was there they kept returning whenever the boat needed repairs.

So it was natural then that they should plan to drop in there briefly during the winter of 1939 as they were taking the boat to Hungerford in Berkshire, where Tom had at last managed to get another job that allowed him to leave the hated Rolls-Royce. His new work was in a foundry, and though it paid less than half what he'd been earning, the priority for him at that stage was to get away from the nightmare of factory life which had ground him down so much. The visit to Banbury was only scheduled to be a short maintenance stop, but in the event it lasted far longer than anyone could have predicted. The weather turned cold very suddenly and *Cressy* became trapped in thick ice which was to paralyse the whole waterways system for months on end.

Tom had begun writing *Narrow Boat* during the honeymoon cruise, provisionally entitling it *Painted Ship* from the reference in Coleridge's *Ancient Mariner*; but he'd found it impossible to carry on with the project while he was working and had laid it aside. Now, though, with time on his hands, he returned to it with a new enthusiasm, writing through the long winter evenings at the desk he had built in the cabin specially for this purpose. Sometimes he read what he'd done to Angela. 'Very occasionally I would make a tiny suggestion or criticism,' she commented years afterwards. 'They were not well received.'

The enforced stop in Banbury gave Tom a perfect opportunity for sustained work: when he left in March 1940 the book was all but finished except for a concluding chapter or two. Angela has left us a description of him working on *Cressy*, hunched over his desk, his face creased in concentration, tapping away fast and fluently at his typewriter using just two fingers. Occasionally he'd get stuck and sit 'chain smoking, lighting one cigarette after another until suddenly the words flowed again'.

Reading her account of Tom at work – brief though it is – always sets my imagination racing and I picture them at Tooley's where in my mind's eye it's always a cloudless frosty night, and there's always a hazy winter moon casting a pale light over the ice, highlighting the thin pall of smoke which hangs over the basin from the chimneys of *Cressy* and the other boats moored there. Sometimes it's almost as if I can feel the acrid coal which is burning in the boat stoves, and which is bitter in my throat; but it's mixed with other sweeter smells too – the odour of different woods: the almonds of rich elm and the sweet resins of pine which are drifting up from the dock.

At first, so quiet is it, and so dark, I think it must be midnight, or maybe even later; but then I become aware for the first time of the clamour of the town which seems so far away, even though it's so close; and I catch fragments of drifting conversation from women in headscarves queuing for buses. Gradually it begins to dawn on me that it must be earlier than I think. I hear the deep, hollow echo of a caulking hammer ringing against the planking of a boat. It is coming from the dock where men are still at work, so that finally I realise with a faint yet disturbing sense of disorientation that it's still only the afternoon, not yet five o'clock and maybe even earlier...

Actually, it wasn't much past seven in the morning but I realised as soon as I stuck my head out of the boat that I wasn't going to be able to get much of a lie-in that day, for the shopping centre wasn't completely finished yet and workmen were still swarming all over the place, banging and crashing together anything that looked as if it might raise the general sound level a decibel or two. I washed, threw on some clothes and walked over to examine the new development, which I'm pleased to report was nothing like as awful as I'd anticipated. Even Tooley's turned out better than I thought it would, since after a good deal of protest the planners eventually conceded to it being kept as a working boatyard, albeit a somewhat unusual one in that it's clean and orderly and covered with an ugly framework that makes it look like a greenhouse. At the time I visited it was being incorporated into a new museum over the other side of the canal; and there were plans to connect it by a modernistic bridge.

Tom Rolt would have hated it. I think he would have found its orderliness too antiseptic. OK, the old place was always a bit of a mess: a sort of cross between a junkyard and a back-street garage. Yet for all that, it was comforting and reassuring, and spoke of another, kinder world governed by a different set of values than those of today.

When I visited what was then the current museum up by the famous Banbury Cross I didn't detect any wild enthusiasm for the new dock development, let alone the new museum. Apart from the fact the latter would probably incorporate posher toilets and maybe a staff canteen, I got the impression that people working there would have been just as happy to have left things as they were. But then maybe it's characteristic of museum staff that they should want to leave things as they are. Perhaps it's in their job description. Anyhow, they were helpful enough to me – remarkably so, given my curmudgeonly request to be allowed to look at pictures of old Banbury since it seemed to me there wasn't much of the real thing left to see.

Sadly, although the museum was fully aware of how important the Oxford Canal once was to the town, and aware too of how crucial Tom Rolt was to the survival of contemporary waterways, it didn't for a long time have any pictorial record of the area around the canal as it used to be when Tom and Angela Rolt were moored there that first winter of the war. Luckily, though, only a short time before I arrived, someone had walked in off the street and donated a set of old black and white photographs of the area taken around the period. They'd been shot with nothing more distinguished than a box Brownie, but you could see by the value ascribed to them by the staff that they'd been pounced upon as if they'd been Daguerre originals.

In the old days, the area adjacent to the canal on the town side was a confusing maze of small streets lined with higgledy-piggledy workshops and warehouses, two- and three-storeys high

– most of them dating, I guess, from Georgian or early Victorian times. Factory Street, where Tooley's was, led from the Market Square to where a lift bridge crossed the canal. It was an extremely narrow thoroughfare – so remarkably constricted that Tom Rolt even commented on it in *Narrow Boat*.

So it wasn't as if I had no mental picture of the place…

Even so, back at the boat, examining copies of the photographs closely for the first time, I was still astonished at the gulf that existed between my imagination and the reality. Factory Street was narrow all right – but much narrower than I'd thought. In fact, it was more like an alleyway than a street – no wider than a car in places. And yet I'd always known it was like that. Why should it have surprised me so much to see pictures of it? Suddenly my mind began racing once more as I played over every scene I could recall that had ever taken place there, painfully struggling to re-impose the characters of my imagination onto their new environment.

There was one photograph in particular that I couldn't stop staring at: a picture taken looking down the street, past Tooley's and the row of half a dozen workmen's cottages which used to stand adjacent to it – one of them, incidentally, where the Tooley family had once lived. It dated from sometime in the early 1960s, later than the other pictures, and not long before the area was demolished. The cottages are virtually derelict and some of the upstairs windows are swinging open so that you can just about make out the ragged edges of broken glass clinging to the surviving frames. Downstairs some of the windows haven't even got frames and have been ripped out; and the vandals have even pulled away parts of the wall underneath, revealing raw courses of brickwork which gape at you like open wounds.

There was something about this image I found oddly compelling. Yes, the mental picture I had of Factory Street wasn't entirely divorced from the reality of what Factory Street was; but the reality as depicted in the photograph was nevertheless a different sort of reality. Like all photographs, it was a moment frozen in time; a single instant in the infinity which surrounded it. But this gave it a strange and melancholic quality that obsessed me in a way I can't account for fully even now.

It was taken in bright sunlight, and the poor contrast this created makes the image difficult to discern entirely, since the foreground is dark and slashed with ominous shadow, while the brightness of the background burns out the detail of the lower part of the street in a sort of ghostly, blanched hue.

Perhaps its irresistibility for me was that it caught Factory Street at the very point of its demise, for within – what, a month or two? – there can't have been much of it left, and today no remnant of it survives at all; and the street, like the era in which it was paradoxically the very focus of the future, has gone forever.

Or perhaps it's the lift bridge that preoccupies me? You can just about make out its balance beams at the bottom of the street, beckoning you like a pair of open arms. I can never think of that lift bridge without sadness for eventually it was to become the setting for the final act of Angela and Tom's relationship – the very spot where she finally left him and where their idealistic dreams of an alternative lifestyle ended in what must have been heartbreak for them both.

The two of them must have crossed over that bridge a thousand times during that first winter of the war when they were trapped in Banbury by the ice. They'd struck up a friendship with an old boatman called Alfred Hone who was moored with his wife immediately opposite, so the bridge would have been the quickest and most obvious path between them. It's been rebuilt recently as part of the redevelopment, but for years there was nothing to mark it except the narrowing of the stonework of the towpath where it used to be.

Coincidentally it was there that I moored *Justice* on my second night in the town.

And a strange night it was too, very disturbed and restless. I'd not turned in until late, my mind burdened under the weight of where I was, troubled with so many imaginings of half-remembered fragments of events of long ago that I tossed and turned until the early hours, unable to sleep. When I finally did, I fancy I must have dreamt about Tom and Angela. I certainly recollect listening intently to some mundane exchange between a man and a woman I took to be them. It was about food, or shopping, or something like that. But then the conversation was suddenly an argument, and there were raised voices, and harsh words, and I heard an angry tearful outburst – though despite the volume, I couldn't understand what was being said as clearly now, and I certainly couldn't understand what had provoked this clash between them. For some reason it made me unaccountably anxious, as if the antagonism between them was being directed at me.

Eventually I woke. I sat up suddenly and abruptly, and I immediately became aware that my dream was actually real – or real in the sense that the voices were real and the argument was real. It seemed to be coming from the towpath, immediately outside the boat. Yet strangely, when I peered out of the windows into the gloom of a night illuminated only by the eerie sodium glow of streetlights, there was no one at all on the towpath. The only people around were two young people – but they were on the *other* side of the canal some distance away. Seeing them was unnerving enough though at that time in the morning, when in normal circumstances when you wouldn't expect anyone to be up.

They were standing against the water's edge in the pallid night-time shadow of the new development, a man and a woman who seemed to be in their early twenties – though in the gloom I couldn't make them out clearly enough to be certain. All I could really be sure of was that before – immediately after I'd woken – I'd heard something that sounded like a disagreement between a man and a woman; but that now the only man and woman in sight were not where I'd heard them and were anyhow silent. They were facing each other eye to eye and playing out some strange, dumb mime which seemed to involve the slow and mystifying movement of their limbs like a t'ai chi dance.

Strange, very strange. Eventually I went back to bed but I couldn't sleep again for a long time, turning things over in my mind. What I'd seen must have been some trick of the light. And maybe what I'd heard was just the distortion of sound, since I'm sure I've read somewhere that this can sometimes happen around water.

I must have dropped off finally, for the next thing I knew it was morning, and the workmen were getting into percussion mode again…

Sadly, Banbury's decision to sacrifice its canal basin for a bus station wasn't untypical of the place. The town dates from Saxon times, but there are few buildings today which are much older than the seventeenth century, so one way or another a lot of Banbury's been replaced over the years, including its famous cross, which is a Victorian replacement for one pulled down in a fit of Puritan zeal during the Reformation. I grant you, you can hardly blame the council for this. Or for two Civil War sieges which left its castle in ruins. Even so, it doesn't say a lot for Banbury's civic pride that the residents pulled down what was left of the stonework to rebuild their damaged houses.

Mind you, that's not untypical either. People in Banbury just don't seem as concerned about their past as people elsewhere. In the eighteenth century they even blew up their parish church rather than spend money restoring it.

Predictably, given the importance it ascribes to such things, Banbury's new shopping centre incorporates a replacement bus station – which is a good deal more attractive than the old one was. Mind you, it would have been difficult for anything *not* to have been more attractive than the old one. Indeed, the only thing that could be said in favour of the old bus station – apart from the fact that it was the best place in Banbury to catch a bus – was that it had a café which served a formidable mug of tea.

Soon after *Justice* was built, when she was no more than a steel shell, we ballasted her at Tooley's after having had a couple of tons of paving stones delivered from a nearby garden centre. It was tough work which involved manhandling the slabs one by one onto the boat up a narrow gangplank. In the specialist jargon of the inland waterways this is known as 'a bastard of a job'; and Em and I wouldn't have had a hope in hell of surviving it but for the sustenance afforded by the regular input of bus station tea. A friend had offered to help us, but in the event he only turned up at the last moment – and promptly ricked his back so badly we had to call an ambulance to cart him off to casualty. I spent most of that evening with him gripping my hand in pain, apologising profusely for the trouble he was causing me.

Unfortunately, with the old bus station demolished, if you want a good cup of tea in Banbury you are constrained to explore the cafés in the centre of the town where the general tendency is to serve you delicate china cups of hot water with bags of wood shavings floating in them. Or worse, delicate china cups of hot water *without* the bags of wood shavings. Actually there is one place in Banbury where you can still get a fortifying cuppa, but it's brewed to such industrial strength you can feel the enamel dissolving on your teeth as you sip it.

It's tucked away in a back street which I had some difficulty finding, because recently – like most English market towns – Banbury has become almost unrecognisable in the summer due to the outbreak around April or May every year of that pernicious disease *geraniumitis*, the main symptom of which is the appearance of a rash of brightly coloured bedding plants on every accessible inch of civic space. In its earliest manifestations, this condition was most apparent in concentrations of inconvenient pavement tubs, placed about knee height and ingeniously positioned to catch your shins as you were passing. Recently, though, the contagion has shown an alarming tendency to spread upwards, with plants at first colonising low walls and window sills, or indeed any area at all which might comfortably accommodate a window box; and then afterwards – as they have in Banbury – spreading higher yet. The current fashion is to suspend hanging baskets from every available lamp-post, slinging them so low that if you find yourself in the vicinity of one without knowing it and turn inadvertently in the wrong direction, you're in danger of losing an eye to a trailing lobelia.

Since I last visited Banbury had become such a riot of plants that I could have done with a machete to hack my way up the high street. Mind you, a machete's a pretty useful tool generally in Banbury in my experience, especially on Saturday nights when the streets become awash with hordes of strapping farm workers from the adjoining villages out for a night on the piss. Even for someone like me, used to the high spirits of London youth, Banbury at the weekend still has the ability to strike the fear of God into my heart. It's certainly a place where you risk more than the health of your liver going for a drink in a local pub.

One night five or six years back I was having a quiet pint when for no apparent reason – or at least not one I could fathom – a brick came crashing through the window and landed at my feet. It shocked me, I can tell you; though I was more astonished by how little this seemed to affect anyone else in the place. It was as if this sort of thing happened in Banbury every day of the week – which it probably did, and probably still does for all I know.

I remember vividly that at the very moment it happened there was a man standing at the bar who had his beer glass to his lips, and who – with the sort of indifference that passes for panache in these parts – finished his long draught without being put off his stride even momentarily. My companion that night was a man with royal connections brought up in one of the nearby villages, and he seemed similarly blasé about what had happened – a response I put down either to his familiarity with the realities of contemporary England, or his sense of detachment from them born out of generations of good breeding.

I suppose I shouldn't blame Banbury particularly for any of this, for if its inclination to want to transform itself into a garden centre in the summer months is a common feature of life in England at the beginning of the twenty-first century, then sadly, so too is the propensity of its young to get arseholed on Saturday nights and start throwing building materials about.

It happens all over the country, and Banbury's no worse than any of a hundred other places in this respect. Though I grant you it somehow *seems* worse because there's something about Banbury – the very name Banbury – which is so connected to nursery images of Fyne Ladies on Cock Horses, and so redolent of a better, less threatening past, that it somehow epitomises the genteel traditionalism that we have come to associate with towns of rural England.

And here's a funny thing: we still want to believe this aspect of our national character still survives, even when we live in rural areas ourselves and know better than most that it's a busted flush – an idea as dead and outdated as saving your virginity for your wedding night.

But Banbury. Banbury! Surely not Banbury, of all places? It's like a redoubt of Middle England falling to the invading hordes. The very idea of it pains me.

They really should have looked after their castle better.

Nine

So if we expect more from a place like Banbury because it's called Banbury, is there really something in a name then, despite all that Shakespearean banter about roses?

Take the word 'zobo', for instance. They might still smell as sweet, but could you really see minor members of the royal family and fragrant romantic novelists being as keen to be associated with them if instead of being called roses, roses were known as zobos?

As monikers go, it's hardly a grabber, is it? And not one with much of an amorous cachet to it either. Valentine's Day? A bottle of champagne and a dozen zobos... it just doesn't sound right for a flower, does it? But then it doesn't sound right for much else either, notwithstanding the fact that on narrowboats we use a grate cleaner on our stoves called Zebo, which is a thick black paste and comes in a container so much like a toothpaste tube that knowing how stupid people are, I just can't believe that at least one living soul in this rich and colourful world of ours hasn't ballsed up at some stage and finished up with incisors the colour of coal.

A zobo is actually a sort of crossbreed domestic ox, related to the yak. It's not what you'd call a glamorous animal. Certainly not one whose name you could see being appropriated for a new perfume – 'Zobo, the new intimate fragrance from Calvin Klein' – that sort of thing. They're not particularly speedy animals either so you'd think it unlikely you'd ever see the Ford Zobo as a 'passport to millennium driving luxury' either. It doesn't seem to have the right feel to it for the name of a car, does it? Any more than for a rose.

Except that there you'd be totally wrong, for improbable though it may seem, many years ago the name Zobo *was* used, at least for a time, as the name for a car – and a very commercially successful one at that, a vehicle still lauded for its elegant, racy lines and sophisticated engineering.

Well, for its elegant, racy lines, at least…

The car was the Triumph Herald, of which the Debsmobile – last left languishing in a garage in Oxfordshire with a crocked clutch – is an example.

'Zobo' was actually chosen as an early designation for the Herald after one of the staff had come up with it as a four-letter project code for a new small car the company was developing. Given that any fool could have seen it was totally unsuitable as a name for a car, it was, paradoxically, an inspired choice for one, because at this point in its history most of the vehicles being manufactured by Standard Triumph were hardly capable of being called cars either, being no more than the equivalent of large sardine cans with windscreen wipers.

The very names of that range are redolent of the post-war austerity years when the words 'British' and 'design' harmonised with about the same compatibility as 'Japanese' and 'prisoner care'. The Standard Eight, the Standard Ten – the Pennant, for heaven's sake, a vehicle that can genuinely be said to have defied all known concepts of aerodynamics. It was so ungraceful it might have been modelled on the lines of an unmade bed. I swear it must have created more wind resistance than the Ferguson tractors the company was producing at the same time. In fact, I'm not certain the company didn't base the Pennant on the tractors. Sadly, its early efforts on the Zobo weren't much of an improvement either, and one of the designers later described the prototypes looking like a 'mechanised bathtub'. Actually, I think he was being a bit harsh. I've seen pictures of those prototypes and they look like cars all right – just the sort of cars you might see in Toytown with Noddy behind the wheel.

It's wrong, though, to laugh at those early attempts of the

British car industry to pull itself up by its bootstraps after the war. The wonder wasn't that the early designs for the Zobo were so dreadful, but that the company was still in the business of producing new cars at all, given the quality of its management. For a long time it was run by a 79-year-old chairman who'd spent his working life as a solicitor, and a managing director who had such an autocratic style he's remembered even now as a 'schizophrenic dictator'.

But times were changing across the whole spectrum of British life, and a new generation forged in the war years was beginning to take over key roles in the country's industrial infrastructure – at Standard Triumph no less than anywhere else. In 1954 there was a boardroom coup, and at what was to prove a significant period in its history the company fell into the hands of a group of people who weren't just talented as managers, but who were talented engineers too – men who'd been brought up with cars and engines, and actually liked them, and knew what they were talking about when they discussed them. Men in their own way not entirely unlike Tom Rolt.

The new managing director at Standard Triumph was Alick Dick, who'd joined the company as an apprentice 20 years before. He was 37 years old, and his appointment to the top job precipitated a whole host of changes as he promoted a group of younger, more enthusiastic men to be part of his team. One of the most important of these was Harry Webster, who was appointed chief engineer, replacing the funereal Ted Grinham who seems to have received some bad career advice in early life since it's said of him that he couldn't see the merit in designing advanced cars. Which is, I suppose, a little bit like saying of an Olympic sprinter that he can't see the use of running quickly.

Webster was the same age as Dick, and like his MD he'd joined the company as a young apprentice. George Turnbull, who took over as boss of the company's experimental department, was in the same mould; and though he was younger – just 30 – he was another former apprentice for whom the promotion represented the beginning of a long and renowned career, one that would eventually take him overseas to Korea where he played a key part in launching the Hyundai company.

These men, and others like them at Standard Triumph, seem to me to epitomise what England was in those days, and looking at pictures of them with their thick-rimmed glasses and their fashionably narrow Italian ties, I can't help but be thrown back to my childhood when all men seemed to look a little like this: when they all smoked untipped cigarettes like Players or Park Drive, and had swept back hair held down with thick swathes of Brylcream, and when they all smelt reassuringly musty in the solid, dependable way that damp tweed does.

My own father was in the hosiery industry and an engineer too, though he wouldn't for one moment ever have used that term of himself, since as far as he was concerned the only people who warranted that designation were men like Brunel or Telford – civil engineers responsible for massive projects which changed the world forever. At the very least they were academics who'd been to college and wore suits to work – which was something my father would never have dreamt of doing, even though, like most working men of that era, he'd never so much as venture beyond the front door without a collar and tie. What you wore to work made a statement about you, you see; it was a signal of where you lay in the hierarchical structures that characterised post-war Britain. My father always went to work in a casual sports jacket of one sort or another, but as soon as he arrived at the factory he'd don a calf-length khaki overall which was like a badge of his trade.

Regardless of what he called himself, my father was still capable of diagnosing and repairing those fearsomely complex knitting machines that were being installed all over the East Midlands during that period. After years of low investment, industrialists had finally realised they had to do something to compete with the Far Eastern countries which were beginning to export cheap knitwear into Britain; so they bought these monstrous things called Comets, like the aircraft, that were supposed to be the last word in new technology. My father used to take me into work with him from time to time at whatever Victorian mill building he was based – for skilled employment in the hosiery industry was easily had then, and he used to move around a lot, sometimes even leaving one job on the Friday afternoon and starting a new one on the Monday.

As a child I found the whole environment completely overwhelming. The din of factories terrified me, and I couldn't understand how my father could show such astonishing detachment controlling these banks of machines that raged and screamed around us. He'd be on his feet constantly, literally running between the narrow aisles that separated the rows of them while they spewed out great colonic tubes of what, he explained, would eventually become socks once they'd been separated and sewn up.

It was a numbing and repetitive process, carried out against such a brutal wall of noise that I wondered sometimes how I'd stand it a moment longer – except that like the people who worked in the place I soon stopped hearing anything after a while. Even so, my father could diagnose by sound when there was something wrong with any of the machines under his charge. He had the skill of being able to predict the advent of a problem by some minute change in tone, or some scarcely audible whine; and when that happened he'd cock his head, concentrating intently for a few moments until he could identify the source of the trouble and decide which of the bank of red switches that controlled their power supply he needed to switch off in order to allow him access to repair the fault. Sometimes if he thought he could get away with it, he wouldn't even bother, and he'd dive fearlessly into the very heart of the beast, emerging later with his face covered in grease, and with flecks of fabric clinging to his hair, the machine repaired and his task achieved as gloriously as if he'd been some knight in shining armour laying siege to a citadel for the sake of a maiden's honour.

Even as a kid I must have been aware of the risks he was running and the danger he was courting, but at the time this just seemed the way that life was. Or at least, the way it was when your only experience of it was through the TV and story books. Everything then just seemed like a game, and the world of grown-ups was the most exciting lark of the lot, filled with excitement and adventure, and untold promise. I couldn't conceive of the darker realities, of course; not at that stage in my life. I perceived everything that happened as if it was taking place in my world where everything was done just for fun and nothing could ever harm you.

Eventually my father must have said something which alerted my mother to what he was doing – or maybe I even said something to her, who knows? But I recall one night while they were watching *Sunday Night at the London Palladium* there was an angry exchange between them which finished up with her in tears screaming at him. My father scarcely reacted to the whole outburst. I remember there was a look of indifference on his face, and everything seemed to wash over him. The argument seemed to come down to money – but then every disagreement between them did in those days. I seem to remember him saying he had to do things the way he did because he could earn more that way.

So he kept working in the way he always had worked – except that if ever I was around and he was repairing a machine that was switched on, he'd give me a knowing, conspiratorial wink as if to seal my lips forever. But, of course, by then my lips *were* sealed forever, even to myself. The fun had gone out of this game, you see. I'd begun to suspect that it was being played for much higher stakes than I could conceive.

He nearly did get his comeuppance, though, for a few years after this one of the hundreds of hooked and barbed needles that lay at the core of the Comets caught a gold signet ring he was wearing and nearly succeeded in stitching him up the length of his arm. Except he managed to wrench himself free in the nick of time and save the limb, not to mention his life. He never worked on an active machine again after that as far as I know. He never wore the ring either, and he gave it to me soon afterwards. I'm wearing it now, as a matter of fact.

The men of that period had skills which to my mind seem so much more real than those we have now. This isn't to undermine contemporary expertise, for I'm sure I could never design and build a computer microcircuit, let alone write a programme that might utilise one; but everything today seems so much less *tangible* than the metal-bashing accomplishments of our recent past. And so much less commonplace too, for when I was a kid there were people like my dad all around me – engineers, mechanics, toolmakers – people who could work machines that made socks and shoes and knitwear and lace; people who could build diesel trains like they did at Brush in Loughborough, or construct cranes like they did at Herbert Morris next door.

No, we just don't play Premier League any more in this country, and it's no use kidding ourselves that we do, or that we ever could do again. Times have changed inexorably and what we did best, no one wants any more. Or they don't want it at the price we charge them for it. Nowadays we can do computer games and pop music, audio visual and a bit of prestige architecture; we can do fine art, design and fashion; and good movie effects. We can even turn a deal or two in the City when the conditions are right. And of course we can pull in tourists by the coachload, flogging them a carefully cultivated image of our past.

But this isn't anywhere near the tabernacle in today's church, and in our heart of hearts we know it, despite all the pap the politicians feed us about being at the sharp end of the new millennium. The problem isn't that those old greasy craft skills are a thing of the past, but that they're a thing of the wrong sort of past. A past that's unmarketable. A past that you simply can't sell to anyone except enthusiasts and no-hope sentimentalists like me.

And anyway, inside a generation, so many of the accomplishments which made us what we are will have died out completely: the process is in its death throes and you can see it happening. Today getting even basic manual work done is a major operation. Forget the cutting edge of new technology, have you tried getting a burst pipe repaired recently? Or a room decorated? In some parts of the country the only people who can actually do these jobs properly are like top international opera stars, booked for years ahead and charging the same sort of rates too. The best that most of us are able to aspire to is the sort of fly-by-night cowboy who thinks he's doing you a favour by deigning to turn up at your house within a couple of days of agreeing to be there.

Certainly there didn't seem to be much in the way of traditional craft skills in evidence in the garage where I'd left the Debsmobile. When I went back to collect it I found I'd accrued an enormously high bill for a new main cylinder in the clutch; yet after I'd paid up and driven away, the car began to play up again in a way entirely consistent with needing a new main cylinder in the clutch. So I turned round and drove straight back to the garage again, only to discover that an instruction that was so express it might have been the 9.03 out of Euston had somehow, in translation, managed to get garbled.

'I thought we'd agreed you were going to replace the main cylinder in the clutch,' I said in such a tone of reasoned moderation I surprised even myself.

'Ah, I must have got the wrong end of the stick,' said the boss who – give him his due – sounded to me as if he was an expert in dealing with this sort of thing. By which I mean an expert in dealing with frustrated and angry customers on the verge of ripping out his throat with their bare hands, the better to suck his blood.

He smiled at me. I smiled back at him.

I said: 'Strange that you should have misunderstood because if you look at your bill here' – I took it out – 'you'll see that you have charged me the equivalent of a couple of useful limbs for what you describe as – how do you put it? – "A replacement main cylinder on the clutch." Puzzling this, wouldn't you say?'

He pursed his lips. This was probably not the worst customer relations problem that he'd ever been called upon to resolve, but even so it was a tricky one.

'You see, you may think me old-fashioned here,' I went on, 'but I'm left wondering if you haven't replaced the part, and yet you've billed me for it, what exactly is it that you *have* done? Am I, for instance, to expect the car suddenly to surge forward with a new intensity as a result of some turbocharger you've inadvertently installed? Or maybe, unbeknown to me, hidden in the bowels of this modest machine is a new in-car entertainment system complete with digital television and 360-degree surround sound…'

Of course, I didn't say anything of this sort, every word of which – if you haven't guessed already – is complete fabrication, and like most of this book, totally fictional.

Instead, I did what we English *always* do in these sorts of situations. I took the car back to the garage somewhat contritely, mumbling about there still being a bit of a problem and, if they could possibly find time, I'd appreciate it *very* much if they could look at it once more…

The man in charge was, of course, totally unmoved by the fact that I'd already paid an enormous bill to have the car repaired. 'I'll try and get someone to have a look at it later this week,' he said, 'but I can't promise…' For which read: another sad sucker of a customer come for another dose of the same. I suppose this time I better at least get it half right.

And half right's about right too, for when I eventually came to pick up the Debsmobile – not later that week, or even the week following that, but the week afterwards when the garage had finally got around to doing some work on it – I found that though this time they'd successfully repaired the clutch, for some reason they'd felt the need to drain the radiator at the same time. And they hadn't bothered filling it up again.

The car began overheating so badly the thermostat was showing temperatures high enough to roast your Sunday dinner. I had to stop at a house along the way to beg for water.

Lucky I noticed really. Another few minutes and I'd have destroyed the engine completely.

Soon after you pass the Alcan aluminium factory north of Banbury, you go under a railway bridge and then pass through a lock. Finally, the canal swings under the M40 which – mercifully – now veers off in a totally different direction, so that you can begin to enjoy the Oxfordshire countryside in the couple of miles or so before you reach the small village of Cropredy.

I was pleased to be travelling again, and pleased to be away from the town and back in the countryside, which even after such a short absence seemed somehow sweeter and fresher than it had before, somehow more luxurious and verdant. It was bucketing down as I left Banbury that morning, but the downpour soon abated and before long the rain turned into a mist so fine it seemed to hang in the air, clinging to the hedgerows and the overhanging boughs of trees; so that later, when the summer sun finally condescended to appear, everything around me began to glisten as if caught in the grip of a harsh winter's frost.

Even *Justice* seemed pleased to be on the move once more, and before long her engine settled into its regular soporific rhythm, like the slow and steady beat of a heart. At times like this she seems to be totally at one with the environment, her bow cutting through the water so gracefully she scarcely creates a ripple on the surface, and her hull undulating so indolently with every touch of the tiller she's like a languorous Latino dancer.

At Cropredy the canal passes under the main village road, and almost immediately afterwards it enters the shallow cutting that leads to Cropredy Lock where there's a tiny humpback bridge at the top of a narrow street of thatched stone cottages facing the village church. For some reason I've never enquired into, the churchyard is at a higher level than the street, and I can never pass it without the grotesque thought that one day it might give way and spill the bones of the village dead over the pavement.

The place used to be a farming village, but the last thing any farm needs is to be sited anywhere near a residential area where queues of impatient traffic will inevitably build up as soon as anyone takes a tractor out onto the road; and where – even if it's been in the same place for centuries – it'll still get criticised for the smell and the noise it creates. Crazy, isn't it? But this has led to the paradoxical situation in Oxfordshire where farms have actually been moving *out* of villages, relocating to purpose-built premises on the fringes as one did in Cropredy just a year or two back. Meanwhile, the old farmhouses and their outbuildings and barns are converted to what are euphemistically termed 'executive homes', that is, overpriced houses that cost a bomb and are out of reach of anyone with a normal job.

For some time I was uncertain how to respond to this process. Part of me felt instinctively that I didn't like it, but this was the part that lives in London and has a Londoner's metrocentric view of the countryside as a place where you go for long walks to get away from the rat race. This bit of me felt that the process was destroying the country village and everything it stood for. But I was born in the country, and brought up in one of these villages, and I know as well as anyone that these rural communities are living, organic places which are constantly changing, and always have changed, and need to change again in the future if they're to survive in any real sense, rather than just become another fossilised fragment of the heritage industry.

Cropredy's not a bad example of the positive way it's possible for villages to develop. Though a casual visitor passing through on the canal might just dismiss it cynically as another rural rest home for the retired on the fringes of the Cotswolds, or at best a commuter town for London and Banbury, nothing could actually be further from the truth. The truth is, Cropredy is a place that's got real soul.

And not just soul either: it's got two pubs, a small supermarket that doubles as a post office, a saddler's, a signwriter, a craft shop and café, a welder, a bronze-casting foundry, a classic car renovation garage, an arts centre and cinema club, a small music studio, a ceramics workshop – and God knows how many electricians, plumbers and builders, not to mention painters of so many different sorts that you'd be as well to be cautious employing one, for you could find yourself with a landscape on your living room wall when all you were after was a coat of magnolia.

Most important of all for the future, Cropredy's got a school of 120 kids, and an environment safe and pleasant enough for them to grow up in. And I'll tell you one other thing: when these kids get older, they won't all be as desperate as I was to get away from the countryside, because villages like Cropredy offer real opportunity to young people. Not just as pleasant places to live – because what youngster in their right mind is looking for *that* in their teens? – but as engaging places to live, places where things happen, and where a night out doesn't have to mean just kicking around the bus shelter, which was about the only option open to me at that age.

It's got a sense of fun about it generally, Cropredy; and once a year, over one weekend in August, it puts this part of itself on display when it hosts a folk-rock festival organised by the band Fairport Convention, who washed up in the village decades ago for a farewell concert and have been holding one every year since with a persistence that puts even Frank Sinatra to shame. Fairport are still capable of turning it on a bit when the mood takes them, and they can attract some class supporting acts, so that over the two days as many as 20,000 people can pile into the village with a resultant colourful clash of cultures as young, dreadlocked New Agers, barefoot hippies and face-painted eco-warriors rub shoulders with the type of Miss Marple characters you find in Cropredy as you find them in every other English village everywhere.

If you visit Cropredy by canal for the festival weekend these days, you need to plan well ahead since the towpath gets packed with boats, and moorings are at a premium; but in the past you could just turn up on spec on the Friday night and find a spot to stop, as Em and I did one year when we cruised up from Banbury with another boat owned by a friend of ours, who was at that time working as a restorer of historic wooden craft.

We arrived about seven o'clock on what was a balmy Arcadian evening; and with the music already filtering down from the main festival stage, we didn't hang around and moored up as quickly as possible next to an old houseboat from Oxford which was up for the festival like us. It was the early hours when we got back, considerably the worse for wear, and the scene that confronted us was dreadful. The old boat we'd moored next to was now listing at such an alarming angle it was apparent it wouldn't be afloat much longer. Standing on top of it was a young guy, almost in tears with panic, screaming for help.

He wasn't in danger, for canals aren't particularly deep; but the boat was his home, and it was enough that all his worldly goods were threatened. In between bouts of hysteria he kept disappearing into the cabin and dragging as many things as he could out onto the roof, which by now was beginning to resemble the scene of a bomb explosion with bedding, lamps and clothes strewn all over it.

Our friend took no more than a second or two to survey the scene, and while Em and I were aimlessly running about hither and thither, bumping into each other and tripping over our feet like characters in a Buster Keaton movie, he'd gone back to his boat to retrieve a pail of that vile concoction called 'charlie', made of tar and horse shit, which wooden boat builders have traditionally used to caulk the timbers of their craft.

Half an hour later, the stricken boat was repaired and floating again; and the distraught owner had calmed down enough to start taking his possessions below deck once more.

Well? Lucky or what? To have your wooden boat sink next to

a man who repairs wooden boats for a living and who just happened to have some charlie on board because he'd been using it himself that day?

I wonder what the odds against that were when at the time there probably weren't more than two or three people in the country capable of repairing a wooden boat?

But that's life, isn't it: random, arbitrary and a bitch if you're not born lucky.

Which I was beginning to realise I wasn't.

I got a call from Em. Some other pipe somewhere in the viscera of the Crumbling Pile had burst asunder, and no more than a month after sorting out one crisis it seemed there was another requiring my attention…

Ten

BEYOND CROPREDY THE Oxford Canal continues its gentle rise from the valley of the Cherwell by way of a series of isolated locks which nestle among the rich and fertile fields hereabouts. It was two weeks later and high summer by the time I got back from London – a considerably poorer man as a result of yet another wad I'd had to hand out to one more dodgy builder for services rendered to the Crumbling Pile. The trees were now in full leaf, so as I cruised through what was still a season of incessant and unremitting rain, it was against the background of a constant hush: a sound like a gently steaming kettle; a soothing monotonous sonata caused by a myriad of raindrops falling softly onto the countryside.

The hedges were high and lush, threaded with dog roses and lined with thick bands of cow parsley; and along the remorselessly green towpaths were sudden vivid patches of yellow and purple where clumps of vetch had strayed from the meadows and now sat uncomfortably isolated, reaching upwards towards the sky for company, their curled tendrils twisted tortuously upon themselves. Cropredy Lock is followed by Broadmoor Lock, and after that Varney's and Elkington's come in quick succession until very soon you arrive at the foot of the short flight of six locks at Claydon which take the canal to its summit level.

There's something perpetually evocative about the names associated with canals, rooted as they are in folk memory. Many of the designations are predictable enough, and it doesn't take an archivist to work out why a bridge carrying the towpath from one side of the canal to the other might be called Crossover Bridge, or why the locks passing close to some village should unsurprisingly be named after that village. But many canal-related names are more reluctant to be deciphered, and they hint at a mysterious and lost past peopled by characters who for different reasons established themselves in their own world sufficiently to be esteemed by it, but whose memory in ours has eroded with time, and whose existence is now only marked by this trivial nomenclature which has survived the years.

Who on earth was this guy Varney, and what manner of man or woman was Elkington? And was Broadmoor a real moor once?

You somehow feel that locked into English names is a coded chronicle of the English past which could tell you so much if only you could crack it. But the same could be said about the landscape too, especially in the heart of these Midlands shires where the ridge and furrow patterns of old strip farming are still indented on the fields, and where the ghosts of a thousand and more abandoned villages lie just below the surface of the soil.

At Fenny Compton you pass through a straight cutting of almost half a mile which is all that remains of what once used to be a tunnel until they took the top off it in 1868. Nowadays, travelling north, it's the last straight of any kind that you experience, for you are at the high point of the canal now, and from here onwards for the next 11 miles the Oxford winds around on itself and back on itself, arcing in a series of agonisingly tight bends so that steering a narrowboat you no sooner extend the tiller in one direction to turn one way, than you have to heave it in the opposite direction to go the other. The reason for these convolutions – as for so much else on the canal system – was the need to save money. Twisting and turning in this way, following the level contour of the land, the canal engineers avoided the cost of expensive locks to carry the waterway up or downhill.

The effect of travelling along a canal of this sort can be most peculiar, for it engenders a strange sensation of unreality in that early on misty mornings, or late in the evening when the onset of night blurs your perceptions, any sense of direction you have seems to dissipate and you can become hopelessly confused as to the way you're going. You pass a radio mast after a while, and this seems positioned to confound you, since when you first catch sight of it, it's ahead of you on your left-hand side; but then it disappears behind a copse, only to appear again behind you on your right.

No sooner have you adjusted to this unusual configuration of the natural world than the damned thing moves again – and suddenly appears in front of you once more! This time you work out that it should be on your left as it just was. Except it remains resolutely and irrationally to your right. This is baffling, and so counter-intuitive that it's weird. So you promise yourself now that you won't take your eye off it to ensure that it doesn't get up to any more of its tricks; but this becomes increasingly difficult as the canal swings around in further tighter arcs until, strangely, what seems to be moving now is not you on the boat, but the radio mast itself, gliding gracefully across the fields…

Spooky or what, eh?

Believe me, it *can* be on those vaporous mornings I'm talking about when the mists swirl in wreaths above the water, playing around your bow like some malign miasma from the nether world. Or on those high summer's evenings after nine o'clock when the sun has set and when the onset of darkness seems halted in that uncertain lacuna between day and night so that the world appears to fracture and distort, and every small movement in the hedgerows becomes a threat, every screech of a bird or rustle in the trees a malicious affront to reason.

The corkscrewing of the Oxford Canal summit reaches its culmination in the journey around the 400-foot-high Wormleighton Hill where, if it's speed you're after, you'd be better leaving your boat completely and taking to foot, since a five-minute walk across the fields will take you to a spot you'd need three-quarters of an hour to get to by water. But it's worth leaving the boat at this point anyhow to visit nearby Wormleighton village, which the guidebooks recommend for its church and the remains of its old manor house, but which I think is a valuable excursion for an entirely different reason since it's the sort of place that can give you a whole new take on the contemporary world.

Now this may come as a surprise to anyone who's visited the village without knowing its past, for on the face of it there doesn't seem to be much bar its prettiness to commend it. A narrow, rather sleepy road winds through the place; and you get the sense that this is about the only thing that connects it with civilisation. There's certainly no reason why anyone from the modern world should so much as set foot in Wormleighton since it's got neither a shop nor a pub, nor much in the way of a population either; but instead sits resplendently severed from everywhere, a perfectly proportioned English village resting soporifically, apparently abandoned, in a sea of Warwickshire pastureland.

But it wasn't always like this. In the thirteenth century in the time of King John its thatched manor house was the focus of a community of forty or so homesteads which probably supported a population of several hundred people. It must have been an affluent place then, and big for its time, and it would have bustled with the industriousness of labour, its fields busy at the quietest of periods, but almost frenetic during the harvest season when everyone who could walk would have been out lending a hand with the crops, and when the surrounding lanes must have been full of horses returning from the fields with heaving cartloads of produce for the barns.

Two hundred years afterwards, though, everything had changed completely. By then hardly anyone lived in Wormleighton. This was because there'd been a boom in the price of wool and the manor had been bought up by one of that new breed of entrepreneur who would inherit, if not the earth, then at least that bit of it in the rich and fertile Midlands plain where they could get rid of the tenants without much opposition and enclose the land for sheep pasture.

'So what happens?' explains Thomas More in *Utopia*. 'Each greedy individual preys on his native land like a malignant growth, absorbing field after field, and enclosing thousands of acres with a single fence. Result – hundreds of farmers are evicted. They're either cheated or bullied into giving up their property, or systematically ill-treated until they're finally forced to sell. Whichever way it's done, out the poor creatures have to go: men and women, husbands and wives, widows and orphans, mothers and tiny children.'

This enclosure movement seems such a distant issue for us today, a thing of such dry irrelevant history, that it's barely possible for us to conceive the raw human suffering it must have caused as families who had no other way of earning a living were cast off the land which had been their birthright, forced to beg or steal, or throw themselves on the parish and the new Poor Laws which had been introduced to deal with the crisis. Except, I suppose, we've seen a little of it in our own recent past as the mining industry has been run down, and pit communities that were once vibrant centres of working culture have withered and perished away with a similar cost in human suffering.

Of course, with the benefit of hindsight we know now, don't we, that like the closures of the pits which prepared our workforce for the new challenges of the information age, the enclosure movement all those years ago created the economic wealth that would fire the Industrial Revolution and create the world we live in today?

Well, yes and no.

Surely I can't be on my own in finding this sort of simplistic explanation of the past a poor apology for history, bereft as it is of any sensitivity to the personal cost of change for individuals who've found themselves trapped helplessly by events and manipulated by social movements that seem to serve everyone's interests except theirs. But that's the trouble with social movements. They're fine while you're sitting on the outside as an observer analysing them. But they're a swine when it's *you* they steamroller.

The enclosures were the beginning of the end for that medieval social contract by which the wealthy, in return for their privileges, recognised their obligations to the common good. And so John

Spencer, farmer, who had bought the Wormleighton estate, became a sheep rustler in the name of progress, and so grew rich on his profits and became Sir John. And 500 years later one of his descendants, Diana, married the Prince of Wales and a few years afterwards gave birth to a child who will eventually become the king, and to whom, if we love our country, we must all pay a fawning deference, honouring this sordid past as a legitimate justification for the present.

My meanderings across the countryside had by now developed their own routine in that after kicking about a day or two in one location, I'd move off – something I always did in the mornings – cruising until mid-afternoon at the very latest, never longer. Then I'd cycle back to wherever I'd left the Debsmobile, load the bike and drive back to the boat. Unfortunately, being such a small car, the only way of actually getting a bike into a Triumph Herald is by taking down the hood and jamming its wheels behind the front seats in such a way that the frame stands up vertically. This makes it impossible to get the roof up again, and since there is nothing more designed to invite rain than someone in a convertible car open to the elements, I regularly got completely soaked, and I count myself lucky not to have caught pneumonia at least once during the summer.

Food became something of a high point of my day. I'd determined from the outset to eat well and avoid the ever-present temptations of canalside pubs and their consistent, if suspicious, menus of cow in various forms, whether cheap steaks, pies or casseroles. I'd got interested in Thai food and realised that as long as I kept a few basic ingredients on the boat, it could be cooked almost effortlessly before I went out for a beer. Or even after I got back if I was taken with the munchies.

Gui Paht Meht Mamuang Himapahn, for instance, is a genuine Thai dish from the central part of the country: it's delicious and quick, and can be thrown together in a wok so there's not much in the way of washing up for anyone cooking in a limited space.

The genuine version is made with chicken, but in the past I've made it with pork; and fish-lovers could just as easily use prawns instead, which I've done too, and which I can warrant is just as delicious if not more so.

Another Recipe

Cut a small chicken breast or small pork steak into strips and fry it with one or two chopped garlic cloves until it's cooked through. Towards the end of the cooking process crumble one or two dried red chillies into the pan along with a small onion cut into quarters. The onion needs to be crunchy when you eat it, so don't worry about cooking it thoroughly, though it does need to colour on the outside, so as to rid it of the worst of its raw taste. When this begins to happen, add a handful of cashew nuts to the pan along with a teaspoonful of sugar. Brown the nuts gently and toss everything around a bit until it's heated. Finally, sprinkle a tablespoon of fish sauce and half a tablespoon of soy sauce over the mixture and stir well. Serve with plain boiled rice.

The drawback to this as a one-pan meal is that it's a bit short of vegetables to be bowel-friendly, so if you're not too wedded to the idea of total culinary authenticity, do what I do and add a few frozen peas to the rice, or maybe throw a few Chinese leaves into the pan after you've added the sauces. Or perhaps some green beans cut into strips, or even a sliced fennel bulb. Actually, you can add any vegetable that's available...

The Oxford Canal summit ends at Marston Doles where a peculiar warehouse with a couple of outside walls built at the angle of an arrowhead marks the beginning of the picturesque flight of nine locks that takes the canal past the foot of the hill after which Napton-on-the-Hill is named. From the top there's a wonderful view of the surrounding Warwickshire Plain; and under normal circumstances I'd find it hard to pass the place without stopping, for it's one of those unassertively comfortable English villages which fit the English way of life like a well-worn old shoe. Napton's pretty enough, but it's not prissy-pretty; and the old houses sprinkled around its narrow streets and village green are mixed with a significant amount of honest new building, so that you get a sense of the place – as you do in Cropredy – as a working village, living without the threat of the conservation order and the kiss of aspic death that can so often result from it.

I have good memories of Napton. Em and I spent Christmas afloat here one year. On another occasion, walking up the hill in the early evening, we watched enthralled for almost an hour as a family of badgers rooted around for food – the only time in our lives that either of us have seen such a thing.

On this occasion I had to pass through without stopping, though. The problem was that after a decade of fighting every bit of brickwork on the system, *Justice*'s hull was beginning to show its age and she was scheduled to go into a boatyard at Braunston eight miles further on where she was to be pulled out of the water the next day for a canal version of a facelift.

Now there's a paradox about Braunston which is immediately apparent the first time you visit, for although it's renowned among the canal community as the capital of Britain's inland waterways system, it's actually rather an insubstantial place, being not much more than a single street stretched along the escarpment of a low hill and bounded on one side by an imposing parish church and on the other by a poky council estate. Braunston's significance to the canal system has come about not because of its relationship to the village, but because of an historical accident of canal development which left it, if not the Spaghetti Junction of the canal world, then about the nearest thing you're ever going to get on water. In other words, it's a place where you at least have to be alert to the possibility of taking a wrong turning.

This is very unusual on canals.

No, I'd go further and say that this is almost *unique* on canals, for with the exception of Birmingham where the remains of old loops and arms can still make getting about a bit tricky, canal boating in England is hardly likely to ever test your map-reading skills. Or putting it another way, among the canon of oft-quoted inland waterways clichés, 'I'm lost' does not exactly figure highly.

Essentially, what canal navigation comes down to is ensuring that you're not pointing south when you should be going north. Or vice versa. This is not exactly an intellectually taxing operation since the northerly direction generally takes you to towns like Leeds, Liverpool and Manchester; whereas travelling south, you generally end up in London – unless you're being inattentive, in which case you might find yourself in Bristol or Bath after a couple of weeks.

On rivers it's even easier. There, if you get confused, there's even a clue to which direction you're travelling since if you're going upstream the flow of the water will generally be against you, while going in the opposite direction it's more often than not in your favour.

Braunston, however, can sometimes be quite a challenge for some crews who arrive there after having journeyed at 3 or 4 mph for sometimes up to weeks on end with nothing more substantial than enormous quantities of beer to facilitate their passage. It lies, you see, along the central arm of the H-shaped junction of the Oxford Canal with the Grand Union, so that boats have the perplexing and unprecedented choice of no fewer than four routes available to them. Even though one of these will be the one along which they've already travelled, and another involves negotiating a flight of locks and a tunnel more than a mile long, you'd nevertheless be surprised at the number of intelligent people, many with university degrees, who find themselves going to Coventry when they thought they were travelling to London, or heading to Leicester when they thought they were on their way to Oxford.

It's because of its geographical location that Braunston became an important canal centre, and it's retained that distinction today;

for in the same way that it was well-positioned for getting to places in the days when the canals were important for haulage, today it's equally convenient to get to by car, situated as it is in the centre of the country close to motorways. So it's become a popular place for people to keep their boats.

And they do. In their thousands.

As a result, it seems that not a week passes without there's a move to dig up another local field as a marina, presumably with the ultimate intention that this bit of Northamptonshire should become a sort of inland lake where boaters who are attracted to the canals can moor their floating cottages without the inconvenience of actually having to go anywhere in them in order to enjoy the authentic waterways experience.

Parts of Braunston are already like a vast caravan site on water, and such is the ethos that pervades the place now that on some weekends in summer it can be like walking through suburbia for all the crowds of people waxing their paintwork and buffing up their already gleaming brasswork to ever greater levels of lustrous shine. Sometimes you can't help but think that there's an incomprehensible game being played out here whereby you establish a sort of social dominance over your neighbour by the luminescence of your boat.

What's been clear to me for a long time is that in the caste system which has become modern canalling, *Justice* lies some considerable way down the pecking order. Even putting aside the question of her battered and gouged hull, the sad state of her brasswork alone would be enough to guarantee her social ostracism at a good many clannish gatherings of canal boats. It's not that boats in Braunston have to be absolutely pristine, more that they can only be scruffy within set parameters. So it's OK if you're thought of as a 'working boat' or can otherwise claim connection – however far removed – to the days of canal carrying. Then you can fill your hold with scrap metal and cover your cabin in engine oil, for a bit of rubbish and a patina of grime will only be thought to add to your authenticity.

But show up in a modern boat which could do with a lick of paint and you'd think you'd farted in church for all the raised eyebrows and averted glances you get from the towpath traditionalists in these parts.

Much store, you see, is set by the authentic in Braunston – or at least the authentic looking, which is a totally different thing. There is much in the way of the application of washers to the hulls of boats as a substitute for genuine rivets, for instance; and much grooving of steel to make it look like planks of wood. There is also a lot of talk about the 'right' way of doing things on a boat, whether it's the 'right' way to go through a lock or the 'right' way to turn at a bend. One of the things it is most definitely *wrong* to do – in fact, it's a heinous crime by canal standards – is to carry your stern rope coiled over your tiller, and there are many and varied arguments advanced by the traditionalists as to why this should be the case, each of them studiously designed to avoid the glaringly obvious fact that it's far and away the most convenient place to keep it.

I *always* keep my rope over my tiller on *Justice*.

I do it mainly to annoy them.

I do it because I can't see the use of maintaining sterile tradition just for the sake of it, especially when it runs totally contrary to common sense and verges on the completely absurd. Like *Raymond*, for instance, a boat which currently sits at Braunston after a long and expensive 'renovation'. For many years *Raymond* was home to Arthur Bray, one of that extinct breed of boatmen known as 'Number Ones' who actually owned their own craft rather than worked on boats owned by carrying companies. After his death there was a move to conserve the boat to commemorate the life of a man who was a link to a past canal age, and who in his final years had become something of a living monument in Braunston, moored as he used to be in one of the most prominent positions in the place, and the sort of bloke who when you were passing always had time for a chat about the old days.

So they started work on the boat, trying to preserve what had survived the ravages of time, and replacing what hadn't. Except it soon became apparent that very little actually *had* survived in any decent state. Certainly no wood from *Raymond* could be salvaged, and this presented something of a thorny problem for the renovation team. You see, *Raymond* was, by and large, a totally wooden boat…

Which is why today when you see her, though she's an exceptionally beautiful craft – one of the few built recently to the design of a traditional wooden working boat – she's hardly what you'd call totally kosher. Indeed, the only parts of her that are genuine are the iron brackets or 'knees' used to fix the sides to the bottom – and, or so I believe, a single cupboard door in the back cabin.

I think Arthur would have seen the funny side of all this. I'm not sure he would have seen the purpose of it, though, given how much it cost.

But maybe it's the fate of Braunston to symbolise everything that's worst about canals in the twenty-first century. And maybe it's the destiny of the place to show the way forward, for unless there's a serious rethink, I can't see that in the long run it's going to be possible to protect Braunston and other places like it from themselves; because for all the planning laws in the world, as canals get more popular, increasingly more people are going to want to live and moor in places like this.

What's more, they'll be willing to pay a lot of money for the privilege of it.

The acid test for us in the future, if we're to rescue anything tangible of an authentic rural England, is whether we are going to be able to manage these commercial pressures for change in the countryside in such a way that it doesn't destroy what we value most in the process. And a good measure of whether we're going to be able to do this is if we can come up with some fresh ideas for how we can plan new countryside communities since at the moment, architecturally, the best that seems to be on offer is either another version of the three-bedroom detached suburbia that we've been looking at for years, or the sort of dodgy postmodernism that began to look outdated the moment Margaret Thatcher left Downing Street.

Maybe in the canals context the best way to start would be by abandoning the pretence that developments around waterways are in any way *countryside* developments so that we stop trying to model them on idealised versions of the English village with the canal as a sort of central landscape feature, like a country brook running through the middle. Instead we should recognise the industrial traditions of the system, and start building to a more industrial scale so that apartments tower above the waterways as the old warehouses used to do, enclosing them and creating the feeling of the canals as a secret world beneath.

I'm not optimistic, though. I'm afraid the pastoral idyll is too indelibly engraved on the English psyche. Recently in Braunston they built some flats in a warehouse style around one of the boatyards, and you'd have thought they'd erected a multi-storey tower block for all the bitter opposition they engendered. OK, so the development wasn't exactly great architecture. Or even particularly good architecture for that matter. The design was all a bit passé and twee, with too much of the Milton Keynes about it. All the flats have their own little lawn the size of a postage stamp, and each incorporates a balcony with iron railings scarcely big enough to accommodate a pot plant.

One evening, not long after they'd been constructed, I watched, totally intrigued, as a couple squeezed their way onto one of these tiny terraces and stood wedged against each other sipping white wine. This might not have been so strange except that it was an icy, dark October evening. The two of them were so cold they couldn't wait to get back inside again, and they were virtually choking trying to empty their glasses. Or maybe they were just hurrying to get off the balcony before it collapsed, since, like me, they probably didn't feel it had been built to deal with anything heavier than a bird box. But I really shouldn't mock: what they were doing was a vote of confidence in the function and fabric of the building – a decision we should respect because they'd backed it with their hard-earned cash.

I wonder what opponents would have preferred for this site instead? Something of uncompromising brutal modernism like the South Bank? Or something more contemporary from Richard Rodgers with its guts hanging on the outside? Somehow I doubt it. Somehow I suspect most people in their NIMBYish way would have preferred no development at all, or if it was forced on them, then something along the lines of the boxes we were building in the 1960s, with maybe a few Victorian features tacked on to the outside to make the whole thing look 'period'.

And if that sounds pompous and condescending of me, well… it probably is. But that's the way Braunston gets to you, especially when you arrive in the place with your hull pummelled by ten years of cruising and everyone else's has a glossy finish you can see your face in because they haven't been further than the nearest pub garden since they were launched.

I was pulled out of the water the next morning, a process that involved manoeuvring *Justice* over a rickety trolley which was then hauled onto the bank up a track like a tram line. It all happened so quickly. One moment I was wondering whether you could trust a boat to this Heath-Robinson contraption and worrying about whether I should have informed my insurance company about what I was doing; and the next the boat was up the bank in a single cloud of exhaust from a Land-Rover.

Out of the water *Justice* was so awkward and ungainly that an upturned bus would have looked elegant by comparison. She towered above me, her hull scarred and stained by her long cruising, and so high that after I'd climbed up onto her by a precarious ladder I could, for the first time in my life, look down my nose at Braunston.

Which at least made a change.

Eleven

As MEETINGS BETWEEN great men go, it wasn't exactly in the Stanley and Livingstone league, though you can't help but think that the effete literary agent and his wife on a day trip from London must have felt they were in deepest Africa. After all, they lived in the heart of Bloomsbury, one of London's more fashionable areas, and in order to get to what must have seemed to them a god-forsaken spot they'd taken a train to Bromsgrove in the West Midlands and walked for more than a mile using a map to navigate their way. They must have made an odd sight as they climbed the steep towpath by the side of the near-derelict locks: her with her bright violet-blue eyes and him short-sighted and deceptively boyish in his heavily framed glasses, the pair of them like a couple of fish out of water away from the city.

It was August 1945, a clear and sunny day, and only a few months after the end of the war in Europe. The place was a flight of locks at Tardebigge, just outside of Birmingham, and the literary London pair were Robert Aickman and his wife Ray, both of them only just in their thirties. They'd come to meet the author of a book they'd read recently which had impressed them greatly.

The author was Tom Rolt; the book *Narrow Boat*.

The Tom Rolt of Tardebigge – this Tom Rolt – was a totally different man from the one who'd left Banbury for Wiltshire five years earlier. A lot had happened in the interim – so much that Rolt himself must surely have been wondering at this stage how it was when everyone else's life had been torn apart by war, everything he'd planned for himself had fallen so neatly and easily into place. He was still living on *Cressy* with Angela, but the despairing and depressed engineer who'd left Rolls-Royce for a new job all those years ago had now become a successful writer, and that 'design for living' about which he and Angela had fantasised for so long had now become a reality.

How on earth had it all happened? And how had it happened so relatively painlessly?

The future certainly hadn't looked particularly bright after they'd arrived in Hungerford and Tom had started the new job at the foundry. It involved reconditioning agricultural equipment, and although he liked the work well enough, the pay was appalling, and he and Angela were often left depending for survival on the small allowance that Angela's father still gave to the daughter he'd disowned in all other ways. At the beginning Tom wasn't any more successful with his writing ambition either, and all attempts to get the book about the honeymoon trip on *Cressy* published failed totally. One company wanted him to print it at his own expense, another tempted him with an offer to buy it outright; but most of the major publishing houses just sent it back to him with the mandatory rejection slip. The final straw came when he sent it to a literary agent who unceremoniously refused to have anything to do with it. After that the manuscript was dispatched to a bottom drawer – though the reality on *Cressy*, where space was at a premium, was that it finished up in a suitcase under the bed.

'Poverty, like the toothache,' Rolt wrote, 'can play havoc with philosophers.' Eventually a meeting with an old friend led to the offer of another job and the Rolts moved back to the Midlands, where despite Tom's distaste for bureaucrats and bureaucracy, he took up a position with the Ministry of Supply. It was a bit of a sell-out for a man of his mettle – and he knew it. But at least it was a sell-out at a good price: his new salary was three times what he'd been earning.

Another bonus of the move was that it allowed him to continue writing, for though his new position as an 'Isolated Technical Assistant' in the dusty-sounding Department TT3 was important enough as war work goes, it wasn't exactly a high-pressure job.

The department was responsible for the manufacture of vehicle spares for the services, and his work involved travelling around the Birmingham area liaising with the factories. After he returned from his site visits he'd write up his reports at his desk on *Cressy*; and then, working under the light of a paraffin lamp, he'd turn his attention to a new project he'd started: a second book, this one a philosophical treatise in which he was trying to marshal some of his ideas on the way that modern technology was destroying the ecological fabric of the earth.

This was a deliriously happy period of his life, and it was a creative one too. As well as the new book, he'd started writing articles for small circulation magazines. His main obsession was still what he called 'the tyranny of the machine', which he believed was altering the old relationship of people to the work they did, and destroying the last vestiges of traditional craftsmanship in the process. But he was gradually beginning to write about other topics too – anything from surrealism to stage design. In short, he was becoming a professional writer, and as such he was starting to come into contact with other writers of the same bent. One of them was the rural author H. J. Massingham.

Harold Massingham has been given a bad press since his death fifty years ago. Most recently Jeremy Paxman had a pop at him in his book *The English*, describing him as 'a townie who'd escaped to the Chilterns', and criticising him for producing 'book after book telling the English people that the Industrial Revolution "had destroyed the true England"'. Well, yes, Harry *was* alarmingly prolific, it's true: more than forty books over his lifetime, and countless articles everywhere from the *Listener* to the *Times Literary Supplement* – not to mention a body of correspondence of such bulk it would put most of us in the contemporary world to shame, despite the way we make such a fetish of our e-mails.

It's true too that Harry's perception of the world wasn't particularly penetrating politically either, being what one critic described as 'profoundly reactionary', and based on 'an unusually bitter detestation of modern, industrialised, urbanised civilisation'. Or as another commentator put it to me more bluntly, 'He was a crypto-fascist.'

This discovery came as no great surprise to me, since despite everything I was fed at school about Churchillian defiance, the thing that has always struck me about the history of England in the inter-war years is just how much ugly extremism lay beneath the surface of thinking then. It may be a bit of a shameful secret, and the sort of thing we don't talk much about in company, but it played its part in creating the conditions out of which the horrors of Nazi Germany were to spring. Even so, I'm sure Harry Massingham visited his mum regularly and was kind to his cat. Revisionist romanticism was par for the course at this time, and not every idealist looking to the countryside for a vision of a lost England kept a pair of jackboots in the cupboard. Indeed, during the inter-war period the mythic past became alluring to intellectuals of far greater weight than him.

And it's not hard to see why. After the First World War ended, the remnants of those who'd survived the blood and the mud of Flanders and the Somme were forced to confront the whole purpose of their existence in a way that is scarcely conceivable to us today. Virtually a whole generation had been wiped out. Those left needed to be able to justify their place in the world and come to terms with what had emerged after the carnage. Yet what did they see around them except a country becoming increasingly despoiled as 60,000 acres a year were being eaten up by massive, uncontrolled housing development and miles of new roads which were being laid to feed the voracious appetite of the increasingly popular motor car.

The fact was, they could see that something had been lost – and it wasn't necessarily all materialistic. God had been lost; and the certainties of the Victorian age had been lost, so that when in 1922 the poet T. S. Eliot came to assemble his cultural inventory of the period in *The Waste Land* all he found was an arid catalogue of spiritual despair. The future didn't seem to offer anything more encouraging either, and as the dictatorships began to rise across Europe, and the world was yet again plunged into the slaughter of war, it seemed a stark choice between Huxley's 1932 nightmare of a *Brave New World* where babies were fertilised in bottles, or Orwell's 1948 vision of *1984* in which every facet of our lives would be monitored and controlled by the political-industrial machine.

> *If I should die think only this of me:*
> *That there's some corner of a foreign field*
> *That is for ever England…*

Rupert Brooke's evocation of the soul of England felt tangible enough to a soldier seeking reassurance in nationhood as he faced the incalculable prospect of death. But what about those who were left behind afterwards? Those who survived the trenches and later the horrors of the second war where some of the worst atrocities hadn't been committed on the battlefield, but in places with silly foreign names like Auschwitz and Belsen where death itself had been reduced to an industrial process?

What price little old England then?

At least there was some certainty in the past. At least there was solace. At least when you looked back you could try and make some sense of what had all gone wrong.

At times Massingham's evocation of England sticks in the craw. It's sweet and nauseating like that mead they used to drink in the Middle Ages – a time he viewed as a golden epoch. But even though he was forever looking backwards, he wasn't necessarily always walking in that direction. Years before anyone had ever heard of Greenpeace or Friends of the Earth, he was warning of the threat to the natural balance of the world posed by chemical fertilisers and pesticides. A long time before the future of the Brazilian rainforests had become an international issue, and before British birdlife had been decimated by modern farming methods, he'd written about the likely effects of deforestation and indiscriminate hedge grubbing. Years before anyone was willing to listen, he'd cautioned about the effects of pollution on rivers and streams.

And he wasn't just playing the Jeremiah either. In a series of books he started writing towards the end of the war he began to outline a series of positive strategies for the revival of sound agricultural practice. Way before Fritz Schumacher argued for decentralised, small-scale technology in *Small is Beautiful*; and years too before traditional methods of organic farming began to be reintroduced as a response to the health risks of modern industrial farming, Massingham was warning about the dangers of rural monoculture and advocating a return to smaller, more controllable mixed farms based on more traditional methods of husbandry.

So, united by the common features of their separate philosophies, Tom Rolt and Massingham began writing to each other in a correspondence that was to last for years and which would become more intimate as time went on. It was in the course of this that Massingham asked with an innocence that could only have been born of genuine ignorance whether Rolt had ever considered writing anything about the waterways... You can imagine the anticipation, not to say trepidation, Rolt must have felt as he salvaged the manuscript of his book from the suitcase under the bed where it had lain neglected for almost four years. He must have realised that with Massingham's backing the manuscript might finally get into print. Which is how it finally turned out, for Massingham recommended it to the publishers Eyre & Spottiswood who immediately accepted it for publication.

This was September 1943. The book finally went on sale in early December the following year in an edition produced to war economy standards, priced 12/6d – twelve shillings and six pence – or just over 62p in today's money. It carried an introduction by Massingham and a frontispiece which contained two stanzas of Rupert Brooke's anguished lament to lost love, 'The Chilterns':

> *I shall desire and I shall find*
> *The best of my desires,*
> *The autumn road, the mellow wind*
> *That soothes the darkening shires.*
> *And laughter, and inn-fires.*
>
> *White mist about the black hedgerows,*
> *The slumbering Midland plain,*
> *The silence where the clover grows,*
> *And the dead leaves in the lane,*
> *Certainly, these remain.*

In his autobiography Rolt describes the jubilation he felt at finally getting the book published after having pretty well given up all hope for it. 'I read through the contract over and over again to assure myself that it was really true,' he wrote. 'And yes, there was my name at the top (hereinafter called The Author) and, believe it or not, the Publishers did "undertake to produce and publish [the] work".'

But getting a book published is one thing; getting people to buy it and read it is something entirely different, and even Rolt himself admitted that he was astonished by the reception *Narrow Boat* received. Not only did it get a series of long and favourable reviews in the newspapers, but the book sold well too. Afterwards he was overwhelmed with fan mail, confirming (if he needed confirmation) that his ideas had touched a chord in the national psyche.

One of these letters was from a young literary agent living in Bloomsbury in London. It raised the possibility of founding an organisation to campaign for the preservation of canals. This wasn't an original idea: there'd been a National Inland Navigation League in 1919, and an Inland Cruising Association which had been founded in Cheshire in the 1930s, but neither had survived, let alone had any significant long-term effect in safeguarding the waterways. Until the publication of *Narrow Boat*, Rolt wouldn't have thought such an idea feasible, but the letters he'd received – including this one – made him think there might be something in the proposal.

He wrote back immediately, inviting the young man to visit him at Tardebigge where he was living on *Cressy*...

I know what Harold Massingham was getting at. *Anyone* who spends time on the canals would know what he was getting at.

Once, years ago, Em and I were cruising in Shropshire when we filled our water tank at a tap in the middle of the countryside provided for the purpose. It was at a place which was near enough to a company selling bottled mineral water for us to feel that we were onto a good thing since ours was free and theirs was 80p a litre or thereabouts. Except that there was a warning posted nearby cautioning people not to let children drink it because of the high concentration of poisonous organophosphates leeching from the overfertilised land.

I didn't fancy it after that.

The bottled water, presumably, is drawn from some naturally occurring spring that flows thousands of feet below the water table and is filtered for trillions of years by the geology of the natural landscape. Or something like that.

All the same, I wouldn't fancy that either.

Neither do I fancy cruising through the countryside when they're spraying crops, for regardless of how often I'm told that these things are perfectly safe, I can't help remembering that they were developed from the poisonous gases used on the Western Front during the First World War. Of course, I may be missing some sophisticated bit of science here, but sometimes it's as well to go with your instincts; and as far as modern agricultural practice is concerned, when I saw a government minister on TV forcing a hamburger down the throat of his daughter, all my instincts told me there was something fundamentally wrong with beef production in this country.

And boy, was I right!

Some basic natural balance seems to have been disturbed, some disjuncture seems to have occurred with the natural world; and cruising the canals you notice it more than from inside a car because at canal speeds you observe at a level of detail the human eye can appreciate and which the human brain can assess constructively. The waterways are a back door to England, and they take you into the heart of the countryside and force you to confront these things.

Try as I might, I still can't get used to cruising in the winter through fields of growing wheat: there seems to me to be something freakish about these crops that buck the ebb and flow of the seasons, green when everything around them is brown, blooming when everything else around is dead. And I still can't get used to these rural prairies which seem to go on forever, especially the bright yellow fields of rape which may seem pretty enough flashing by from a motorway, but which can have you heaving with the smell of them after the first few minutes of a passage that by boat can sometimes take you up to half an hour to complete.

But I suppose we'll have to get used to all this and more, for the prospect ahead looks to be one where whole parishes, nay whole counties, will be given over to single crops, and where those crops are likely to become ever more exotic, with genetic engineering no doubt providing the means whereby breadfruit, mangosteens and tropical pineapples will become a common sight in the English countryside.

Or that failing, perhaps fields of mangoes doctored in such a way they grow into organ parts such as kidneys or lungs.

Mind you, we mustn't complain, I suppose, for at least this way we'll be able to claim again as we once did, that the very heart of England lies close to the soil.

My time in Braunston was mostly spent with my sleeves rolled up painting the hull of the boat with the thick, black bitumastic us inland waterways types slap on anything vaguely metallic. In the evenings after I'd cleaned up and eaten, I'd take the Debsmobile into the deepest countryside, searching for the perfect English pub – a job which I saw as a basic part of my research for this book.

Now in all truth I can hardly claim that this task promised to be onerous work. Even so, I didn't expect it to be all holiday either, for I was pessimistically anticipating that most decent country pubs – like a lot of the best pubs in cities – would have been destroyed long ago in the name of progress and that I'd be condemned to spend a succession of miserable nights in the middle of nowhere relying for my entertainment on my ability to engage bilious rustics in conversation about turnip yields or ploughing techniques.

Urban prejudice or what?

In village after village I kept finding a succession of remarkably unspoiled places, some of them genuine and untouched, and most of the others restored with a sensitivity to taste and tradition far beyond anything I'd anticipated. The people I met were exceptionally friendly too, I found, a good deal more affable than in London pubs where sullen detachment often seems an intrinsic part of the urban drinking experience. Certainly if I did meet any initial reluctance to talk to me as a I travelled around, it was only because the sight of a battle-worn traditionalist from a canal boat driving about in a 30-year-old Triumph Herald was anathema to people whose natural inclination is more towards top-of-the-range BMWs or fuck-off big bits of farm machinery with more horsepower than a set of Newmarket stables.

The beer was good too – a lot better than you'd have got years ago at the height of the 'Red Revolution' when the ubiquitous Watneys Red Barrel was being sold at a strength only a little higher than might legally have been given to children as a soft drink. But nothing so emphasises the sentimentality which we English harbour for our traditional way of life, and yet so highlights our reluctance to defend it, as the fight we had to ensure that we could get a decent pint in our pubs. Other countries went to the barricades for life, love and liberty; for human rights and the freedom of man. We campaigned for real ale – but we only did that grudgingly after we were finally persuaded that the breweries weren't exactly playing fair by us charging more than a pound a pint for piss water.

So in inimitable fashion we muddled our way to victory, though it's as well to remind ourselves that it was a damn close-run thing, and that without the intervention of a few enthusiasts we might have been drinking highly expensive fizzy mineral water like the continentals. Yes, of course I know that nowadays we *are* drinking highly expensive fizzy mineral water like the continentals. But that's... well... that's our choice, isn't it? And a lot of it's *real* mineral water which is an entirely different thing altogether.

In those far-off days when messing about on the canals marked you out as a radical as much as long hair did, enthusiasts used to navigate the system less by maps than the pathetically slim *Real Ale Guide to the Waterways*. This at least ensured that at the end of the day you met up with similarly hirsute people who would almost certainly share one of your preoccupations, whether for hard drinking, soft drugs or the primitive traditional music we listened to then, which was played on acoustic guitars and was such a painful experience all round that even those who sang it had to stick their fingers in their ears to avoid the full consequences of what they were doing.

But my, those real ale places were few and far between! And sometimes even when you sought them out after walking for miles across fields and along no-hope country lanes, all you'd find was a pub like any other pub except that stuck away at the far end of the bar would be a single dusty hand pump that had virtually rusted up for lack of use. So you'd be forced anyhow to have a pint of tasteless pasteurised keg, and you'd thank your lucky stars for it, since the licensing hours in those days were so restricted that to arrive anywhere with alcohol in that critical window when it was actually on sale required planning of almost military precision.

Of course, there *were* good pubs then, and some outstanding ones close to the waterways. The Anchor on the Shropshire Union, for instance: a traditional unspoiled canal inn where once the old boatmen used to stable their horses overnight. Or the Bird in Hand on the Macclesfield Canal just outside Kidsgrove which was like a country kitchen with just a single scrubbed wooden table in the middle of the small room which passed for the bar. Except there wasn't a bar as such in the place, and they'd fetch up beer from the barrels in the cellar in a chipped enamel jug. And the Black Lion at Consall Forge in Staffordshire on the Caldon Canal where I've spent many happy hours since at one time you couldn't conveniently get to the place except by water which meant that closing time could be – how shall we put this so as not to upset anyone? – sensibly flexible (will that do?).

Sadly the Bird in Hand is closed now, the elderly lady who ran it for years and who was said to be an old music hall star long since dead and buried. And they've built a road to the Black Lion too which has altered its character fundamentally. The Anchor has altered as well, though perhaps not so much in its fabric as in the clientele it now attracts, since what is antiquated and decrepit and once thought somewhat folksy, has these days become such a commonplace of contemporary style that the place is filled with mid-management marketing types who've copied it in their homes.

So don't let's get sentimental about English pubs of yesteryear: this lot was the best of the bunch and going for a drink in those days could be a grim experience. It's easy to forget that the reason the breweries were so keen on serving us pasteurised beer was that there were so many pub landlords who were completely incapable of looking after the decent stuff. Ordering a pint then was a lottery in which you might – if you were lucky – get something bright, sharp and flavoursome; but where you'd an equal chance of getting a glass of something murky and flat that tasted like tooth suckings and looked as if it had been bucketed up from the Tyne.

And, believe me, some of the people that you used to find in those places were like characters out of *The X-Files*. And I'm not talking Mulder and Scully here, either.

Trust me, I speak with authority on this topic, for in the determined pursuit of alcoholic oblivion I have been constrained to spend countless dispiriting hours amongst the sad and disinherited of Mother England, many of whom still appear in my nightmares smelling of beer slops and wreathed in misty clouds of stale cigarette smoke. The difficulty is remembering them all, for the merely unusual ones have faded from memory and it's only the totally grotesque that I recollect with any clarity.

Like the guy in one pub near Stoke-on-Trent who waited until I'd sat down and then drew up a chair directly opposite me at my table. He had eyes like the comedian Marty Feldman, and as I began to sip at my beer, he fixed me as best he could with the only one he could keep stable. Then, while the other went for a wander around the bar, he watched attentively until I'd drained every last drop from my glass. Eventually, in a lugubrious voice that might have been out of central casting for *Hammer House of Horror*, he said, 'Nice that was, was it? It is nice to drink a pint of beer when you've a thirst on you, isn't it? Perhaps I could be allowed to get you another one, could I?'

If it hadn't been that it was daylight and there were one or two people around so that at least I wasn't alone, I think I'd have run screaming for the door in search of a crucifix, wooden stakes and a mallet.

At another pub I visited near the Welsh border I stood for what seemed like hours before the landlord so much as deigned to look up from a group of people he was with. They were all bunched around a one-armed bandit in the corner, and it seemed that whenever I coughed self-consciously to get attention, or shaped up to start whistling 'Molly Malone', the machine would suddenly burst into life, shrieking and flashing like a fairground carousel, and they would all begin frenziedly feeding it with whatever spare coins they could dig from their pockets.

I suppose you have to expect to be ignored in pubs close to the Welsh border. In fact, it's part of the preparation for actually going to Wales where as an Englishman they make a point of ignoring you all the time. Even so, enough is enough. The landlord finally did clock me, but just as I was beginning to get excited that he might actually get around to serving me a drink, he turned away... and walked off... straight out of the pub.

Don't ask me – I never found out what it was all about either. And I never got my drink. All I know is, you just couldn't get away with that sort of thing running a pub now. Or if you did, you wouldn't get away with it for very long because when your customers are paying a small fortune for a pint, they expect a bit more for their money than to be treated as if their presence is somehow an imposition on the routine of the place.

In fact, the opposite is the case, and as a customer you now get *too much* attention from bar staff. They're always insisting on giving you a clean glass every time you ask for your old one to be filled up and forever wiping down your table and clearing away your crisps bags as if you were some patient in a nursing home suffering from dementia. It's virtually impossible to have a quiet drink in a pub, for if the staff aren't fussing around you like so many clucking hens, they're pestering you for details of your private life with the sort of doggedness that would be considered impertinent, not to say downright rude, by the practitioners of any other profession, doctors included.

'Come far, have we, sir? Going anywhere in particular? Staying long? Had oral sex recently?'

We English seem to have lost the natural discretion we once had in talking about ourselves. It seems only yesterday that our sense of propriety prevented us from even acknowledging a personal crisis publicly, let alone making a big deal of it the way we do now. You might have had everything you ever owned destroyed in a fire and everyone you ever loved killed in a bus crash; even so, if anyone asked you how you were, you'd be classed as hysterically overemotional if you replied in any more demonstrative fashion than asserting you 'mustn't grumble'. In those days it was a maxim of life that everything could get a good deal worse than it was, and so most people just kept their heads down for fear of tempting fate to take a pot at them in the shooting gallery of life.

In this day and age, though, it seems you only have to break a fingernail or lose a button off a blouse to be openly emoting and in need of a therapist to help you through your pain. This is another area where pub landlords can sometimes be a strain, since if they're not offering counselling with the beer they sell, then they're expecting you to listen to them while they bang on endlessly about some problem or another that *they* have.

I came across a publican like this in one of the small villages around Braunston where I washed up on one of my excursions in the Herald one afternoon. The pub was empty, and the landlord fixed on me like a surface-to-air missile, insisting on buying me a drink and leading me off to a discreet corner where, without so much as a by-your-leave, he regaled me for at least half an hour with all manner of details about his personal life.

I didn't know where to put my face. I'd only just met the man, and here he was confiding intimate things about himself I wouldn't even tell my best friend. Eventually I felt the onus was on me to say something, and I hesitated the opinion that perhaps a lot of his problems might be down to stress and overwork. After all, it was a tough job running a pub that was open every afternoon and evening.

'Oh, but I don't open afternoons,' he said brightly. 'Well, not in the week anyway. I just left the door open today for you.'

'For me?' I said. 'But how did you know I was...?'

But I didn't finish. I didn't need to. There was the sound of pennies dropping, and a silence fell between us you could have cut with a knife.

He began to turn a deep shade of scarlet.

'You mean... you're not the bloke Colin arranged for me to see?' he eventually stuttered.

Twelve

ENGLAND OF THE mid-1950s was far from an ideal world for the Standard Triumph motor company. Though the austerity years were drawing to a close and there was an explosion in the demand for small cars, the company just wasn't in any position to take advantage of market conditions. The boardroom coup which saw the young lion Alick Dick become managing director had led to a clutch of bright young men rising in the hierarchy, but the previous dynasty had left them with a lot of baggage that was hampering their ability to plan for the future.

The root of the problem lay in decisions taken at the beginning of the decade when it had briefly looked as if Standard Triumph was going to get totally squeezed out of the small car market by the likes of the Morris Minor. To avoid being left behind, the old management had been compelled to commit to the development of a totally new car based on a redesigned engine and a brand-new gearbox.

That car was the Standard Eight. It was launched in 1953, the year the Queen was crowned, and though it was successful enough in its own way and sold 70,000 a year at the height of its popularity, it was – to say the least – a little basic. So basic, in fact, that with a refreshing lack of political correctness, if appalling taste, the early versions were nicknamed the 'Belsen line' after the notorious Nazi concentration camp. They cost a bit over £480 and for that you got rubber mats on the floor and a hole in the front instead of a radiator grill. A heater cost you an additional £17 10s (£17.50) and you even had to pay extra for wheel hubs.

This was Standard Triumph's main production-line small car which Alick Dick inherited when he took over his job. It just wasn't good enough, and he knew it. At 37 he was a young man himself, and he realised more than anyone that the aspirations of the young were rising, especially where cars were concerned. He saw that in order to compete in the marketplace he was going to have to do something, and do it quickly. But his options were limited. There was no time available to go through the preparation which in an ideal world would precede the launch of a new car, no time for painstaking research and careful development, no time for conscientious planning and protracted months of design.

And there was no money either. Tooling up for the Standard Eight had cost so much that in order to get a return on their colossal investment, the company was stuck for years to come with the engine and gear box they had already designed. The only choice left was to modify them as far as possible and use them in another car. A slightly more sophisticated car. A car that would sell as much on style as performance.

That car was the Zobo: the Triumph Herald.

I have to confess that all this was a long way from my mind as I stood on the grass verge adjacent to the church in the tiny village of Lower Shuckborough near Daventry, watching a small pool of oil form on the road surface from a regular drip which was emanating from my engine. The engine of my Triumph Herald, that is. The Triumph Herald which I'd been happily driving only moments before, until I'd been brought to an abrupt halt by an emergency warning light on my dashboard. I lifted up the bonnet which, as any aficionado of the Herald will know, opens out the whole front of the car so that the complete engine becomes totally and instantly accessible. The reason for the oil leak was all too clear: a small draining screw in the base of the sump had corroded and worked loose, and I had run out of oil.

This wasn't any big deal. In fact, it was a tiny problem, the sort of thing you get used to dealing with virtually every day of the year driving a classic car. It was an inconvenience, yes. And a pretty irritating inconvenience too since, unusually, it was a lovely afternoon, and I had the roof down, basking in the warmth of a mysterious orange planet that had inexplicably appeared in the sky where normally there would be cloud cover. But I knew I'd be able to get a replacement easily enough, and in the interim I could top up with oil and use a bit of old anything as a plug to prevent any further leakage.

Except, of course – and isn't this the way life goes? – I hadn't got any oil with me.

Now precisely *why* I hadn't got any oil with me, I couldn't say. I'd got spare petrol with me, and spare filters and fan belts too. I'd got spare spark plugs and a spare set of points, and spare condensers and spare wiper blades. I'd even got a spare petrol-tank cap, not to mention a breathtaking variety of other bits of bodywork of all shapes and sizes. In fact, I'd got so many bits of spare car in the boot, I could probably have built myself a new Triumph Herald from scratch if I'd wanted one. But of oil, I had not one drop, not anywhere, not even a renegade teaspoonful sitting in the bottom of a can awaiting this moment for its hour of glory. And yet... and yet I had this recollection that I'd only just bought oil – what, a couple of weeks before? Less? I'd put it in the boot. I clearly remembered putting it there. I even remembered *where* in the boot I'd put it. Damn it! I even remembered *how* I'd put it in the boot. But however many times I went back to the boot, desperately trying to convince myself that even in a space as small as that I'd somehow missed it, or overlooked it, or somehow otherwise misplaced it, I just couldn't for the life of me see any sign of it.

Clearly it was Em's fault. It had to be her fault. No one in their right mind would break into a car just to steal a couple of litres of oil; and besides, no one *had* broken into the car: the car was intact and unviolated. Even so, the oil had gone; there was no getting away from it. And since I hadn't moved it, there was only one other person who would have done. It was probably her idea of a joke. I went back to the boot again just to check once more, but I still couldn't find what I was looking for. I slammed the blasted thing closed, convinced beyond persuasion that Em was to blame for all this. She must have taken it the last time she'd visited. She'd done it... well, she'd done it just to annoy me, why else? I took the opportunity of checking the boot one last time. The boot was still empty. Now I was absolutely convinced. This was all definitely Em's responsibility. There was absolutely no doubt about it.

There was no alternative – I'd have to go to a garage. Luckily I remembered passing one a while before, and so swearing death, damnation and divorce, I grabbed my coat and started on what I just knew was going to be a long and unpleasant trek. At that very moment, as if to confirm my cynical pessimism, the sky completely darkened as a whole regiment of cumulonimbi gathered on the horizon as if they were a cosmic football crowd at half time, and I was their nearest urinal. Before I'd walked more than a hundred yards the rain had started falling on me with that provocatively fine drizzle that mocks you by not appearing to be rain at all, even though it takes but moments to permeate through to your very Y-fronts. Minutes later it was hammering down.

An hour or so later I got back to the car with a gallon can of oil. By then I was literally soaked to the skin, and my mood was so thunderous that the weather paled by comparison. It was at that point, throwing my sodden coat onto the back seat of the car, that I noticed, tucked away behind the passenger seat where I immediately remembered leaving it... another gallon can of oil.

Now, I may have been outside a church, but my behaviour at this juncture was not exactly of an ecclesiastical tenor. Nor was my language. It must have attracted attention from inside, for in no time at all I became aware of someone I took to be a clergyman pressing his nose against the car window very close to my face. He'd no doubt heard me screaming. He probably thought I'd had an accident and needed the last rites instantly.

He was, I remember, waving around a large set of garden shears.

Seeing him like that was a shock. With his face distorted through the glass by the rain, and the shears making him look like Edward Scissorhands, I thought I'd got locked into *The Twilight Zone*. Which is, thinking about it, probably what he thought too, confronted by this shrieking idiot dementedly battering his head with the palms of his hands.

Afterwards I felt the least I could do was visit the church – which was fortuitous, since in the state I was in I'd probably have gone straight back to the boat and missed the place which would have been a great loss. The fact is, it's a little treasure: a beautiful example of Victorian Gothic characterised by the most delightful spire set on top of an ornate six-sided tower. Once I'd got my bearings, I realised that I actually recognised the building and had passed it many times before, most recently just a day or two before as I was coming into Braunston, for you can see the back of it from the canal.

Its most impressive aspect is from the front, though. From this elevation you see its full splendour across a small green where many years ago the village stocks used to be sited. Beyond that, leading to the church door, is a path bordered by the most enormous and unusual avenue of yew trees shaped like great teardrops. The man I had taken to be a clergyman was actually the verger, and he'd been trimming the yews until he'd been disturbed first by the rain and then by me.

Inside, the church is just as remarkable, especially the vaulted roof of the tower which is decorated with star-spangled tiles that seem almost bizarre in this setting. In fact, the author of a book on churches around Daventry comments that the first impression they give is of a Hindu temple. This was exactly my reaction too, and odd enough for any English church in the middle of the English countryside, but somehow odder here, for the more I looked at the verger, who was now acting as my guide, the more it seemed to me that there was something of the Indian about him too.

Perhaps part of it was his colour, for his face certainly had a weather-beaten tan about it which gave him the complexion of someone more used to the climate of Rajasthan than Rugby. But most of it was his bone structure. Though he was well into his seventies he was an extraordinarily handsome man, fit and lean, with a head of hair like a 20-year-old and the most strikingly high cheekbones which gave him a proud, aristocratic bearing.

He showed me a spot in the church where the floor had given way, disclosing an unknown crypt which, he said, he'd had the devil's own job getting any expert from Warwick to come and investigate since as far as they were concerned they'd already surveyed the church once fifty years ago and found everything that was worth finding then. As I was leaving he pointed out another structural failing – this time a massive indentation in the path where only a few months before a piece of stonework had dislodged from the tower and come crashing down.

'The whole place is just falling to bits,' he said. 'There's not the interest in these old buildings the way there used to be, you see. They cost too much to maintain and nowadays people just aren't willing to…' he trailed off, shaking his head sadly. 'I don't know what's going to happen to the place when I go,' he said finally.

There was a total lack of any sentimentality in his voice.

It turned out that he'd been involved with the church in some capacity for most of his life. 'My father too,' he said, proudly, 'and my grandfather before him – after he'd got back to England.'

'He was in the army,' he explained, seeing the curiosity on my face. 'India. In fact, my grandmother was an Indian. He married her and brought her back to the village. I can still remember her in her sari telling me stories when I was a child.'

Even after so long he could remember these stories with some clarity, for the world she'd described to him – her world – was a strange and faraway land of gleaming marble palaces and thick jungles where man-eating tigers stalked; and it touched his imagination deeply. She'd talked to him of dusty villages too, where wild-haired holy men sat, their bodies smeared with strange red dyes; and of towns with great markets full of exotic fruits; and of snake charmers, and elephants, of great wide rivers and expansive deserts; and most of all the constant burning heat which made you feel slow and heavy, and caused the world to become richly aromatic, and the air to shimmer as if in constant anticipation of the future.

It was obvious listening to him that these stories were a precious part of his childhood years. And it was clear too that his biggest disappointment was that his own family didn't embrace anything of this personal history; in fact, he gave me the impression that they may have been somehow intimidated by it, fearful that when a child was born to any of them, it might somehow turn out 'coloured' and a throwback to what they seemed to consider something of a shameful family episode.

Eventually, it seemed something of this sort might have happened. One of his grandchildren was born with a dark patch of skin across his back which had caused some concern until the doctor had reassured the family that it wasn't anything to worry about, and that it would fade with time.

Actually I got the feeling that he wouldn't have been too upset if the mark had been permanent so that there might have been some tangible reminder of the past; but perhaps I'm investing him with my own romantic nostalgia, and people on narrowboats who drive around the countryside in old convertible cars should beware of invoking nostalgia in any form. They should also beware of wearing sunglasses with mirror lenses, or donning baseball caps, especially those where the peaks tend to gravitate unstoppably towards the rear. Dispassionate cool is the image we're chasing here, not postmodern self-parody.

Besides, this new century's already too dictated by style, and there are too many people like me ranting at what they should be trying to change; and too many people like the verger's family railing against what they should just accept. The truth is that though things seem to alter with extraordinary speed, attitudes are far more deeply entrenched in England than we think they are, and they change much more slowly than we think they do too – especially in the English countryside where people need much longer to come to terms with change.

My mate Dave and I dropped into the Blue Bell not so very long ago. This is a pub in the village where I was brought up, and where the two of us squandered a large part of our youth on the basis that since drink was the equivalent of 10p a pint and would never in our lifetimes be as cheap again, we were justified in the name of thrift getting as much of it down our throats as we could in the shortest possible time. The Blue Bell in those days was considered quite a posh pub; and you could always tell posh pubs because they had carpets on the floor, served you bitter in dimpled glass jugs with handles, and took exception to you throwing up in the toilet. It hadn't altered much – in fact, if anything it had got even ritzier and had now spawned a restaurant where among other things you could enjoy a selection of pies of various types topped with towering crusts of puff pastry.

In all other respects, though, the village had changed totally.

In my day it was a somewhat dour place with a grey council estate built of pre-fabricated concrete, and an equally dismal primary school where I got bullied for breaking the first rule of the playground and learning how to read. It was a utilitarian place, with a lot of utilitarian terraced housing, a few small utilitarian factories and a row of utilitarian shops grouped around the war memorial on a utilitarian village green.

Not any more, though.

Little did I know it as a youngster, but lurking underneath all that, like a butterfly waiting to emerge from its chrysalis, was a modern English village. All the terraced houses have now metamorphosed into cottages with Quality Street-style bijou bay windows; and the ubiquitous geranium is as much in evidence here as in any market town. The school still just about survives, but all the factories have gone, knocked down to be rebuilt as 'executive' housing estates of the same three-bedroom design that you see everywhere today from Newcastle to Norfolk. Even the council estate's rocketed up-market because, of course, most of the houses are now in private hands; and though you can't altogether hide the aura of post-war municipalism, you can do a great deal to conceal it by the judicious planting of climbers from the local garden centre.

Even the fish and chip shop on the green has changed beyond recognition and (absolutely true this) it's now got a couple of tables inside where they'll let you drink wine with your cod and mushy peas. Wine? With fish and chips? When I was a kid, wine was something you drank once a year with your Christmas dinner. And then it was sweet Sauternes.

It was early in the evening in the Blue Bell, and the pub was virtually empty but for a scattering of locals standing around the bar. One of them stood on his own, a little removed from the others. I'd been aware of him watching me from the moment I'd arrived, but now he turned towards me and I realised with an unpleasant frisson of recognition that I knew him from nearly forty years before. And I hadn't liked him then. We nodded at each other stiffly, and though we didn't speak, it was clear that the next time I went to the bar, I couldn't avoid having to acknowledge his existence and say something to him.

But exactly what could I say? I toyed with the idea of 'It's been a long time,' but a period of four decades is self-evidently a long time, and I thought that it might be a shade unimaginative. 'Fancy running into you, then,' I dismissed too, since my memory of him all those years ago was that he spent more time in the Blue Bell than Dave and I did – and I guessed since then, not exactly being the pioneering sort, he'd probably never wandered very far from it.

'Are you well?' wasn't favourite either, since it risked the danger of him interpreting what I was saying as a genuine question which warranted a reply. Similarly something anodyne like 'You OK, then?' risked hitting an entirely wrong note, for as far as I knew he could have been suffering from some ailment like chronic constipation or athlete's foot which he might have been drawn to talk about at great length. Eventually I fixed on a straightforward 'Good to see you again,' which, whilst not exactly being the epitome of truthfulness, did at least have the advantage of being short, pithy and uncontroversial.

In fact, I needn't have worried, for he got in first. No sooner was I within earshot than he said something that left me absolutely speechless.

Remember, this was a guy who'd never lived outside the parish boundaries but who had doubtless enjoyed a totally contented life, believing not just that this village was the centre of *his* universe, but that it was centre of *the* universe – a place from which no one with any sense would ever wish to venture far, but to which those who did would not be long in returning.

He said simply, and with the conviction of one who had never doubted that I would, 'You've come back, then.'

They dropped *Justice* back into the water after three days, her hull now impeccably pristine and even her livery looking sprucer than it had for ages thanks to a pot of touch-up paint and a coat or two of wax polish I'd found time to apply. I started up the engine and edged off the precarious trolley on which she'd been balanced, carefully moving away from the slipway and navigating towards the centre channel so as not to risk damaging her glossy new finish against any moored boat.

When I met oncoming craft I steered as far away from them as possible to avoid the slightest risk of collision, and, passing through the narrow bridges leading out of Braunston, I slowed almost to a stop so as to avoid scuffing her hull against the edging stones.

Justice was like a proud queen, dressed for a coronation, and I was determined to ensure that she stayed that way.

I steered her like no other boat had ever been steered before. I steered her with a consummate, unparalleled precision that was a joy to behold. I steered her with care and rigour. I steered her with complete concentration and meticulous attention to detail.

Then at the first lock I came to I steered her straight into the wall and gouged a scratch down her side half the length of a car.

But by that stage Braunston was far behind me, and somehow it didn't seem to matter any more.

Thirteen

THERE COMES A TIME in life when you have to take stock of yourself. There comes a stage when you need a clear sense of purpose and a goal, a point at which you have to be clear about your ambitions and aspirations.

It's the same with boating.

Like life, it's invaluable to have some idea of where you're going. It's useful too to have some vague notion of how to get there as well. Otherwise, in the same way that you can finish up in some office shuffling papers when you thought you were going to be a brain surgeon, so on canals you can arrive in Braunston when you were actually going to Bristol.

You may recall that going to Bristol was actually my original plan for this trip, and that the only reason I'd gone north was because I'd left Oxford in a fit of pique and an avalanche of dog shit after being delayed so long from getting on the Thames by the rain. But in going north I'd taken a route that was in an entirely different direction to Bristol – which somewhat ruled Bristol out as a destination for the trip, and ensured that this whole confused mess was turning into a far better metaphor for existence than it was a journey.

But the question still remained: where on earth *was* I going?

'Stratford,' said Em with some conviction.

'Stratford?'

'Stratford-upon-Avon – birthplace of the Bard, the home of the Royal Shakespeare Theatre and a town…' she faltered.

'A town built on the River Avon, maybe?' I suggested.

'Something like that.' She glowered at me. 'What do you think anyhow, Mum?' she asked.

'Mum' was Chris, Em's mother, who had joined us for a holiday cruise. She's an 80-something – a small, alert woman with meticulously kept pure white hair and sharp eyes which dart about constantly like a bird's. Actually, she didn't really care where she went because she was determined to have a good time whatever.

She said: 'I don't really care where I go; I'm determined to have a good time whatever.' And with that she poured us all a glass of the very good malt whisky she'd brought with her as a gift.

The two of them had arrived on the boat that morning in high spirits, looking forward to a holiday break from the routine of London, but as if on cue the rain, which had been in brief respite, started hammering down again, playing out such a rhythm on the top of the boat that you couldn't sit in it long without feeling you were trapped inside a drum. It was about the only incentive we had to go anywhere. Except that we hadn't been able to work out *where* it was we wanted to go.

Now, with the mention of Stratford-upon-Avon as a destination, we were galvanised into action. Suddenly a new energy infected us all.

'Stratford it is then!' said Em. 'Let's get going this very moment. I'll put my coat on.'

'And I'll clear up the glasses,' said Chris.

It could have been the pure elation at finally making a decision. It could have been the promise of the freedom ahead; the prospect of enjoying miles of sylvan canals set in the unspoiled landscape; the anticipation of endless days of lazy cruising and the nights of conviviality which lay before us. It could have been just pure *joie de vivre* and nothing else…

Then again, it could have been the whisky.

One way or another, we were all fired up, so I went and fired the engine up too. It was nice for a change to have some company on my travels.

Going west from Braunston the canal architecture changes

suddenly and radically. Gone now are the narrow seven-foot-wide locks of the Oxford Canal which accommodate a boat like *Justice* with just a couple of inches to spare on either side. Gone too is that sense of Georgian twee, with warehouses and cottages built to the scale of dolls' houses. As you turn onto the Grand Union Canal, the waterway widens and straightens and everything becomes so much bigger and more industrial. One immediate change is the banking, and from now on brutal concrete edging stones installed in the 1930s line the canal with instructions set into them for the dredging depths required to accommodate the commercial traffic that was still plying its trade then.

There's still significant haulage trade on Britain's rivers and canals, and over recent years there's been considerable development of the infrastructure of the waterways around Sheffield and South Yorkshire, and the River Trent. But the investment in this route between London and Birmingham in the years leading up to the Second World War was the last time that money was spent with any real hope that water transport might take its place with roads as a part of an integrated system of moving freight around England. Even then it was a pretty forlorn hope. Until it unified in 1929, what we know as the Grand Union Canal today was owned by a rag-tag of different companies. The improvements were too little, too late, and in the long run the main beneficiary of them would turn out to be the leisure traffic that began to expand in the 1950s in the wake of *Narrow Boat* and the foundation of the Inland Waterways Association.

You can see the change clearly at the three locks at Calcutt, the first you meet after the turn. You're going downhill now, dropping into the valley of the Avon, and they look absolutely huge as you approach them: each of their gates as wide as a small lock and each with an immense, delicately balanced beam like the pointing finger of a great dark fist. The whole scale of the thing is totally different to the Oxford Canal locks, and there's a whole different system of paddles to manipulate the water flow too, for in place of the rudimentary cogs and ratchets of the narrow canals is a hydraulic system necessary to release the 250-ton weight of the 56,000 gallons of water that each lock holds.

Chris was quite enamoured of this system because although it all looks a bit macho and rufty-tufty in a hairy-arsed sort of way, the paddles are like little pussy cats when you start to play with them; and it's not brute force they need, just the persistence to keep winding a lock key, or windlass, for long enough, something easily within her capacity. We were soon past Calcutt, and a couple of miles later we arrived at the first of the eight locks that compose the Stockton flight. By now we were all well into the swing of things, back into a routine of locking which we've done so many times over the years that the technique we use hardly seems like a technique at all, so much is it second nature to us. In what seemed no time at all we'd negotiated the flight and were cruising through the empty countryside that carries the canal towards Warwick.

We moored that night just outside of Leamington Spa, in the bosky basin below the lock at Radford Semele, between the humpback bridge which carries the village road from Offchurch, and the high-level railway viaduct on which the long-since abandoned line to Rugby once ran. It's an alluring spot, adjacent to the River Leam which runs parallel at this point; and it's so thick with trees that despite being close to the town, and despite the occasional noise of a passing car, the kingfishers feed with impunity, nesting around the crumbling chamber of the adjacent narrow lock which was replaced and abandoned as part of the 1930s improvements.

There's a certain melancholy feel about the place, though. Before *Justice*, Em and I had another boat which we kept for along time in Leamington during those heady years of the 1970s when we'd cruise up to Radford with friends at least once a month for one reason or another, be it a search for hallucinogenic mushrooms, or long weekend parties when we'd have the kingfishers cowering between bouts of Pink Floyd or the Rolling Stones as we partied through the night. The memory of Radford is all tied up with those times, and the memory of friends, some who had toddlers then who've since grown up and had toddlers of their own, but some who've just drifted out of our lives the way people do, and some who are sadly no longer with us any more. So there's an eerie but pleasurable poignancy I always feel mooring here, especially when the evening closes in and the light begins to play tricks with the world, so that you can almost see the past playing out before you as if in a half-formed but somehow palpable dream in which you almost expect to glimpse long-lost faces emerging from the shadows to greet you again.

We were moored at Radford many years ago the night that a friend Malcolm took us to a party in Warwick and we borrowed his car to get back because he'd decided on the spur of the moment to stay late. At the time Malcolm was living on his boat in town which was only a couple of miles away. 'I'll just walk up the towpath tomorrow and pick it up,' he said. 'Don't worry about it.'

It was the early hours when we got back, and we decided to have a nightcap before turning in, and somehow the conversation turned to talk of the bizarre and the supernatural, the way it sometimes can on the canal when you're in the middle of nowhere and the fire's flickering behind the stove glass; and when there's a wind gently rocking the boat, and outside there's the creaking of a branch, or some other more inexplicable noise that makes you feel uneasy, yet at the same time reassures you that you're safely cosseted against the world.

We had a guest that night, and she'd just finished telling us that chilling tale which was doing the rounds then about the couple whose car broke down in the middle of the woods the night a notorious psychopath escaped from a local asylum. You remember the story? Surely you must? He was responsible for a dozen or more vile killings, and the couple realised that they were in grave danger, so when the man decided to take a risk and go for help, he gave his girlfriend strict instructions that she should lock the car doors behind him and under no circumstances open them to anyone. Under no circumstances.

An hour went by but he didn't return. Two hours passed and still he didn't reappear. By now she was beginning to panic. At one stage, desperate to believe he was safe, she thought he *had* come back, for she could have sworn she felt the car move slightly, as if he'd tried the door handle and found it locked... But it was nothing, just a trick of the wind. Except that soon afterwards she become aware with horror of a faint scuffling on the roof just above her head. The scuffling eventually became a gently rhythmic banging – Bang! Bang! Bang! – and the banging became louder and louder and louder yet, a persistent terrifying hammering so that she felt it could only be moments before the roof gave way under the pounding it was receiving, and whoever – or *what*ever – was causing it finally got to her as surely was the intention. She would have screamed except her lungs had constricted in an icy terror. She would have bolted except that her boyfriend's last words to her still rang in her ears.

'Don't, under any circumstances – *any* circumstances at all – leave the car. The car is your only hope of safety.'

Suddenly, like a curious nightmare in which events are out of kilter with the natural world, the whole forest lit up about her, bursting into a harsh white light. Once her eyes had adjusted to the blinding brightness she could make out the blurred core of arc lights positioned all around her, on every side, as if this were a film set and she were somehow the star of the scene. She could make out figures crouched beneath the trees, figures kneeling and – strange this, she thought – looking as if they were carrying guns – rifles – tucked into their shoulders and trained in her direction.

A megaphone burst into life with the voice of a policeman. She knew it was a policeman even before she could make out the outline of his uniform through her squinting eyes.

'Leave the car,' he said. 'Leave the car NOW. Walk towards

me slowly. Do not panic and do not look back. Under no circumstances look back.'

She was in a daze now, so totally bewildered that she was in no position to exercise any will of her own; so drugged with fear that when she rested her hand on the catch of the car door, it wasn't her hand which pressed it down, or her strength which pushed the door open or even her body which hauled itself from the car…

'Just walk towards me,' the voice kept saying through the megaphone. 'Walk slowly. Do not look back. Under no circumstances look back.'

But how could she avoid looking back? How could she resist, even at the moment of her greatest terror, that ghastly appalling curiosity which impels us all to probe the deep and dark recesses of our soul?

So she glanced behind her briefly, and the glance was enough, for in that passing moment she saw an image that would be burnt forever into her memory; an image so acute that in future years when it returned to her in odd unguarded moments, it would still have the power to choke her with fear at the hideous remembrance of it. It was the image of the psychopath sitting on top of the car, cross-legged like a recalcitrant child in a nursery school, banging a broken toy on the roof.

Except this was no broken toy he was banging. It was the severed head of her boyfriend, the ghastly gap of his mouth frozen in the rictus of his last bemused smile.

It was at that very point – as the three of us sat in the boat at Radford Semele in the early hours of the morning, frightening ourselves with this story – at that precise moment after the story had finished, but before we'd had time for the gratifying chill of it to wear off, we each of us clearly heard a bang on the top of the boat roof.

We were all struck dumb. We looked at each other as if seeking confirmation of what we'd experienced. It was as if we were expecting that one of us would come up with some rational explanation of the sound, some interpretation of it that we could all happily accept as the truth and laugh at for having thought so menacing. Maybe a broken fragment of a branch had fallen on us? Possibly some pine cone had dropped from a height? Or maybe one of us was just playing a trick on the others?

But then it happened again: a regular banging now, at first soft, but as persistent as in the story. And then becoming louder and more unrelenting yet. I remember looking at the other two wondering whether my face had turned as white as theirs. Or if their mouths could be as dry as mine.

Despite what some people would claim about TV and films coarsening our sensitivities, most of us have got a clear notion of the dividing line between imagination and reality; and we're aware that it looks pretty uncool to be seen flapping about under our seats in the multiplex just because some splatter movie is getting a bit gory. By the same token, we've all been genuinely terrified at some stage in our lives by something we know is real, whether it's been something spectral that we've not totally understood or something that we've understood all too well, like nearly getting ourselves killed in a road accident, or having to sit in front of the TV watching Tony Blair give us his take on sincerity.

But when you're frightened like this – especially frightened after telling stories the way we'd been doing – there's a curious half stage which is neither one thing nor the other, neither fact nor fiction, but between the two; and it was into this lacuna we were all plunged that night on the boat at Radford as we all sat visibly blanching while the knocking we listened to slowly began to move up the length of the boat towards us. We knew that what was happening to us was real enough, but it was so divorced from what we expected of the natural world that we couldn't *believe* it was real and so felt – strangely – that we must somehow have become trapped inside the story.

Eventually, of course, Malcolm, in a half-whisper, said, 'Hello. Anyone awake in there? Hello… hello…'

And when I opened the door to him and he came inside and realised how much he'd terrified us all, even he realised he couldn't make a joke of it, so he just sat apologising for what had happened as if it had been some schoolboy jape that had gone horribly wrong. 'I got a lift, you see,' he kept explaining. 'I thought I'd save myself the walk tomorrow to collect the car...'

So it all ended happily – or if not happily, then at least explicably. Which is more than can be said for another experience Em and I had in Wales a few years after this which, even recalling it now, still makes my flesh creep with horror.

We'd been for a drink in a pub in the small village of Froncysyllte on the Llangollen Canal near Thomas Telford's famous towering aqueduct, which carries the canal across the valley of the River Dee. It's an extraordinary structure, even by today's standards, yet it's really no more than a narrow iron trough the width of a boat which rests crudely on 19 stone piers. These are more than 100 feet high, though, and they taper towards the top so that the whole edifice looks surprisingly graceful and delicate. It's remarkably resilient as well. It was built in 1805, the year of the Battle of Trafalgar, and it's still carrying thousands of people across the valley each year, for not only is the Llangollen the most heavily cruised canal on the whole system, attracting boats from all over the country, but the aqueduct's also become a tourist attraction in its own right and draws sightseers from all over the world.

Our moorings that night were at Trevor, so we had to walk over the aqueduct to get to the pub. It was getting on a bit when we set out, and late when we arrived, so we couldn't have been there particularly long – an important point to make, since there's no question that either of us were drunk, or anywhere near drunk, when we left. It was after closing time, though, and with little or no moon that night, dark enough to need the torch we'd brought with us for the purpose. In fact, we could have done with more than one torch. The towpath then was overgrown and too awkward for two people to walk side by side comfortably, so we were compelled to walk in Indian file with me at the front using the torch to glance briefly ahead of me before swinging it behind me in an arc so as to allow Em to see where she was walking too.

It was in this way we eventually arrived at the beginning of the aqueduct where a path running up the side of the valley joins the towpath. From this path – and entirely unremarkably, since I suspect it's a common short-cut locally – a young man appeared and began to walk across the aqueduct in front of us. He was – what, maybe ten or twenty yards ahead? Certainly no more. The towpath as it crosses the valley on the aqueduct is actually a good deal less intimidating at this time of night than it is during the day, especially for someone like me who suffers from vertigo so badly that even climbing to the top of a double-decker bus is a bit of an ordeal. During the day you've a clear view for miles across the Welsh hills, and there's simply no avoiding the fact that 1) you're very high up; and 2) the only thing that prevents you plummeting the sheer drop to the river and immediate death is a frail-looking waist-high fence forged of cast iron. At least at night, when darkness limits your visibility, you've no conception of how high up you are, and the worst you think you risk is tripping up and falling into the canal on the other side.

Mind you, on a chilly autumn night as this was, that's hardly a prospect to be relished, and so we were both walking carefully, still in Indian file, me carrying the torch and Em following closely behind. I'd take two or three paces during which I'd swing the torch forward, allowing me to survey the ground immediately ahead. At the highest point of the arc I'd briefly catch sight of the young man walking in front of us, and then I'd begin swinging the torch back again towards Em, lighting her world and darkening mine for the time it took for me to take another two or three paces, at which point, once again, I'd swing the torch forward until it once more illuminated the figure walking in front of us.

Three paces of light and a glimpse of the man ahead, then three paces of darkness. Three paces of light and a glimpse of the man ahead, then another three paces of darkness. Three paces of light and a glimpse of the man ahead, then – inexplicably – he wasn't there any more! He'd suddenly vanished.

Totally disappeared.

At this stage we were towards the middle of the aqueduct and both of us immediately froze. I scanned the torch forward now so that it illuminated the whole of the rest of the path ahead. But there was no sign of him, and I could feel my blood beginning to curdle. Em, I remember, was clutching my arm so hard that it hurt.

'He's gone,' was all I could think to say before grabbing her hand and running, my only aim at this stage to get us both off the aqueduct and back to the safety of the boat as fast as possible.

Later that night we compared notes on what we'd seen, and we went through the options of what might have happened. For a start it was clear that our recollection of the incident coincided in every significant respect, for as I'd swung the torch forward, Em had been watching the beam of light too, and she, like me, had been aware of following the figure ahead of us. She'd been conscious of him disappearing at exactly the same moment that I had too. And she knew as I did that, on the surface of it at least, there wasn't any obvious explanation for his disappearance.

'Could he have just run off fast?' she suggested.

'No way! Not in the brief second or two of me swinging the torch. Not even if he'd been an Olympic sprinter.'

'Well, he couldn't have fallen in the water,' she said. 'We'd have heard him splashing about.'

'Or fallen over the edge,' I added. 'Not with us being so high up. With a drop of that distance, even if he'd been committing suicide, he'd have cried out involuntarily…'

We looked at each other blankly. Barring a local practical joke of torturous complexity designed to terrify tourists, there didn't seem to be any satisfactory way in which we could account for what had happened.

Or at least one that wasn't supernatural.

'What was your impression of his clothes,' I asked, reluctant for the moment to concede to that possibility.

'Modern, light-coloured, white – nothing special. Nothing to make him stand out.'

'And nothing special about the style of his hair either,' I said. 'Or his shoes…'

'In fact, nothing special about him in any way,'

There was just one small detail that we could recall that we both thought was unusual, though to call it that rather exaggerates matters. Even so, the two of us had been struck by the fact that when he'd first appeared on the towpath he hadn't so much as glanced in our direction, so that neither of us ever saw his face.

'I think if I'd been coming out onto a dark towpath on my own at night and seen a couple of people walking behind me, I'd have at least *looked* at them,' Em said. 'You never know, do you? They might be robbers or murderers…'

'Or even ghosts, perhaps?' I said.

There must be an intrinsic link between the waterways and the supernatural, for it sometimes seems as if every mile of the canals is associated with some spectral happening of one sort or another. Certainly every self-respecting cutting or tunnel has its own ghost, and so our experience on Telford's aqueduct was in keeping with the best elements of canal tradition. Even so, all this paranormal stuff goes over your head most of the time. The fact is that cruising on a canal boat you spend a lot of time in the middle of nowhere, more often than not mooring deep in the countryside at night; so that if you're the sort who's going to need a change of underwear every time you hear some small furry mammal scrabbling around in a hedge, then it's unlikely in the long run that you'll find boating particularly up your street.

Perhaps it's because we're so generally resistant to things that go bump in the night that us canal types need a more imaginative diet to get our blood moving a bit, and it is remarkable how many people associated with the waterways seem to have been infatuated with the paranormal and written fiction focused on it. Tom Rolt, among his other work, produced a book of ghost stories set largely on the canals. And Robert Aickman was so obsessed with the occult that as a young man he slept overnight at the infamous Borely Rectory, a place said to be the most haunted spot in England. After a start like this it's no surprise that he went on to publish seven books of what he called 'strange stories', as well as editing a further eight anthologies of ghost stories by other people.

In later life, and without any training whatsoever, he even set himself up as an amateur therapist counselling those 'disturbed by psychic experiences'.

But that was Robert Aickman all over: a man who, without the slightest cause for it, was endowed with such overwhelming self-confidence that there was nothing he believed he couldn't do. Once he'd met Rolt at Tardebigge and got his blessing for the idea of an inland waterways association, there was no stopping him. His wife Ray was conscripted to the cause and their Bloomsbury flat completely given over to an office from which in no time at all he was firing off letters and arranging meetings with anyone prestigious enough to further the cause. He worked with a frenetic, almost manic, energy; and at such a prodigious rate that those close to him couldn't help but find him awesome.

You wonder what his secretaries must have thought. He had a knack for dictation and used to reel off letters and reports by the page, picking up his train of thought effortlessly whenever he was disturbed by the telephone. But Aickman wasn't an immediately likeable man. He lived in a distorted world of his own, at one and the same time bereft of self-doubt and yet paradoxically plagued by it. You feel that the perspective of his vision must often have made him resistant to other people's ideas. It certainly made him pompous about his own.

One secretary couldn't stand the pace and the fussy meticulousness of his working methods and resigned after just a couple of weeks of him. Afterwards Aickman enlisted the services of a 24-year-old who was desperate for work after having just upped sticks and walked out on her husband and her 4-year-old daughter. Her name was Elizabeth Jane Howard, a woman eventually destined to become a writer of great force and vision, perhaps one of the most underrated English writers of the century. She was halfway through her first novel at the time, and was paid £2.10 shillings (£2.50) for a couple of days' work a week.

If, as Milton maintains, beauty is 'Nature's coinage', then at this point in her life Jane (as she was generally known) was rich indeed. She was quite simply drop-dead gorgeous, with delicate yet powerful features, high cheek bones and a mass of fair hair which tumbled down her back and which in later years earned her the nickname 'Wog' because of its similarity to the tangled tresses of a golliwog.

Unfortunately her attractiveness would always be a destructive force in her life: it made people of both genders desire her for her appearance, not for what she was. And it made her too vulnerable to the sort of men who were dangerous for her.

Of course, it wasn't long before her and Aickman finished up in bed.

Fourteen

SOME MARRIAGES, they say, are forged in heaven. Which, if it's true, implies that others must be roughly stitched together somewhere deep in the bowels of hell.

Maybe it's a toss-up either way, for as far as relationships are concerned, things aren't always entirely under our control. Often the way things happen seems preordained – if not exactly in the stars, then at least somewhere in the events of our past, perhaps engendered in something that happened way back in our family history. This may have been the case with the marriage between Robert Fordyce Aickman and Ray Gregorson.

It would certainly be one way of explaining it – and this is a liaison that needs some explanation since the two of them were so clearly unfitted to each other it was a catastrophe that they should ever have come together in the first place. They were both too damaged as people to marry anyone, let alone each other: the whole thing was bound to end in tears eventually. You just wonder why they couldn't see it themselves.

It was like booking a passage on the *Titanic*, knowing that it would hit the iceberg. Worse, it was like shackling yourself in leg irons to make survival more difficult when it did.

Fundamentally Robert Aickman was a loner, a man who only really needed other people in order to reinforce his image of himself. Marriage, in the sense that most people understand the institution – as a union between like-minded people who love each other sufficiently to share their future together – was impossible for someone who was essentially so narcissistic you doubt he could ever have felt that level of affection for anyone, let alone felt it strongly enough to commit himself to them for life. Who knows why some people are like this? Perhaps it's something rooted in the experience of childhood, some mechanism they generate as a defence against the world which then becomes corrupted and finishes up like a suppurating wound infecting their sense of themselves and distorting the way they relate to others.

There is certainly something in the union between Aickman's parents which strikes a contemporary observer uncomfortably. For a start, there was a disparity of more than thirty years between his father William and his mother, who was just 23 at the time of the wedding, and apparently so naive that she seems to have been unaware of what it involved physically. Indeed, Robert claimed he'd been conceived as a result of his parents' one and only coupling. But the way the match had come about in the first place would be thought distasteful too in our modern world, since the whole thing was arranged by Robert's grandfather who had met William in the lavatory of the South Coast hotel where they were both staying, and from then on seems to have manipulated matters to get his daughter off his hands as quickly as possible.

After their wedding the Aickmans settled in the countryside near Stanmore, north of London, in a five-bedroom house called Langton Lodge, which I always imagine as one of those rambling old piles which lends itself as a location for a classic English murder mystery. It can't have been a particularly pleasant place to be brought up as a boy, for it was large, cold and draughty. Robert's father was a loud and dominant man with the sort of idiosyncratic personality that suggests mental imbalance, and his son lived in dread of him. He had no concept of time, and would turn up for work in the afternoon, or at theatres during the second act of a play. He was an architect, and this sort of behaviour can't have helped his practice. The family was always short of money – another element of an upbringing which conspired to prevent Aickman from ever making friends, so turning him into the maverick he was to remain for the rest of his life.

Ray Gregorson was cast in the same sort of mould, and though she came from a wealthy family where money was never a problem, her upbringing had nevertheless been blighted when her parents had separated and her mother – with an absurd sense of farce – had run off with the chauffeur. Less amusingly, that relationship ended in a suicide pact which you can only think must have had a deep and enduring effect on Ray, making her in her own way as emotionally unstable as Aickman.

The two of them met through a common friend called Audrey Linley, a rich and pretty 19-year-old student at the Royal College of Music with whom Aickman – as was his way – had become hopelessly infatuated. He invited Audrey to go to the opera with him, but she suggested instead that he took Ray, a childhood friend of hers. This was probably less a favour to Ray than a way of getting Aickman out of her hair, for Audrey didn't reciprocate his feelings in any way. Indeed, she probably found him a bit of a pain since at this stage in his life, and without any evident embarrassment, he was in the habit of declaiming how he saw the opposite sex in terms of 'poetry' and 'free love' and other such nonsense, custom-designed to make any self-respecting woman run a mile.

The affair with Ray, you feel, developed more out of their shared sense of insecurity than as a result of any immediate attraction between them. Certainly it's the case that after their wedding in 1941 – they were both 27 at the time – Aickman wrote to his new bride making it clear with startling insensitively that he'd married her not for love, but out of sympathy; a move which surely allowed him to believe he was acting selflessly whereas you always suspect the truth with Aickman was that he really never acted at all unless there was something in it for him.

One way or another, the functional accommodation between the two of them which passed as marriage was hardly an emotionally charged liaison, let alone the sort of cerebral meeting of minds on which long and enduring relationships can sometimes be built. So by the time Elizabeth Jane Howard appeared on the scene you can't help but feel that their five-year-old dalliance was already on the rocks, and that the Aickmans were both in their own way ready for an injection of passion.

In Elizabeth Jane Howard they both found it.

Jane Howard was born in 1923 into a family that would instinctively have attracted a man like Aickman since it was both wealthy and intellectual, and would have appealed to his worst pretensions. One of her grandfathers was a successful timber merchant; the other the distinguished composer and musician Sir Arthur Somervell. From the outset she had a passport into a rarefied social circle.

So it was that in Easter 1940, in the early months of the Second World War, she found herself a guest at Fritton Hythe near Great Yarmouth where an old family friend, Kathleen Young, had invited her to stay as company for her son who was down from Stowe School for the holiday. The house – actually a bungalow – was set among the woods overlooking the lake; and there at the same time on sick leave from the navy was Kathleen's older son Peter, from her previous marriage to the polar explorer Robert Falcon Scott – the famous Scott of the Antarctic who had perished in 1912 in an unsuccessful bid to become the first man to reach the South Pole.

Jane was just 17 at the time, and flattered to the point of being overwhelmed when the 31-year-old Peter began to pay her attention. They soon became lovers, though the relationship was a difficult one, constantly blighted by the spectre of Kathleen who exerted a considerable (some might say unhealthy) influence over her son until the day she died.

Kathleen was a formidable personality in her own right, and in an era when women could scarcely leave home unchaperoned, she had studied at the Slade and afterwards earned for herself an international reputation as a sculptor. She had worked on the Left Bank in Paris and knew Auguste Rodin. The young Picasso was a friend too, as was the dancer Isadora Duncan whose first illegitimate child she had helped deliver. Later in London, Kathleen's flat and studio on the site of what is now Victoria Coach Station attracted a glittering procession of the rich, famous and powerful of her time.

The Prime Minister and womaniser Herbert Asquith was a regular visitor, and though it's not certain that he actually had an affair with her, he visited her often enough for it to be true. Lloyd George was another Prime Minister who visited socially, as was Stanley Baldwin and later, Neville Chamberlain. President Franklin Roosevelt was there on one occasion as were an array of musicians, painters and writers, ranging from Bernard Shaw, who would cradle the baby Peter in his arms as he spouted about art and literature, to Rudyard Kipling, who would hold up matches for him to blow out.

Perhaps unsurprisingly for a woman of such experience, Kathleen had strong views on how a child of hers should be brought up. Indeed, her choice of husband had been determined by the single criterion that he should be a man worthy of being the father of her son, for it never seems to have occurred to her for one moment that she might have given birth to anything *but* a son. When eventually she got pregnant she took to sleeping on a beach in Devon living on a diet of nuts and wild fruits; and after Peter was born, she brought him up – equally idiosyncratically – after the fashion of a Spartan, starting his day with a cold bath and hardly allowing him to wear any substantial clothing at all. Instead she used to send him out without shoes in bizarre short-sleeved tunics which had been specially designed for him.

A relationship with a man who had a mother as single-minded as this was always going to be a problem for someone like Jane Howard. Despite the lack of self-esteem that characterised her early years – and has been a feature of much of the rest of her life too – she has nevertheless always been capable of being stubborn and self-willed. So from the outset there was a bitter but quietly fought head-to-head between the two women. Kathleen thought the flighty young thing who had attached herself to her son was 'rather pretty' and 'sweet' but a bit of a flibbertigibbet – or 'airhead' as I think we might say nowadays. Mind you, you can see Kathleen's point: she thought Jane 'might possibly develop into something' but at that stage all she'd done was spend a few terms at a drama college so that in terms of life experience she was little more than a child.

Peter was not only older, but also a positively glamorous icon of his age. He was an officer in the Royal Navy; a graduate of Trinity, Cambridge; an Olympic bronze medallist at sailing; the author of a bestselling book; and a successful wildlife painter who'd exhibited in both London and New York.

Paradoxically, though, in their letters, it is Peter – named after Peter Pan, the boy who never grew up – who emerges as the younger and more indecisive of the two. The young Jane is uncertain, yes; but she always seems to know her own mind and where she is going. Peter, to give him his due, recognises that in Jane he's got involved with 'someone very strange and rare and outstanding', but he admits he's 'scared' of her because, as he says, there's so much inside her waiting to burst out. But also because you get the sense that despite her patina of vulnerability, Jane's clear sense of purpose and her sophisticated emotional intensity threatened him.

But then, there aren't men who wouldn't be threatened by Jane Howard's emotional intensity. Even today.

Though it's dangerous ascribing the source of any novelist's work to their personal experience, there's a lot of the relationship with Peter Scott in Jane's first novel, *The Beautiful Visit*, which tells the story of a love affair between an alluring unnamed heroine and a Scottish army officer, Ian Graham. It is set at the time of the First World War, and Jane's ability to get to the emotional core of her characters with an almost forensic precision strikes the fear of God into me. It makes me feel as I would talking to someone who could read my mind. 'Haunting' is the adjective most frequently used of the book, and it's true: it's the sort of story that you find coming back to you in flashes years after you've read it.

Peter Scott responded to Jane's particular intelligence by doing as men often do when faced with women who they care for, but who unsettle them: he patronised her. At times this irritated her immensely. 'Please *darling* Peter pretend I'm not twelve,' she burst out in one letter to him, 'if you don't I shall come in plaits and... you'll have to keep giving me ice creams even though it's snowing.' Kathleen patronised her too, to the point of humiliation, but here you sense a darker agenda, as if Kathleen was determined to find some pretext on which to assert her authority. At one party that Kathleen gave in her flat during the war, Jane for some reason had carelessly thrown off her shoes and left them in the drawing room.

'I had to tell her to put them on,' Kathleen comments caustically in her diary, the very mention of such a trivial incident indication enough that she ascribed to it an importance greater than just a matter of the shoes alone.

'If she ever hurts him I shall kill her,' Kathleen comments at another point in the diary.

And you believe her. Literally.

Jane Howard and Peter Scott married in April 1942 in London, a reception for 300 being held afterwards in Claridges. There is a wedding picture which shows them coming out of the church, him in his naval uniform looking somewhat tired at the whole business; her, as tall as him, in a broderie anglaise dress, tight at the bodice and waist, and with broad, padded shoulders that wouldn't be out of place in a City boardroom today. Their daughter Nicola was born within the year. For Jane, it wasn't an easy pregnancy, and the birth was excruciatingly painful; but then nothing associated with this marriage was easy, for by now Peter's naval career was taking off and they were drifting further and further apart as the war progressed and he was away increasingly often on active service.

It would have been difficult for any woman alone in wartime

London with a young child and history happening around her, but it must have been harder for Jane Howard, whose insecurities would always lead her to rely overly on men as a means of confirming her own worth. Perhaps inevitably, she had an affair. Unfortunately the man she chose to have it with was Peter's brother, and worse was that the two of them insisted on confessing their forbidden love. Afterwards Jane got involved with another man, maybe more, for there was a period of 12 years in her life when she had so many affairs she admits she was a 'tart for affection'.

'I had very, very brief affairs with people I never want to see again,' she once told a newspaper, 'but I always hoped they were going to be much more serious than that. Several times I thought I was very much in love with them. It's very interesting looking back on it – if one's really honest, you know the ones you weren't really in love with. You wanted to be, it all seemed to be what you'd like, you'd go for it, but actually it wasn't true.'

The dilemma of a loveless marriage is one she explores in her second book *The Long View*, published many years after these events, when she once again brings her formidable skill to the close analysis of a relationship as she dissects the marriage of Antonia and Conrad Fleming. Like the Flemings, Jane and Peter attempted to patch up their differences after adultery; but unlike them, their attempts were destined to failure. In the summer of 1947, with only £10 in her pocket and carrying only a suitcase of clothes and her half-finished first novel, Jane upped and bolted, leaving Nicola behind her. 'Bolting' is the word she uses herself for the way in which she leaves relationships that she cannot stand any longer or cannot handle any more: she did it with her next two husbands and she did it with Aickman too, though I suspect that the process was never as hard as this first time when the emotional turmoil she was suffering seems to have led her to the edge of a nervous breakdown and into therapy which she's had on and off for most of her life.

On the physical level it's difficult to understand what Jane might have seen in the young Aickman, for whereas she was breathtakingly good-looking, and becoming more so as she lost the puppy fat of her early years, he was nerdish, fresh-faced but serious, with lips tending towards the thickish and a nose too delicate for the heavy-framed round glasses he was obliged to wear for his severe short-sightedness. He was a powerful personality, though, and while she so entranced him by her beauty that he once claimed that 'little in the way of completely normal business was possible... when she was in the room', you sense that equally he must have captivated her by his confident decisiveness and natural authority.

Besides, they had a lot in common. Aickman had never gone to university, something which throughout his life would be a chip on his shoulder. Jane had even less formal education, and had only been to school for a couple of terms during which she'd been badly bullied. Afterwards she was handed over to a governess who taught her an 'eccentric' curriculum, but one that at least included Greek and Latin – subjects at which Aickman excelled. Both were from problematic families too, and if Aickman's father was a burden to him, then so too was Jane's mother to her. She'd lost a child – another girl – the year before Jane was born; and whether she somehow believed her surviving daughter partly responsible for this, or resented her for being a reminder of it, Jane eventually came to believe that her mother never really wanted her, and preferred her brothers, so that she was always searching for a maternal love which she never felt she received.

'There are certain experiences you need to have had by a certain age; and if you don't have them, you're stuck in a time warp either waiting or experimenting or reacting the wrong way,' she once said. 'One basic one is feeling quite sure your mother loves you.'

But it was not just a lack of love Jane felt from her mother: she experienced active resentment from her too – what she described as 'straightforward jealousy'. Jane was a modern woman, with the choice both of pursuing a career and having children – a freedom never available to her mother and one which may have engendered a bitterness in the relationship. 'What on earth makes you think anyone would ever want to publish anything you wrote?' her mother said disdainfully when she learnt of Jane's literary aspirations.

This ambition to become a writer was the main thing Jane shared with Robert Aickman. He always maintained that he'd deferred his writing career to become chairman of the Inland Waterways Association, and whatever the truth of this, it is the case that he always thought of himself as a writer and knew that sooner or later it was what he would do for a living. While they were working together they collaborated on a series of ghost stories, *We Are for the Dark*, which was her first book and for a long time his only published work.

Strange then, that for two people who could work together so creatively, there was so much destructiveness in the relationship as well.

So much that their affair would almost ruin the nascent Inland Waterways Association.

Back on *Justice* life had become very much more complicated since Braunston when Em and her mother had arrived hotfoot from London in the household's Mighty Metro. This was yet another vehicle to add to the growing convoy which was moving inexorably westward across the countryside towards Stratford-upon-Avon like some twenty-first-century wagon train.

Theoretically, of course, the presence of the Metro should have made things so much easier, since before its arrival I'd had to use the bike to get from wherever I took the boat to wherever I'd left the Debsmobile. This was a process that had sometimes involved a substantial amount of cycling – not exactly easy-peasy stuff for a 50-year-old whose last experience of unmotorised two-wheel locomotion had been around the time of puberty. It did at least have the advantage of simplicity, though. Once I'd got back to the car, it was a straightforward task to fold down the roof, stuff the bike behind the rear seat and drive back to the boat.

With the Mighty Metro, of course, it *should* have been even easier. With two cars we *should* have been able to ferry ourselves around at will, taking the cars to wherever we planned mooring that night, leaving one there and driving back in the other. And with two cars, once we'd got to our evening mooring, we *should* have been able to drive back in one car to pick up the other. This *should* have been relatively uncomplicated stuff. Not exactly rocket science. Except, of course, life is never that elementary. It's a mistake to think you can plan for it.

For a start, with a crew to help me, I was travelling further now. On my own I'd been pottering along, cruising for no more than a couple of hours a day and staying for weeks on end in the same place. Now, with Em and Chris on board, we were moving upwards of seven or eight hours a day, which even at a rate of three miles an hour, and even with locks, still meant we were shifting considerable distances.

So in order to effect the cunning strategy with the cars we had to drive the two of them to our final estimated destination first thing in the morning, sometimes as far as 30 miles away, a total distance for the two cars of 60 miles. Then we'd leave one car and drive back to the boat in the other – another 30 miles. Total distance travelled: 90 miles – with the same again required to get the cars back together again in the evening. This was arduous enough along country lanes, but once you got anywhere near a town – as we did around Leamington Spa and Warwick – the hassle factor was further exacerbated by rush-hour traffic jams and incomprehensible systems of inner ring roads.

OK, so Warwick may not exactly be up there with the big boys in terms of the irrationality of its road planners – it isn't exactly a Reading or a Milton Keynes, I grant you that. But it can still spring enough surprises for me to have come close to believing one evening, having passed its castle four times in as many minutes, that actually there was more than one of them in the town.

And then there was the whole question of what you could do

if you didn't get to your planned destination, or if you got to it too early and wanted to press on a little further that day. Canal travel, as anyone who's done much of it will testify, is a totally unpredictable method of getting around. You only need a stretch of shallow water to slow you down, or a floating fragment of debris to wrap itself around your propeller, and then the very best-laid plans of any crew go totally awry.

When that occurred I had to take to the bike again, and that took matters to a whole new level of complexity which I'm not even going to bother trying to explain since it's worse than those brain-teasers we used to tell each other as kids.

You know the sort of thing: Farmer Giles is on one side of the river with a fox and a chicken and a worm, and a boat that will only carry any two of them at the same time. The fox will eat the chicken, and the chicken will eat the worm, so how can he get them across so they all survive the journey? Take it from me, puzzles like that are a trifle to me now after having done this trip. I spit on their so-called complexity and solve them in my sleep.

But why on earth did we do it? What could possibly have been in our minds? Well OK, having a car always available theoretically meant that we could get around and visit other places – except, of course, that apart from shifting cars, we didn't get around at all, and anyhow we didn't want to visit any other places because we were on a boating holiday and perfectly happy on the canals, thank you very much. I suppose – my excuse for having the Debsmobile in the first place – having a car did at least give us the advantage of not needing to worry about shopping since we could always get to a supermarket. But the gloss of that attraction soon wore thin after the first transition from the tranquil peace of the towpath to the frenetic trolley-rage of the canned vegetable aisle. After that I'd have been happy enough to survive on a diet of dry bread and water just to avoid the coronary stress of it all.

Eventually we threw in the towel and did the sensible thing. We decided not to bother about cars. From now on we would be free again.

Well, free after a fashion, for the Debsmobile had gone on the blink again and I spent a frustrating afternoon high on the smell of petrol fumes as I drove around attempting to find a replacement for a diaphragm which had split in the carburettor. It wasn't easy, but eventually a helpful garage traced one for me from a mail order parts catalogue in Kazakhstan or somewhere like that. It cost me the princely sum of £3.46, including postage, but it meant I couldn't drive the car even if I'd wanted.

Then I realised why the garage had been so helpful. They charged me thirty quid for the privilege of parking in their forecourt until it arrived.

That night we moored at Cape Locks on the northern outskirts of Warwick, and the following morning we cast off early for the endurance test which passes for Hatton Locks – 'the 21 steps to heaven' as the old working boatmen used to call them.

Now Hatton isn't the longest flight on the British canal system, that accolade being more accurately applied to Tardebigge on the Worcester and Birmingham Canal where a total of 30 locks (36 if you count Stoke Locks, which are practically part of the same flight) lift the canal from the River Severn to the hill on which Britain's second city is built. Neither are they the most difficult locks on the system either, that cussed honour belonging in my opinion to the 21 locks at Wigan where the chambers are horrendously uneven and where each paddle has to be inconveniently unlocked with a special key because of the oiks who regularly used to open them and flood out half the town as their idea of constructive social debate.

Even so, arriving at the bottom of Hatton is an awesome experience. Once you've got yourself into the swing of things by cantering through the first three or four locks (phew – difficult? *Pour moi*?) you round a bend to be confronted by the next dozen or so sweeping intimidatingly up the hill, their gates like colossal steps to... well, to heaven, I suppose (gulp!). Even with a well-drilled, disciplined crew up for the task, you're looking at a minimum two or three hours of hard graft to get to the top. And 'well-drilled' and 'disciplined' were not precisely the adjectives that readily sprang to mind when I cast my eye appraisingly over the crew of *Justice*.

Up for it? Downcast by it might be a more accurate way of putting things.

For a start there was me, who for the last two months had been ditch-crawling from Oxford at a rate of knots so slow that to have gone slower would have entailed me moving backwards, and who was still feeling somewhat shell-shocked at all the activity since Braunston. Then there was Em, whose idea of exercise is occasionally walking down the escalators on the Underground, and who thinks she's Sporty Spice if she gets to the bottom without falling over. Even Chris, who under normal circumstances is the most athletic of us all, seemed somewhat daunted by the prospect of the flight; and apart from a bit of well-meaning wafting of the lock key in the general direction of a paddle, she pretty well went AWOL, having played the age card and decided that there were far more interesting things to do than locks on a summer's day, even one that was overcast and drizzling.

Nevertheless, by some means or another, we made the beginning of a disordered ascent until we chanced fortuitously upon the rare discovery of another crew going in our direction. They seemed motivated to about our level of enthusiasm – which is to say not motivated at all and counting down the time to the top when they could finally get the kettle on and have done with this sweaty manual labour stuff once and for all. Pete and Sarah – I won't give their real names – had not long bought their boat, and it was at that meretricious stage of adornment which to the cynical eye like mine all but declares they paid five grand over the odds for it.

Pete was much concerned about its decorative state, and at first he was a bit cagey about us travelling together and sharing locks. Until the penny dropped and he realised that at the rate he and his wife were moving, and with their holiday time being limited, it was more than likely they'd get to the top of the flight in just about enough time to turn round and come back down again. After that, he reluctantly conceded to the inevitable, though stipulating that we should go into the locks first so that he could follow us.

Well, I don't want to be overly critical of Pete's steering skills, which, with time and practice, I am confident will improve significantly. At our first lock together he hit us stern on, and at the second he took us out broadside. By the third he'd developed an amusing little variation on our *pas de deux* whereby he could hit us both stern on *and* broadside in the same move. Eventually all this became too embarrassing even for him, and he handed over to Sarah who, because she knew she couldn't steer, was amenable to one or two suggestions from Em; so that by the time we got to the top, the two of them were moving together in graceful balletic concert that was a joy for everyone to behold.

Well, everyone except Pete, that is. He was still nursing his wounded pride.

'She seems to have tightened up a bit, your missus,' he commented uncharitably at one lock while we waited for the boats to enter.

'Tightened up a bit?'

'Her steering, I mean. It was all over the place earlier, wasn't it? She seems to have got the hang of it now Sarah's with her. Still, that's women for you. Give 'em half a chance and they'll be showing off…'

Our mooring that night was beyond Shrewley Tunnel at that extraordinarily beautiful spot where the canal perches on the high embankment which overlooks the fields and the small village of Rowington. About five in the morning I woke breaking my neck for a pee, but after I'd done what was needed, I lay fitfully, tossing and turning until it became clear that I was beyond sleep now, and that out of fairness to Em I might as well get up. I dressed and stepped out onto the deck where the mist was lying impenetrably thick over the water as it often does in summer this time of day. I watched it swirling enigmatically in the calm windless morning, and gradually it began to lift, melting away gently like a soft fall of snow in the warmth of sunshine. Suddenly, and without warning, the sky became luminous with a deep reflected purple as the rays of the sun, not yet risen, began to touch the underside of the blanket of cloud which was lying across the sky. As I stared – totally entranced by now – this cloud cover shifted and fractured until there appeared behind it a sharp splinter of perfect azure blue; and after that, resplendent in its sharp outline – so clear I swear you could see flames leaping from its surface – a most magnificent, spectacular, breathtaking sunrise.

I stood almost hypnotised for as long as it took daylight to finally break upon the world – fifteen minutes, maybe twenty. As I did the birds began to stir, at first a cautious wood pigeon in the trees nearby, then another calling to it, and then another so that in no time at all it seemed there was a choir around me, cooing its welcome to the morning. At length, a remote cockerel crowed, and a second soon answered it from far-off across the fields. Then thrushes and blackbirds and a whole cacophony of birds and creatures seemed to wake, hopping about the trees and scratching in the hedgerows with a presence that I could sense all around me.

The new day had begun. But in a way I'd never experienced before.

Which I thought was odd – since though I've been oblivious to it, it's happened much like this every single day of my life.

Fifteen

FOR A CHANGE, it had started raining again.

The same as it had rained as we'd come through Leamington and passed Warwick. The same as it had when we'd left Braunston, and before that, when I'd been alone, and when it had rained every blasted, god-damned day I'd been on the boat from the moment I'd first arrived in Oxford. In fact, further back than that; for it seemed to me it had been raining non-stop since my adolescence – before that even – since I'd been a kid at school – and maybe even earlier than that as well. Indeed, the more I thought about it, the more it seemed to me that it had been raining from the very moment of my birth, for as I sat in the boat listening to it hammer on the roof, it seemed to provoke some deep primeval memory which might have been of the rain hammering on the hood of my pram, or even of my pregnant mother sheltering under an umbrella.

And the records were falling as inexorably as a drug-fuelled Olympics. At first it was the wettest spring of the century, then the wettest since 18-something-or-other, and then the wettest summer since records began... Every day, it seemed, the weathermen were struggling for new levels of hyperbole until I came to believe that I was living through the wettest period in British history – the wettest ever – since the very dawn of man when the first hominids crawled upon this, our island home.

At least all this was positive in one respect, since when it gets as wet as this, you just stop caring about being wet at all. Wet becomes the nature of your universe, and being constantly saturated becomes as natural to you as being surrounded by air.

When it's *that* wet you forget about ever being dry. You even forget about falling into the canal as well – and that's unusual, since even though no one admits it, the idea of taking a tumble into the water is a niggling worry for anyone who spends any length of time on a boat. Regardless of how experienced you are, or how careful, it's a constant concern: it's just one of those things that you know will happen sooner or later – and generally when you least expect it.

There you'll be, sitting on the deck quietly reading or contentedly leaning against something or other sipping a cup of tea in the sunshine when – glug! – suddenly you've been deposited as if by sorcery into some cold netherworld of frondy plantlife and strange creatures with fins.

At Kingswood Junction, about five miles from the top of Hatton, the Grand Union links with the Stratford Canal at a tricky little junction which connects through a short spur and which brings you out in the middle of the Lapworth flight of locks. You're back on a narrow canal again now, a waterway like the Oxford Canal which is equally as pretty. It's characterised by bijou little cantilevered split bridges built of cast iron, designed to allow the tow ropes of horse-drawn boats to pass through a gap in the middle without having to unharness; and there is also a series of charming cottages with barrel-shaped roofs said to be constructed from the wooden scaffolding which was used to build the canal's distinctive humpback bridges.

The Stratford Canal has been a bit of disaster area for Em over the years in terms of falling in. Once we were cruising along it, engaged in quite a heated discussion about something or other, when I looked away from steering only to find that… she'd gone. Totally vanished! Disappeared from the face of the earth! Instead – for reasons that are even now not entirely clear to me – she was thrashing around in the water at a point the boat had passed a few moments before. She was, I seem to recall, shouting a lot. More specifically, she was shouting at *me*, and from what I can remember of what she was saying, it was distinguished by a note of profanity that I don't think was entirely justified by the context of our conversation…

Another summer we stopped at one of the locks to buy a window box from an adjacent cottage which had a lucrative seasonal sideline selling to boats. It advertised itself by covering the whole of its frontage with flowers, trailing them around its doors and windows, and hanging them in baskets from its brickwork so that it was a riotous blaze of colour. We bought a mixture of the most glorious blood-red geraniums, great garish pink petunias and clumps of ice-blue lobelia. Em put them on the bow of the boat and took a pace or two backwards to admire them…

And stepped back straight into the water.

I seem to remember getting sworn at then too, but that time I probably deserved it. I found the whole thing so improbable – so like a scene from a slapstick comedy – that I literally collapsed on the ground in helpless laughter, scarcely able to gather myself enough to stand on my own two feet, let alone help her out of the water onto hers.

I've fallen in myself from time to time, but for pure theatrical spectacle the best I ever managed was once after using the boat to go out for the night at Hawkesbury Junction at the very end of the northern Oxford Canal not far from Coventry. Sutton's Stop, as it's also known, is a busy place: there's one pub on the waterside and another nearby; and it can sometimes get hectic – especially on warm summer evenings when the boisterous crowds at closing time congregate in groups around the basin, reluctant to admit it's time to get off home to their beds.

Until recently there weren't any drink-drive regulations on canals, and when it was time to go it didn't occur to me for one moment that cruising at night with large quantities of beer swilling around my gut might not exactly be the most sensible thing I could have chosen to do. I pushed the boat off from the bank without really thinking about it. It moved almost imperceptibly at first as heavy things do in water, but then it began to accelerate at a rate far faster than I was ready for in the state that I was in. In what seemed no time at all I found myself suspended over the water, my feet on dry land and the balance of my weight on the boat. Things go into slow motion at times like that. You get a sort of out-of-body experience which allows you to see yourself as others see you. There was really only one way this could end…

And sure enough, I gradually lost my tenuous hold on dignity and sank into the murky black water as gently and gracefully as a newly built ocean liner sliding down a slipway.

I wouldn't have minded so much if I'd been on my own. But I wasn't on my own. Far from it. The crowds turning out from the pub had seen what was going to happen long before I had.

And as I disappeared under the surface every last one of them burst into rousing applause.

When Em and I first cruised the Stratford Canal it was owned and administered as a totally separate waterway from the rest of the system by the National Trust, an organisation which is doubtless unsurpassed when it comes to the appreciation of the finer detail of eighteenth-century English country houses, but which isn't exactly up there with the world's best when it comes to its expertise in water management. In fact, so little did the Trust know about the business in those days that it took years for it to grasp some of the basic principles of the process.

Like the fact that in order to move a boat on water you first need water.

In those days the canal was so poorly dredged that there was barely enough of the stuff to float a toy boat, let alone a real one. The locks were in awful disrepair too, with some gates leaking so badly you hardly needed to open them, and others literally falling off their hinges so that you couldn't anyhow. All this wouldn't have been so bad, except that to cruise the Stratford Canal then you had to buy a separate National Trust permit, which was a prohibitively expensive business for young people like us who were struggling to afford the basic British Waterways' licence.

But for all its failings, this route to the River Avon probably wouldn't exist today without the National Trust; for when the canal was threatened with closure in the late 1950s the organisation stepped into the breach and restored it on a shoestring using any labour it could get hold of, from volunteers to serving prisoners. At a time when waterways restoration is the flavour of the month, with newly renovated canals being opened almost annually, and other new lengths actually being built totally from scratch, it's as well to remember the importance of the Stratford Canal which was the first major project of its sort in modern years, and the pattern for much that would follow. It's as well to recall too that in those days saving a waterway wasn't exactly a piece of cake.

For a start, the canal was only brought back into use in the teeth of official intransigence, since Warwickshire County Council had decided to seek a closure order rather than spend a few thousand pounds repairing a bridge which crossed it at Wilmcote. Stratford Council was no better either, and at one stage there were plans to fill in Bancroft Basin – the terminus of the canal and the junction with the Avon where today thousands of visitors to the town gather around the gardens on summer days to enjoy the boats.

They wanted the land to extend the bus station. Like they did in Banbury.

Thankfully common sense prevailed, and eventually the restoration was completed in the astonishingly short time of just three years, with the opening taking place in 1964 to coincide with the four hundredth anniversary of Shakespeare's birth. It was a personal triumph for Robert Aickman who had encouraged and inspired the campaign; but it was an archetypal English victory for the muddled forces of amateurish enthusiasm too, and as such it was a close-run thing. Or as David Hutchings, the man mainly responsible for it, said in words that have inspired the waterways restoration movement ever since, 'None of us were experts, or we should have known it was impossible.'

To make ourselves comfortable as we travelled down the canal in the driving rain, we'd turned on the central heating and lit the cast-iron coal stove in the back cabin. This is set at the level of your feet, just below where you stand to steer, and it generates such an immense heat there can be an Arctic storm raging outside and you'll still be cosy.

These back-cabin stoves were what the original boatmen depended on for their livelihood. They not only provided a source of warmth that meant they could keep going in all sorts of extreme conditions, but they were little cookers too – small Agas – which ensured there was always a hot meal at the end of the day. In Dorothy Hartley's classic *Food in England* she gives a traditional recipe for what she calls a Bargee's Pail – a meal cooked in a galvanised bucket which is used like a medieval cauldron, with soup, main course and dessert all simmering away in the same pot.

If the recipe's genuine then it must date from the early days of the industrial revolution when the job paid well enough for boatmen to afford to keep a separate home for their families, and when they had to fend for themselves while they were working. In later years as the rates for the job dropped, their wives and children were compelled to join them on the water as crew; the women taking over the responsibility for cooking, preparing meals at the same time as they steered the 'butties' – the second of the two boats which were worked together as a pair, one towing the other.

The women were also responsible for looking after the kids. And doing the washing. And the cleaning. And helping with the locks. And unloading cargo too, which meant them rolling up their sleeves and – literally – shovelling out coal from the hold.

It wasn't an easy life for anyone then working on the water –

men, women or children. But it was particularly hard for the women.

Even so, I suspect that when they were on board the food would have been more imaginative and creative, if for no other reason than for the sake of economy. I imagine the women would have made more use of available ingredients, whether seasonal vegetables they could have grubbed from the fields, or the sort of fruits like sloes and crab apples, or herbs like thyme and chervil, that you can still find growing wild around towpaths. This recipe for Shin of Beef in Ale has absolutely no historical provenance that I can attest to, though for some reason I always think of it as a traditional dish, possibly because until relatively recently shin was one of the cheaper cuts of beef and within the reach of poorer folk; and possibly because I always think of the recipe in the terms I've described it, the meat cooked in traditional 'ale' rather than modern 'beer'.

Or then again, maybe it's because I imagine the recipe to be one of those dishes the boat people in Victorian times might have cooked as they were moored in London at Limehouse or East India Dock, close to where ocean-going ships would have berthed to unload their cargoes of spice and demerara sugar from the Caribbean, and where there was always the possibility of something finding its way out of the hold, no questions asked.

Whatever its background, it tastes just as good in an ordinary oven as it does cooked in a saucepan on the top of a stove; but there's no doubt in my mind that it tastes even better cooked in a coal-fired oven, and best of all cooked on a back-cabin stove on a narrowboat on a wet day in Warwickshire with the rain driving horizontally under a sharp wind. That way, when it's cold and inhospitable, you can get it simmering first thing in the morning and have it bubbling away gently all day, tempting you with its rich and delectable smell whenever your spirits are getting low.

The Third Recipe

Though these days the price differential between shin and other steak may be less than it used to be, don't be tempted to cook this with anything except shin since you won't get the taste. Besides, any better quality meat will break up to an unappetising mush during the long cooking the recipe requires. Shin of beef is sinewy, but so packed with flavour and goodness that it's what they used to make beef tea for invalids in the past. It lends itself to this sort of dish.

For four people you need about 1–2 lb of meat – though my inclination would be to go for less and buy organic. You can eat it with rice or potatoes, and any green vegetable in season, so there's no danger you'll go hungry. Dice it into largish chunks and sear it quickly in a small amount of lard until it goes brown on the outside. Better still, if you're on a boat and want to avoid washing up, sear it in the fat left in the frying pan from the breakfast bacon. When all else fails use vegetable oil which, yes, I know is healthier, but which just doesn't taste anywhere near as good.

Transfer the meat to a casserole dish and fry a large, roughly chopped onion in the remaining fat until it begins to brown at the edges. Put that into the casserole too, along with three or four thickly sliced carrots, a stick or two of diced celery, and a handful of the chopped celery leaves. Then – the magic of cooking this – add two teaspoons of demerara sugar, and a heaped teaspoon of mixed spice. That's right – the same mixed spice that you use in cake recipes. Mix all of these ingredients together in the casserole along with a tablespoon of flour, a teaspoon of mustard powder and a generous sprinkling of black pepper. Then cover the contents with beer.

Now, if you want to impress your guests, you could at this stage be very particular about the beer. You could use only Legless and Hangover's 9 per cent Special Rotgut Easter brew. Or Stagger and Fallover's malt-based Throw-Up bitter, brewed at the Old Cobblers Brewery using only the finest 100-year-old Wiltshire gusset yeast. You could do this – and then try to convince your guests that this is what makes this dish taste as good as it does.

Actually the truth is, it doesn't make a heap of difference what beer you use. I've cooked it with best Shepherd and Neame bottled bitter at more than two quid a throw, and with cheapo French lager at 10p a gallon. I have made it with live Worthington Shield India Pale Ale, including the sediment from the bottom and – when it was the only thing available – with Guinness past its sell-by date. I have even made it with the salvagings from a rather good party the night before, including fag ash from the bottom of old cans for all I know.

And all I can say is, it tastes good every which way.

Cook it in an oven at a lowish heat, or on the top of the stove at a slow simmer. Either way, ensure that you keep it topped up with beer (and maybe a little beef stock if you have it) so that it doesn't dry out. It will be ready to eat in about two to two and a half hours, though in a damped-down back-cabin stove it can cook for twice that time and longer without spoiling.

That night we stopped near the small village of Wootten Wawen, which straddles the A34. We moored up just a few yards short of one of the three aqueducts – no more than cast-iron troughs – which are as characteristic of this canal as the bridges and the cottages. Afterwards we went for a walk to a nearby farm where the out-buildings have all been converted to shops and where we bought some splendid home-made sausages for the following day's breakfast.

It was a strange evening, for after the awful weather of the day there was an unmistakable sense of change in the air, but change for the worse – as if the rain that we'd been suffering was really just the beginning, just the harbinger of something much darker and more threatening. Great purple clouds made stately procession across the sky, and the atmosphere felt heavy and ponderous; and even though it was cold, there was a damp clamminess in the air of the sort you occasionally experience in the tropics.

I thought it was building up to a storm. I thought it was going to be the mother of all storms.

Funny how wrong you can be sometimes, for overnight there was a meteorological miracle, and when we woke up the sun was so fierce that before ten o'clock the thermometer was almost touching 90 degrees.

Summer had finally arrived on the waterways.

Sixteen

I'VE NEVER MANAGED to get my head around this contemporary cult of the designer where virtually every mundane object you buy is autographed, stamped or branded in some way. OK, designers have always been with us, and someone at some time must have actually fashioned all the commonplace items of my youth like cups and crockery since they didn't spring ready-made off production lines in Stoke-on-Trent. Neither were the patterns for them somehow ordained by God and handed over to Moses on Sinai: 'Here are ten commandments on tablets of stone – and while I'm thinking about it, I've thrown in a few prototypes for fluted porcelain mugs decorated with a Bouquet-of-Spring-Flowers design.'

Yet in the past no one seemed to feel their professional reputations depended on being personally associated with every banal and prosaic household item on which they worked; and certainly no one felt the need to proclaim their creativity to the world by slapping their name on every item they touched. However, you just can't get away from it anywhere any more: clothes, furniture, domestic appliances – it's all the same. Designers are like a pack of dogs on heat, and they feel the need to piss their identity on everything in sight and charge you a fortune for the privilege of it.

Even if you attempt resistance and try to save a bob or two by buying the things you've always bought like those chunky dimpled glasses you used to drink milk in when you were a kid, or those ineluctably uncomfortable cottagey kitchen chairs which seem destined to wobble whatever you do to stop them, then all you'll find is that they've been re-branded as 'classics' and their price hiked anyway.

The fact is, people nowadays don't value things for what they *are*; they value them for how they *look*.

This preference for the visual appeal of an object over its intrinsic value has now got to the stage where you only have to pick up a Sunday supplement and open the lifestyle pages to be regaled by an astonishing array of tacky crap which you just know will fall apart in your hands the first time you touch it, and yet which costs the equivalent of the GNP of a small African country. And why? Simply because it looks good. Simply because it's been designed by someone who's so famous that you've almost certainly never heard of them.

I suppose I could just about live with all this, except that now we've started applying the same principle to people. OK, maybe you expect it in my industry, television, which as a visual medium is so driven by appearances it should come as no surprise to anyone that talentless bimbos of both genders are given jobs just because they have a cute face or a prominent embonpoint. But it comes to something when you've got to conform to a certain appearance even to become a political leader – which is how it is at the moment since everything else that used to be associated with the job like idealism and commitment are today treated not as the essentials they used to be, but as accessories to be taken up, tried on and discarded, as you might do a hat in a boutique sale.

The diaphragm had arrived for the broken-down Debsmobile, and I went off to the garage early next morning to collect it. Installing it in the carburettor was a job of just a few minutes, and, with the car back on the road again, I felt inordinately pleased with myself – a joy out of all proportion to the work I'd done. Driving back that morning in the warm sunshine I began musing on these matters of design: a train of thought triggered to a large extent by the fact that so many of our contemporary views on style originated in the car industry where, for better or worse, the Triumph Herald played such a critical part in getting us to the point we're at today where it's generally accepted that the car you drive says more about you than a DNA profile ever could.

To be blunt, if harsh, the Herald couldn't have been made by a more appositely named company since its whole concept represented a triumph of sorts – even if it was only the victory of style over performance.

What else could the company have done, though? At the time it was saddled with a series of outdated models powered by engines and gearboxes in which it had invested so heavily that it hadn't got the resources to go back to the drawing board and start again from scratch. It had no option but to design around what it already had, even though this effectively meant putting a new body shell on the top of the old components.

The trouble was, how could it even get a new body shell? As the early 'bathtub' design for the Zobo had shown, the company's design department was uninspired and pedestrian; and anyway, it was in total disarray following the 1955 Earls Court Motor Show when its head Walter Belgrove had a blazing row with the technical director and walked out in a fit of pique.

It was at this chaotic moment of its life that Giovanni Michelotti fortuitously walked into the company's history books. Or to be more accurate, a Captain Raymond Flower did. Flower was an entrepreneur in the days when making cars was almost a cottage industry, and he was planning to go into production with an economy model of his own for the Egyptian market in which he wanted to install Standard Triumph engines. Except that during negotiations it came out that he hadn't as yet actually got a design for the car! This was, to say the least, a little unusual. Even more extraordinary was that this didn't seem to particularly bother him since he claimed to know a designer who could get a prototype knocked together in a few months.

A few months?

This was post-war Britain, and these were the austerity years.

It was a period in our history when it could take you hours to do the simplest thing like buying a half-pound of bacon from the butcher's. That's always assuming there was bacon to buy. And that the butcher's hadn't been taken out by the Luftwaffe. The idea that you could get *anything* of significance done in just three months, let alone design a prototype for a new car, was laughable, and... well, simply unbelievable. The bosses at Triumph Standard certainly didn't believe it, anyhow, and they challenged Flower to back up his claim by producing a fast-turnaround design for a sports car they were developing.

Ten days later, despite everyone's cynicism, Flower returned with a selection of sample plans; and a few weeks after this – comfortably within the deadline for the challenge – a painted and trimmed body shell was delivered to the company's astonished executives at their Coventry headquarters.

All through this process the canny Flower had refused to disclose who was doing the work for him. Unfortunately, when the body shell was delivered, by some oversight on his part, it arrived in a truck owned by an Italian company, so that it didn't take much sleuthing to discover the workshop from which it had been collected, and thus trace the designer who had conceived it. Within a short time the company had fixed up a freelance contract with Michelotti in which, among other things, he agreed to take over the styling of the troubled Zobo project which the company were ambitiously hoping to complete in time for the 1958 Motor Show.

It was a tough assignment. For a start the styling work that had already been done on the car didn't particularly help Michelotti; in fact, it seemed to handicap him, impairing his natural creativity. The only existing prototype was shipped over to him in Turin, and he agonised over it while virtually every weekend the company's chief engineer Harry Webster drove to Italy to monitor progress – no mean feat in itself in the days when motorways were virtually unheard of, and when cars were far less reliable and powerful than today.

Michelotti worked from a small penthouse studio on the tenth floor of an anonymous office block, and it was there in the summer of 1957 that matters came to a head. The fact was that if the company were going to have sufficient time to meet its deadline on the new car, then the decision on styling needed to be taken by August at the latest. Yet by that month the designs for the project were no further progressed than when Michelotti had come on board. As it happened, Harry Webster was holidaying in Sorrento that year with his wife and daughter, and on his way back to England he decided to pop in to see how Michelotti was getting on. He didn't expect the visit to be long, and he left his wife and daughter waiting for him in the car outside.

In truth, he wasn't anticipating much in the way of progress. And he wasn't wrong.

'Nothing! It was hopeless,' Webster recalled later. 'I said, "We are wasting our bloody time! Look! Suppose you could start again from scratch, here in Turin, to begin with a clean sheet of paper, what would it look like?"'

Michelotti was a hyperactive, headstrong man; an impulsive, energetic genius who would eventually kill himself with overwork. There's a picture of him taken outside the corrugated-iron walls of a factory somewhere, and you can almost feel his irritability at being taken away from his work for the sake of such a time-wasting irrelevance as photography. He's clutching his hands together as if to constrain them into inactivity, and what at first sight seems to be a weak smile on his angular face, on closer examination, turns out to be an impatient grimace. There are a row of three pens in the breast pocket of his natty suit. You feel he can't wait to take one out and start drawing something.

To a man of his bent, a question of the sort Harry Webster posed was like waving a red rag at a bull: it was a challenge to everything he held dear. Within a few minutes the Italian had sketched out the outline of a new car. It was a design similar in almost every detail to the Triumph Herald we know today. He immediately started transferring the drawing to a full-scale draft on the wall, and with Webster alongside him and the creative juices flowing, the two men worked on solidly for the next nine hours until around midnight, when Webster suddenly remembered with a shock that he'd left his wife and daughter outside.

He found them both curled up in the car fast asleep, and went off to book them into a hotel.

Meanwhile, totally obsessed by now, Michelotti worked on alone through the night on other versions of his design so that by the next morning he'd drawn not just the coupé model, but also the saloon, the convertible and the estate version too. Webster delayed his return to England for another 24 hours, and when he eventually set off he was clutching a complete set of one-eighth scale drawings of the whole of the Herald range.

Even so, back in Coventry there was still a good deal of scepticism that Michelotti could actually deliver a physical prototype of his plans on time as he was contracted to do; and as the clock ticked closer towards Christmas, the next relentless deadline in the production schedule, tension in the company mounted to breaking point. In those days, when we had industry in England, it was the custom for most major manufacturers to close down their operations over the main holiday periods in order to save on the costs of overheads, and it wasn't until 24 December – the very day of the shut-down – that to the great relief of everyone another Italian truck finally rolled up at the factory gates.

Inside was a completed prototype of the Herald coupé in black and gold which Webster and his managing director Alick Dick wasted no time in having transferred to a turntable in the styling studio. Everyone who saw it agreed it was a magnificent design, and even today, nearly fifty years later, when you look at its low wheelbase and its sleek, narrow lines it's impossible not to be struck by the pure aesthetic beauty of Michelotti's creation.

In Coventry at the Standard Triumph factory they all knocked off early and went for a drink. Back in Italy, you can't help but suspect that Michelotti was probably still at his drawing board…

We all went off for a drink too in Stratford once we'd got the boat moored. We deserved it, for after the miraculous overnight change in the weather, it had been a long and sweltering day, so blisteringly hot that in the couple of hours it took for Em and I to work our way through the flight of locks that lowers the canal down to the level of the River Avon, Chris had managed to get herself badly sunburned. She'd dropped off to sleep in a chair on the front deck, shaded by the overhang of the cabin; but unfortunately as we'd moved she caught the full force of the sun so that with her white hair and her eyes protected by her sunglasses, she finished up at the end of the day looking like a peculiar albino panda.

The first critical decision you have to make when approaching Stratford by water is where to moor. There are two alternatives: the first, Bancroft Basin, is the town's equivalent of Piccadilly Circus, except that where the London tourist magnet is grubby and tending towards the squalid, the basin is anything but, overlooked as it is by the Royal Shakespeare Theatre and surrounded by meticulously tended flowerbeds and neatly manicured lawns. It's just as busy, though, and in the height of summer, it's always crowded. Even assuming you can find a place to moor, you often have to disturb people picnicking on the grass in order to tie up.

But if you are fortunate enough to find space, Bancroft Basin is the last word in convenience – in fact, it's so convenient that it becomes *in*convenient. It's true the place is so close to the town centre that you can virtually go window shopping from your deck, but the fact is some of the boats in the basin are actually shops themselves, and so it's not unknown for crews mooring here to be woken at night by tourists who've mistaken them for hamburger stalls or a floating restaurant.

Privacy? Forget it. In the high season it's unfeasible to leave any curtain in your boat open for people shamelessly peer in at you; and I've even known tourists to clamber unselfconsciously on board in order to get a closer view, as if boats were just another visitor attraction.

Which, thinking about it, is what I suppose they've become.

The alternative is to moor on the river, and even if you decide to do this you're not exactly out of the way either. The best mooring spots are directly facing the theatre, where if you take in a show you can check out your boat from the balcony of the bar while you're having drinks in the interval. Even so, although you're just the width of the river away from the main part of the town, you virtually leave the tourists behind, for visitors to Stratford are in the main creatures of the herd, and the overwhelming majority of them seem never to venture over Tramway Bridge, despite the fine recreation ground and splendid river walk there.

But don't go running away with the idea that just because you're further away from the tourists, you're completely insulated from the crowds. You may leave the human sort behind, but Stratford's river is teeming with wildfowl, and there's been an internecine war raging on the waterways between different species for more than fifteen years now, and nowhere better encapsulates the tensions at the heart of hostilities than this reach of the Avon.

The conflict has its roots in the eighteenth century when county landowners laid down ornamental lakes on their estates and began to import exotic birds to live in them. One favourite was the pale Atlantic-coast version of the North American wild goose, the largest of the species and absolutely unmistakable with its black neck, white face patch and mottled feather pattern. It's called the Canada Goose, and as late as 1953 a survey found only 1,500 or so pairs in the whole of Britain. Today, on a good summer's afternoon, I reckon you'd find that many of them in Stratford shitting on the grass between the bridge and the bandstand, with as many again on the bank opposite jostling for bread from tourists, with another predatory flock perhaps twice as large just cruising the river looking for any chance to cause trouble.

They *are* rather beautiful creatures, though, with their deep-black, pleading eyes that somehow hypnotise you into giving them what they want. They certainly seem to have mesmerised our indigenous white farmyard goose, much familiar from childhood stories, for today around Stratford-upon-Avon the two species seem to have mixed and mated with impunity, each imparting to the other its worst characteristics. To say the indigenous English goose was never a particularly friendly creature is a bit like pointing out that Attila the Hun never signed the Geneva Convention. Yes, English white geese were always bad-tempered, aggressive birds, despite their Goosy Gander nursery image. But they did at least have the good grace to keep themselves to themselves – as opposed to the gregarious Canadian breed which think nothing of moving in on you mob-handedly if they suspect you of harbouring anything remotely edible.

Unfortunately some of the unusual hybrids currently populating Stratford's waterside are aggressive *and* gregarious, so that they not only come looking for food, but are quite capable of taking off your arm if they don't get it.

Meanwhile, all this has left the graceful Stratford swan – the traditional monarch of these waters – on its webbed back foot. OK, swans haven't exactly been slow on the mating front either, and there seem to be so many more of them in Stratford than there ever were when I first visited the place years ago on a school trip to see *Hamlet*. But even so, I sense in these parts that their elegant, gliding progress through the water is sometimes less confident than it may appear on the surface, and I fear that despite their showy style many of them are subconsciously traumatised by the fear of suddenly getting mugged by their North American cousins.

And violence happens, I can testify. When the tourists have

finished for the day, their supply of stale Hovis and Mothers Pride exhausted, the Avon reverts to what passes for normality; and any boater who casually throws anything into the water, even a discarded cigarette, is in danger of precipitating a major ornithological incident with so much squawking and flapping and irritable pecking of feathers on all sides that you wish you were back in Bancroft Basin for a bit of peace and quiet.

We finally decided to moor on the river, but either place would have been a wonderful spot since they're both locations you couldn't pay to stay, simply because there isn't anywhere except a boat where you *could* stay, regardless of how much you were willing to pay. There's no hotel or guest house hereabouts, and none would ever be allowed; and in this, Stratford is similar to many places on the waterways where there are moorings at unique sites over which you claim a short but intense ownership. It's one of the delights of cruising.

Where else apart from on water would you be able to sleep under the city walls at Chester, or adjacent to Henley Bridge on the Thames? Or deep in the hills on the very Pennine Way where hikers trek? Or in Bath facing Poultney Bridge which is like the Ponte Vecchio in Florence with shops along its length?

Stratford gets a bad press, unfairly in my view since it's not hard to imagine the Disneyland clone that could have resulted if the whole Shakespeare thing had been allowed to get out of hand. OK, so there are a few tacky tourist shops and a couple of hamburger bars, and now they're getting impatient to develop the theatre itself, which some say is looking a bit shabby. But on the whole the place is looked after, and the gardens and parks are kept reasonably clean and tidy.

Extraordinarily, a great deal of the credit for this lies not with Stratford Council, but with Cheltenham some thirty miles away, for under the mysterious magic that regulates local government in contemporary Britain, Cheltenham is actually responsible for maintaining Stratford's parks and collecting its rubbish. Indeed, for all I know Cheltenham may also have the job of looking after

Stratford's roads and educating its kids as well. In fact, if a town in Gloucestershire can be responsible in this way for clearing up chip wrappers in a place in Warwickshire, I suppose it's just about feasible that there isn't a Stratford Council at all, and that everything to do with the town is run from Cheltenham – though I somehow doubt this, since in my experience local government affords so much natural opportunity for provincial aggrandisement and the expression of parochial pomposity that I can't for the life of me ever imagine a town willingly giving up the rituals of the council chamber.

Even so, I think there's a promising idea here and one that hasn't been explored nearly far enough. For surely if Cheltenham can provide all of Stratford's services, why stop at just Stratford?

Just look at the white stucco façades of Cheltenham, look at its population of retired military men and ageing colonial administrators, look at the acres of land on the outskirts covered in military buildings, the existence of which the authorities resolutely deny even though everyone this side of Beijing knows that they're the headquarters of Britain's electronic spying network (though since the Cold War ended no one seems to care much one way or another).

Cheltenham is clearly a town that needs a new purpose – and maybe it's found one. Maybe in the twenty-first century Cheltenham should provide *all* the country's services – everything from defence to environmental health, financial control to consumer affairs. Just look at the benefits of it, for if Cheltenham was able to handle, say, overseas development with the efficiency it handles the flower beds at Bancroft Basin, there'd soon be commodity brokers all over the Third World, and Ethiopia would be the market garden of the world. Just imagine! We could even abolish that bear garden of the Commons since if the whole world can be administered with Cheltenham's quiet efficiency, with the practical decisions about the things that really matter to us in life based on pragmatism rather than untidy emotional idealism, then – as Stratford Council has discovered

– what need is there for the messy processes of democracy to foul everything up?

We went to the theatre that night and saw an absolutely dire production of *Romeo and Juliet*, the quality of which you could judge by the numbers of tourists who, the moment the curtain fell, leapt to their feet in thunderous applause as if to congratulate themselves at having got through the performance without falling asleep. Mind you, it served us right since all tickets for that night had been sold out and I'd only managed to get us in at all by calling in a favour with a friend who knew an actor in the company. Would that all attempts at similar social string-pulling like this could end in such dismal failure, and who knows, the world might be a better place?

To be fair, though, perhaps the way we responded to the play said more about us than it did the production. We all felt a little doleful because the next day we were going home: Em and Chris's holiday was over, and I needed to go back to London to clear up the latest problem that was plaguing the Crumbling Pile. It seems that while it had been left uninhabited a small fissure had appeared in some guttering and water had soaked through an outside wall, leading to an outbreak of familiar cotton wool-like green mould across the wall of one of the bedrooms.

After the performance we walked across Tramway Bridge for the last time. The lights of the town were reflected on the rippling river, and through the uncurtained windows of the theatre you could see the staff as they busied themselves cleaning the bleak bars and restaurants which had now emptied of the crowds that had earlier been milling around inside so cheerfully. It was a sultry evening, and a lone busker stood on the bridge strumming out some melancholy ballad which we could make out echoing across the water when we got back to the boat, and which we could still hear tucked up in our beds as sleep came upon us.

Seventeen

Jane Howard has never really understood the power of her looks, or the effect they have had on men. It's something that's always made her feel deeply uncomfortable about herself, and so she's professed never to believe that she has been, and still is, so graceful and handsome; or to ascribe beauty itself any value.

'I realise now that a lot of people took up with me because of what I looked like and didn't know anything else about me at all, or want to know,' she admits now, a little sadly. 'It was a kind of awful trap because I never liked my appearance very much.'

Throughout her life her striking demeanour has regularly been the cause of problems in her relationships with men. Robert Aickman saw her as Zuleika Dobson, the heroine of Max Beerbohm's eponymous 1911 novel whose pulchritude led the young men of Oxford to queue up to drown themselves in the Isis out of love for her. 'Jane's presence,' he said, 'had the effect of making everything else in life seem worthless and absurd beside her radiant identity. By merely existing, she promoted loves and hates which, through no fault of her own, left some who felt them fevered and wasted.'

He was obsessed with her, and the three mornings a week they worked together must have been charged with a painful emotional intensity for them both, especially since for most of the period they knew each other, the Inland Waterways Association used as its office the living room of Aickman's small London flat where he still lived with his wife Ray, and where as well as running their literary agency, she did occasional work for the organisation herself.

On the surface at least, Ray seems to have been indifferent to their affair; indeed, in some ways she welcomed it since, as she told Jane, Robert was depressed and it was good for him. When they were away, she looked after the office; when they were around, she cooked for them. She once remarked that she didn't mind Robert and Jane having a relationship – she just drew the line at having to take them breakfast in bed. 'He exploited Ray frightfully,' Jane has said of this period, in a way that seems to deny that she herself might have had any part in events. 'He recognised in Ray that there was somebody who would type his letters, wash his clothes, do the housework and cooking, be a sort of First Lieutenant which she certainly was.'

The claustrophobic incestuousness of life in this Bloomsbury bohemia wasn't helped by the fact that Jane's estranged husband Peter Scott was also involved in the IWA as a vice-president. At the time he was in the process of setting up the Severn Wildfowl Trust (subsequently the Wildfowl and Wetlands Trust) at Slimbridge in Gloucestershire, on a site just a half mile or so from the Gloucester and Sharpness Canal where he kept a narrowboat called *Beatrice*, modelled on Rolt's *Cressy*, which was used as overflow accommodation for guests.

Robert Aickman was attracted by celebrity, and Scott – among his many other achievements – had not long before commentated for the BBC at the wedding of the young Princess Elizabeth and Philip Mountbatten. He was a nationally famous figure, and Aickman soon identified him as being a potentially useful contact, so that in no time at all – his affair with Jane notwithstanding – Aickman struck up a close working relationship that soon developed personally. To complete the circle, Scott subsequently employed Ray on *his* staff as his organising secretary.

As anyone who has ever experienced these things knows, romance in the workplace, however well managed, usually causes nothing but pain to those involved and upset to the organisation concerned. Jane Howard and Robert Aickman's affair was no different to any other in this respect, and difficulties soon began to occur in the nascent IWA after the two of them took a boating holiday together on the Thames. Perhaps ill advisedly, they went during work time. And they left without Aickman saying anything to Tom Rolt, who was not only the IWA honorary secretary and, nominally at least, jointly running the organisation; but also a man who, as an instinctive traditionalist, might have been expected to have strong views on this sort of thing.

Until this point Rolt and Aickman had been close, not only as two individuals who were themselves friends, but also as part of two couples who all got on with each other intimately. The Rolts had often been guests of the Aickmans at their home in London, and the Aickmans guests of the Rolts on *Cressy*. The two couples had holidayed with each other, and partly because the Rolts lived on a boat and hadn't got a phone, and partly because they were a generation – the last one – for which it was commonplace, there was a period during which they corresponded with each other on a regular basis.

Aickman's romance with Jane Howard made things very difficult, though you can't help but think, as so often in circumstances like this, that what actually brought the two men into direct conflict was of less importance than what had been festering under the surface between them for sometime beforehand. Rolt fired the first shot by writing to Aickman complaining that while Jane had been cruising the Thames, he'd been 'deliberately misled' into thinking she was in the office. There's little doubt that what he was feeling cut a good deal deeper than this, though, for he added disingenuously – almost as an afterthought – that, of course, he 'could not care less' how Jane had spent her holiday and *who* she'd spent it with…

Really? So if he cared so little, then why did he mention it at all? And if *this* wasn't bothering him, then what *was*? Jane being out of the office for a few days when she'd not taken a holiday in a year? The marginal inconvenience to the IWA that this might have caused? The trivial drain on the funds of the organisation?

Clearly there was a lot more than Jane's absence at issue here, and Aickman focussed on this when he replied to the criticism.

He admitted he'd known Angela and Tom wouldn't be happy about what he'd done, but he argued that Jane had been working for the IWA for a long time without ever having been on the waterways. As if this somehow justified him taking her away. As if this somehow detracted from the simple truth of what had happened which was that the two of them were having a passionate affair and had decided to go away together.

Rolt wasn't satisfied. 'I do not think that this was right,' he said bluntly, 'and, as I said before, it damages the feeling of mutual confidence without which a concern like (the) IWA cannot carry on, at least not happily.'

This had become an openly moral question now, a matter of right and wrong; but who can ever know the extent to which someone's ethical perspective can be distorted, consciously or unconsciously, by other factors? Did Rolt just find the liaison unacceptably distasteful? Or was there something more deeply psychological in his response? Was he, for instance, somehow attracted to Jane Howard himself? Or did Aickman think he was?

Perhaps behind Rolt's response was a sort of jealousy, for around this time, Robert had started a flirtatious relationship with Angela which didn't go down well with anyone, and which may have tempted Tom to take liberties with Jane in a way that wasn't completely natural to him. There's certainly an intriguing incident that takes place a little after these events when they had patched things up and gone away together on another boat trip – this one arranged legitimately as part of the IWA's campaigning activities. Rolt for some reason had plaited Jane a boatman's belt out of long grass which she is reported to have 'swung provocatively around her hips, infuriating Robert'.

What on earth was all this about then? Was the provocation a consciously sexual one? Or was the real affront Rolt's? Was his gift of the belt made knowing Jane well enough to predict how she would respond to it? And was it made anticipating how Aickman would respond to *her*? Either way, why *did* Aickman react so angrily? Was this covert sexual jealousy, or something even more complicated, something rooted in Aickman's own muddled morality which allowed him to bed women with impunity while at the same time expecting them to act like prim Victorian virgins?

Correspondence between the two men continued, with Aickman becoming increasingly more defensive about Jane in a way that seems to have taken the form of a growing aggressiveness towards Tom and Angela as a couple. It was as if the gloves were suddenly off between them. Soon Angela pitched into the fray. 'I *do not hate* Jane,' she wrote bitterly in one of her letters. 'Indeed, I admire her brain and her beauty immensely but, from the day we all four went to the opera together, Jane has never spoken a civil word to me… Apart from one conversation with Ray (which I now regret) I have never discussed Jane with anyone… Why you should think that Tom and I want to interfere in your affairs, God only knows…'

So they 'all four' had gone to the opera together? Two couples as they had always been, except with Ray Aickman now replaced by Jane Howard? It is not hard to see how uncomfortable this outing must have been for the Rolts, and how hard especially it must have been for the emotionally voluble Angela who always found it difficult to hide what she was feeling. Not hard either to see why, out of loyalty if nothing else, she might have felt obliged to speak to Ray about it later. Or why, knowing this, the insecure yet self-willed Jane Howard would have responded the way she did to Angela.

Aickman felt that the Rolts were messing too much in his personal life, and he was right: the fact is that his affair with Jane Howard deepened the rift with Tom, ensuring that they'd never again be able to work together with the same degree of trust in each other. From now on the relationship between the two men would always be prickly; and although Tom Rolt always professed himself a deep admirer of Robert Aickman's organisational abilities, from this point onwards he seems never to be able to resist bickering with him about something or other, whether the state of the IWA's book-keeping, or the way he believed Robert was using the organisation for his own self-aggrandisement.

You can't help but wonder if driving a wedge between the two wasn't in the back of Angela Rolt's mind all along; for just as Robert Aickman's relationship with Ray was rocky at this time, so her own marriage to Tom was beginning to come under strain as their 'design for living' increasingly became subsumed by the burden of Tom's IWA responsibilities. Eventually they began to think of themselves as tools of the Gower Street office.

Which was another way of saying tools of Robert Aickman.

A couple of weeks after Em's holiday, I returned alone to Stratford-upon-Avon from London, so covered in fungicide from all the remedial work I'd done to rid the Crumbling Pile of mould that the very mushrooms I prepared that morning for breakfast were wilting before I could get them into the frying pan. Mind you, there was no doubt that I'd killed the mildew. The trouble was, I seemed to have killed a good deal more besides. Every pot plant in the house had given up the ghost, and even a bunch of Sweet William inadvertently left in a vase in the living room had reduced to a display of monochromatic husks like a three-dimensional X-ray. After I finished I swear even the roses on a set of flowered curtains in the bathroom looked noticeably withered.

My brother Jay was scheduled to join me on the next leg of the journey to use up a couple of days' holiday he had owing, and because his time was limited we cast off very soon after he arrived, even though it was late in the day and evening had already set in. As soon as we slipped her mooring lines and she was released to the river, *Justice* surged forward with the downstream current, her propeller responding to the exceptional depth of the water beneath her. In this, as in so many other ways, navigating a river is a totally different experience to being on a canal. A river is nature's creation, a live creature with its own will, and with its own moods and foibles. It's also much more dangerous and unpredictable than a still water channel, especially at times like this when there's been a lot of rain and it's 'running fresh' as us boaty-types say.

Weirs can rush powerfully, you see; and the river can build up alarmingly behind the narrow archways of bridges. It can get assertive and unpredictable too as the accumulation of water leads to confusing cross-currents that can buffet you in all directions. When the water's high and you're travelling downstream, the best thing is to use natural forces as far as you can so that you literally 'go with the flow', working in a sort of partnership with the elements, albeit sometimes a rather uneasy one.

All this is a totally different experience to steering a boat on canals, which are human constructions – physical manifestations of man's success in asserting himself on nature. Compared to a river, canal water is inactive and lifeless – like a block of plastic against a plank of wood – and you're not so much travelling on it, as moving through it – ploughing your course with a sort of dogged perseverance.

Speed is the one thing you notice most in open water. Released from the drag factor of canals, a moving narrowboat sits differently in a river: it drops at the stern and rises more steeply at the bow so that it slips through the water with less resistance, reaching 7 or 8 mph, or even more. Now I grant you, heady speeds like this wouldn't actually impress on your local by-pass, let alone at Hockenheim or Silverstone. But on a racetrack you're not steering a vehicle which can be up to 70 feet long and which can weigh anything up to 20 tons; and when you're driving on the roads at least you have things called brakes, which, generally speaking, are useful to have at your disposal if you need to stop quickly.

The best you've got on a boat is your reverse gear.

Try using that on a fast-flowing river when you're in danger of smashing into another boat, or of being swept into some dark threatening place where the water's gurgling and eternity beckons you with its ominous finger. Of one thing I can assure you: you won't stop quickly.

At the very best, making your propeller go backwards might be enough to bring you to a halt in 20 or 30 feet, but that sort of stopping distance is hardly enough to inspire confidence. Which is why – like death and the prospect of relegation if your team's having a bad season – it's best not to lose too much sleep contemplating those aspects of existence over which you have only minimal control. Things like the weather, for instance...

Predictably, after a few consecutive days of sunshine, the British summer had drawn to a close; and having thrown aside whatever items of clothing they decently could in an attempt to work up a good melanoma, the people of this country had reverted to a more traditional summer garb of shell suits and light sweaters, the better to flaunt their peeling noses and flame-red complexions. Not that this sort of stuff is much use at any time in our weather when the priority should always be keeping dry; but protection from the elements is hardly the purpose of English summer apparel which is donned less as a response to the climate, and more in the way of a stubborn statement of nationalism.

Anyway, you could tell the overseas tourists easily enough in Stratford. The tourists were the ones prepared for the rain; the English were the ones walking around looking like drowned rats.

As soon as we started it began to rain with a light drizzle which we endured for half an hour or so until it began to blow up windy as well, making the boat lurch around unnervingly in the swell. At this we decided to throw in the towel and stop at the next lock where there were a series of well-appointed moorings, which I suppose would have afforded a pleasant outlook on the water had you been able to see it through the unpleasant murkiness which by now had fallen on the river. Of course, no sooner had we tied up and abandoned any hope of going further that night, than His Honour Lord Justice Sod decided to lay down the law. The weather cleared immediately and it became, if not exactly the end of a flaming June day, then at least the beginning of a half-decent summer's evening.

So we decided to go hunting for rabbits.

Now, the concept of killing bunnies is something I am aware may well shock the more urban-minded of my readers for whom a brisk walk past the chilled-meat counter at Sainsbury's is probably the nearest they ever get to blood sport. In mitigation I have to confess that my shooting skills are so poor they threaten little beyond my own rather pathetic view of myself as the sort of hunter-provider who in a perfect world would be spending more time banging on drums in the woods with his mates. In ten years, my total tally with the air rifle that I keep on the boat has been a few Coke cans I've seen bobbing around in the water, and a pigeon that I left traumatised outside Whitchurch in Shropshire one year after I'd pulverised the crab apple it had been unenthusiastically pecking.

And my brother Jay isn't even as good as this.

However, in the past both of us have noticed that our appearance at a local farm requesting permission to have a pot at a few rabbits has given us instant countryside credibility, since in some places they're a complete scourge on the land, and a genuine pest. They are also a rather tasty pest, which can't be said of crows, for instance. Or foxes for that matter.

Before long we were nestled down in the fold of a nearby meadow, taking turns at blasting off at a drove of rabbits that had assembled in such numbers I can only think there must have been some special event taking place – maybe the appearance of some furry celebrity, a sort of Zoe Ball with long ears, there to open some new warren or another. Certainly our presence didn't cause much of a stir, for though we peppered the air with pellets, it was clear none were getting close enough to their mark to make us even objects of curiosity, let alone threats to health. Eventually one rather tatty and bruised old beast did fix us in his gaze, rising provocatively on his hind legs in such a way that to have attracted our attention more he'd have had to pull on a sweater decorated with target markings.

In fact he made himself so obvious that a passing dog ran at him which sent the whole colony scurrying for cover and left us looking pretty stupid lying there aiming at buttercups in the gathering gloom.

'Disturb you, did he?' the owner of the dog asked somewhat unnecessarily. He waved his arm towards another field belonging to the same farmer, which, he said, backed onto a large modern bungalow. 'You'll find twice as many of the things there. All around the pasture and running wild in the garden. The lady living there used to feed them, you see – but then she was from London, she was,' he said, as if this explained such eccentricity – which, of course, it did.

'She's dead now, though; died just last month,' he added, giving us the sort of look that communicated precisely how fitting he thought this fate was for anyone from the capital, regardless or not of whether they had a penchant for cuddly creatures which hopped around a lot.

Jay and I went to the place he suggested, and sure enough we found an even larger assembly of what seemed at first glance to be several hundred rabbits, if not more. There were rabbits all over the place: rabbits hopping about aimlessly, rabbits playing with each other, rabbits doing... well, doing what rabbits do. Some of them were spilling from the field through a hedge and into the bungalow garden where they were gorging themselves stupid on the thick, uncut grass of the lawn. Not that any of this mattered much to us, though. However many rabbits had been around that evening, it felt as if we'd be incapable of hitting one if it had been tied to the barrel of our gun making rude faces at us. After another half an hour of desultory shooting we were just about ready to pack it up for the night.

Then Jay had a lucky hit. It *must* have been lucky since by this point it was almost dark, and anyhow at the time he was lining up his target anyone who wasn't blind could have seen that his aim was totally cock-eyed. One way or another, a young buck which had been grazing close to the hedge with a group of other rabbits suddenly stopped in its tracks and double somersaulted straight out of the field and into the middle of the bungalow lawn where it dropped like a stone. This had absolutely no discernible effect on its erstwhile colleagues which continued feeding dispassionately around where it had once been as if nothing had happened – much in the manner of a gaggle of teenage girls disturbed nibbling chocolate in the middle of their favourite soap.

At this stage in the evening, a certain note of absurdity began to characterise proceedings, for two things then happened at so nearly the same time as to be intrinsically connected in my mind.

The first was that a lamp suddenly went on in the bungalow kitchen, flooding the lawn with light and emptying it in an instant of everything except the grey silhouette of a single dead rabbit. A figure appeared – a man – and I watched nervously as he glanced towards the lawn. Finally, to my relief, he turned away and began preparing a meal.

The second was that a Scotsman walked by in full regalia – kilt, dirk and bagpipes – the full monty.

'Good evening,' he said. 'Bit drier now, isn't it?'

'Yes,' Jay replied automatically. 'Much nicer.'

A little later we heard the strains of 'Amazing Grace' echoing from the direction of the river. Afterwards the tune changed to 'Mull of Kintyre'.

'What the hell are we going to do now?' asked Jay.

'Just grit your teeth. It'll end soon,' I said.

'I didn't mean the music – I meant the rabbit.'

Ah. The rabbit? Yes. The rabbit. This was a trickier problem. 'Well, we've shot it – we can't just leave it,' I said eventually.

'And we can't go marching across his lawn to pick it up either,' said Jay. 'It was one of his dead wife's pets.'

Eventually, after some discussion, we agreed that to avoid drawing unnecessary attention to ourselves Jay would take the gun back to the boat, and I would lurk in the darkness waiting for some opportunity to run across the lawn to collect what I'd already earmarked as the following day's dinner. Jay wasn't entirely happy at this – which I put down to the fact that the death of the rabbit was probably beginning to play on his conscience. The evening had almost turned into night by now, you see. Suddenly Jay didn't seem comfortable in the dark. Not a happy bunny, you might say under different circumstances.

Perhaps he expected his victim to rise up and haunt him, pointing at him accusingly with a bloodstained paw in the manner of Jacob Marley confronting Scrooge.

'Maybe I'll wait for you, after all,' he mumbled.

'And maybe you won't!' I said. 'Just bugger off. If we get clocked, it'll be cheese sandwiches tomorrow.'

Jay set off down the path back to the river, and, as I learnt later, he immediately ran into the Scotsman, who apparently was engaged every night to play a couple of songs to American tourists on a trip boat as it turned back towards Stratford at this, the furthest point of its journey.

'Any luck?' he asked, seeing Jay with the gun.

'Er – no – not at all. But then, you wouldn't expect it, would you? I mean, it's not as if I've been shooting, is it..? Oh, no… well, not at rabbits, anyway. Especially not rabbits. Oh no, I would never do that…' said Jay, who was startled by the meeting, and by now was so nonplussed by events he wasn't going to admit anything to anyone – or at least not until he'd had a stiff drink or two.

Regrettably, I passed the Scotsman on the same path just a short while afterwards. He was on his way home, swinging his bagpipes in his hand. I was on my way back to the boat, proudly swinging the rabbit which I'd just managed to retrieve after a breathless dash across the lawn.

He gave it – and me – a very strange look as we passed, but he went on his way without saying a word.

He probably thought the whole thing was very odd. But I

suppose when you walk around in a skirt with a sheep's stomach slung across your back and an offensive weapon in your sock, you get used to keeping your mouth shut about the peculiarities of other people.

It's easy to prepare a rabbit, and if you hang it by its back feet and rip its skin off downwards, then its fur will peel over its head making its decapitation a more agreeably anonymous business. Gutting it is not difficult either since the weight of a rabbit's entrails virtually strips them itself once you've split the thin membrane of the stomach which holds them in. Cleaning up can be messy, true; but if you're doing this outside in the countryside then it's hardly worthwhile bothering since the foxes will almost certainly do the job for you if the crows don't. There's a balance to all this which I like, a naturalness. The rabbit becomes a food to nourish different species and nothing of it gets wasted.

This sort of thing bothers a lot of people I know, but being brought up in the country I learned early on that there was a connection between the animals around me and the food on my plate; and so even now I find it difficult to account for the squeamishness of those who eat meat regularly and yet somehow deceive themselves about what it actually is and what's involved in its production and preparation. Certainly I have less moral scruple taking out a rabbit which has lived its life freely and organically than I do eating a slice of bacon from a processed pig that I know will almost certainly have suffered a diet of daily indignity and antibiotics along with its putrefying swill.

In that sense killing is part of the food preparation process. Or as every medieval recipe for rabbit always started, 'First catche yr rabbit.' Here's the recipe for how I cooked this one; it was made up on the spur of the moment from what happened to be in the galley.

The Fourth Recipe

First catche yr rabbit. Cut it in half, carefully jointing and reserving the thick hind legs and the back or 'saddle'. Marinade these in red wine, black pepper and thyme and leave them overnight. Meanwhile simmer the sparse front portions in a large pot with an onion, some dried mixed herbs – or whatever fresh you can muster – a couple of carrots and a litre of water to make a pint or so of light stock. Always be careful when jointing rabbit since their bones are like needles and can be both dangerous and unpleasant.

The next day cut up two or three rashers of smoked streaky bacon or similar, and fry them slowly so as to sweat out the fat. Be careful not to burn them. Dry off the marinated pieces of rabbit with a kitchen towel, dust them with flour and brown them lightly in the bacon fat. Afterwards put them into a pot with the bacon pieces, another coarsely chopped onion, a large roughly sliced carrot, some more thyme, black pepper, the wine marinade and the stock, all of which should comfortably cover the rabbit. If not, make up the volume with water. Bring this all to a steady simmer and add a can of chopped tomatoes or, if you have them, three or four roughly chopped fresh ones that have gone past their best. Simmer all this, without covering the pot, for about an hour or so or until the rabbit has become tender. But be careful. Once rabbit has cooked, it disintegrates very quickly and falls off the bone in a sort of textureless mush that tastes OK but looks unattractive.

At this stage if the cooking liquid has formed a rich and thick sauce, the dish may be ready for eating – in which case season it finally and sprinkle it with coarsely chopped parsley of any sort. However, if it's too liquidy remove the rabbit pieces carefully and reduce the cooking stock. Similarly, if your simmer hasn't been gentle enough you may need to add more water to the pan. Don't worry about this. And don't worry either if the cooking time is longer than indicated since you may get an older, tougher rabbit which many maintain tastes better, but which may need more time in the pot. For this reason, since you can only accurately estimate the cooking time by the individual rabbit, this is a good dish to cook and serve heated through the following day when it seems to improve in taste.

Eighteen

YOU DON'T GET MUCH for free in the world today – which is why mooring on canals is such a good deal. Apart from in locks and at water points, you can pretty well stop where you want anywhere on the towpath side; and even though, sadly, more and more restrictions are being applied to how long you can stay in any one place, the whole process is still about as laid-back and hassle free as you find anywhere in this increasingly regulated society of ours.

Not on rivers, though.

On most of them you couldn't moor if you wanted to because the banks are too high and overgrown to be able to land. But even if it *were* possible, you wouldn't be allowed to anyway. Rivers are very much older arteries of transport than canals, and the riparian rights have been jealously guarded and squabbled over since time immemorial; so that even if you saw a good place to pull up for the night, you'd probably find the only people allowed there were the fair-haired second sons of parish cobblers who'd been granted some charter or other by Henry II in 1161 or thereabouts.

The only alternative is to stump up some exorbitant sum to a farmer to stay on their land – a source of income which on some reaches of the Thames is every bit as lucrative for them as an EU subsidy. Otherwise you have to compete with every other boat afloat to get one of the rare mooring spots provided by local councils, where these days, nine times out of ten, you'll probably find yourself having to shell out anyhow.

Actually the Avon isn't too bad by the standards of other places, and there are generally enough free spaces to be had even in towns like Evesham where the night after the rabbit hunting, Jay and I moored just a little away from the town centre opposite what I suppose you have to call the lock-keeper's 'cottage' – though that's a poor word to use for what is such an unusual structure. It's built on a contemporary A-frame design, bridging the chamber of an old lock and a weir stream that once used to feed a mill here; and it looks a little like an Alpine ski chalet which is the more intriguing for being so totally out of place in somewhere which in most other respects is a traditional English market town built in the classic Georgian style. I'd liked to have seen more of the place, but after a night sampling the local beers, we woke late the next morning and were keen to get off as soon as possible.

Evesham marks the traditional boundary of the Upper and the Lower Avon, a distinction which is far from academic since even today both of these sections of river are administered separately from one another, and from British Waterways which runs most of the rest of the system; and both require boats to pay an additional licence fee in order to cruise them. This division of the two parts of the river goes back centuries, and the Upper Avon – the section we had just cruised from Stratford – was at one stage owned by the Great Western Railway, which in the 1860s stopped charging boats tolls for passage.

Predictably, this bit of Victorian corporate altruism wasn't as generous as it might have seemed, since by this strategy the company avoided all its maintenance obligations. Within a decade the river had deteriorated to the point where it was all but unnavigable, thus leaving the way clear for the Great Western's new-fangled steam engine thingy to pick up lots of profitable freight business – which, of course, had been the intention all along. For the next hundred years or so the river steadily went to the dogs until by the 1960s many of the weirs along the Upper Avon had completely collapsed and most of the locks were derelict.

However, with the foundation of the Inland Waterways

Association, the idea of restoration became feasible; and very soon a head of steam built up to open the river to navigation once more – not just for its own sake, but as an important through route to the Severn, from which other canals linked to the rest of the network. In 1950 a trust was set up with the aim of renovating the lower part of the river, and with the support of Robert Aickman among others, remedial work started on the back of voluntary labour, so that by 1962 it was possible for the first time in years to take a boat from the Severn *up* the Avon to Evesham.

It still wasn't possible, however, to do what Jay and I had just done and take a boat in the opposite direction *down* the newly opened canal and *into* Evesham. For that, enthusiasts would have to wait another ten years until 1974 when a second charitable trust finally succeeded in completing work on the river, opening it in its entirety for the first time in more than a century, and effectively laying the foundation for the national restoration movement which would explode into activity over subsequent years as increasingly more people became aware of the economic and leisure potential of the waterways.

The small town of Pershore is about ten miles from Evesham, and because there's a reliable bus service to Stratford where Jay had left his car, we decided to make it our goal for the remaining part of his short trip. There are about a dozen or so moorings here which lie dappled by willow trees adjacent to a park and only a step or two away from the town centre, famed for its pubs. This alone would make it an attractive enough proposition as a place to stay for a night or two, even if it weren't for the fact that – like the Evesham moorings – the ones at Pershore were free too: gratis and buckshee.

They get crowded, though, and so to avoid disappointment we thought it would be wise to stake a claim on one as early as possible. The journey from Evesham is a short one, and we planned to arrive at Pershore before four o'clock which we were confident would give us the pick of the best spots. So certain of this were we that at the lock near the intriguingly named Wyre Piddle, not far from our destination, we were happy enough for a cruiser to overtake us – even knowing that he was heading for Pershore too and that this would give him priority over us. It didn't seem to matter, though: the rain of the previous day had cleared the air, and though it wasn't warm, and the wind was blustery, it was at least dry and bright, and we were feeling good about the world and our place in it.

Except that Rule One of rivers is never to count your moorings before you're actually in them. When we arrived, astonishingly, every single available space was occupied. Well, all of them except one – and that was just about to be taken by the cruiser we'd allowed to overtake us which at that very moment was manoeuvring snugly and smugly into position.

There was, it is fair to say, much cursing on *Justice*. There was also a degree of fraternal recrimination as to whose crap idea it actually was in the first place to let a bloody boat overtake us… Then we spotted another mooring space. It was at the end of the line in what would have been an ideal position except that it was about 20 foot too short for us and to stop there would have meant us tying up with our stern poking into the river like some badly parked Nissan taking up two bays in a municipal multi-storey.

Still, beggars can't be choosers, and, with no other option available, I began to nudge the bow of *Justice* forward until I remembered Rule Two of river cruising which is never to believe when you see a patch of water that it will necessarily be deep enough for you to manoeuvre a boat. *This* patch of water certainly wasn't. In fact, strictly speaking, it wasn't water at all: more a sort of sludgy mudbank in which we soon found ourselves inextricably stuck despite my very best attempts to reverse us off. In fact, all my efforts in this direction made matters a good deal worse, for the river current caught us and started corkscrewing the boat so that within no time at all we were facing upstream in the direction from which we'd come, having somehow completed a 360-degree pirouette.

What was worse was that all this cavorting about, accompanied as it was by much revving of the engine and the emergence of much black smoke from the exhaust pipe, soon began to attract the attention of other craft moored along the bank, confirming – as I inevitably knew it would – Rule Three of the river, and indeed every other waterway too. This states that you shall never commit a balls-up without there being an audience of at least a dozen people to witness you making a complete prat of yourself.

Again, there was much bickering and mutual recrimination on *Justice*, during which the ties of brotherly love between Jay and I wore so exceedingly thin they were in danger of snapping in a hail of increasingly ill-tempered banter. Fortunately, before things could degenerate further, we suddenly found ourselves drifting off the mud, and at the same time – as if on cue – another narrowboat which had been moored immediately in front of us pulled out into mid-stream, giving us easy access to a perfect mooring spot into which we fitted without any problem whatsoever. It was the best spot on the bank. In fact, it was the place we'd have chosen ourselves if we'd have had first pick.

As if to compound our joy, we discovered later that the space taken by the cruiser we'd allowed to pass us – the one we'd have jumped at if we'd had half a chance – wasn't anything like as good as it seemed from the water. In fact, the reason it was the last mooring to be taken was that it straddled the concrete mouth of a small weir designed to allow excess water to run off from a brook in the park, and it wasn't a very pleasant place at all.

Looking back, I suppose Pershore was an example of the perverse way that life can sometimes pan out when it's not being a complete bitch; for sometimes things don't exactly happen in the way you want them to do, but all the same they happen for the best. Something similar occurred for a second time later that day when Jay and I sat in the beautifully tended garden of one of Pershore's fine pubs nursing some rather good bitter which had been brewed on the premises. We had long since kissed and made up, and we were talking about my plans for the following day after he'd left. I'd brought along some maps which I'd spread out on the pub table, and we were examining the options of where I might go. I suppose at this stage I was thinking that once I'd reached the confluence of the Avon with the River Severn, maybe I'd head upstream towards Worcester and from there perhaps swing around towards Birmingham…

'But you said you were heading for Bristol, didn't you?' Jay said. 'Why have you given up on that idea?'

For a second or two I looked at him blankly. It wasn't that I didn't understand what he was saying, it was just that what he was saying seemed inexplicably stupid. 'But that was a plan I had when I was in Oxford. That was months ago and a million miles away. That was when I was thinking about going down the Thames and on to the Kennet and Avon Canal… I can't do that now. I can't go back to where I started.'

'So what's wrong with the back way, then?' he asked.

Once again I looked at him blankly. 'There isn't a back way, or any other way to Bristol apart from down the Thames and along the Kennet and Avon…'

Jay pulled a map towards him and pushed it in my direction. 'So what's that then?' he said, jabbing his finger onto the sheet. 'Scotch bloody mist?'

'Surely if you go *down* the Severn,' he explained, 'onto that canal – there – what's it called? – the Gloucester and Sharpness – then you'd come out here. That'd get you to Bristol, wouldn't it?'

I looked at where he was pointing, and I took a long swig of my beer. It was as much as I could do to avoid laughing in his face. But you have to expect this with my brother – he has no experience of canals and can't be expected to know any better.

'That,' I said, speaking slowly, so that there couldn't be any misunderstanding between us, 'is the Severn Estuary. It is probably the trickiest and certainly the most dangerous estuary around the coast of England. It is characterised by a savage set of complex and dangerous currents, a constantly changing weather pattern and a tide range of up to 45 feet, which is the second highest in the world and which strikes fear into the hearts of round-the-world yachtsmen, let alone people like me, cruising in a boat which is little more than a sophisticated steel box.'

Jay looked at me for a moment or two.

'So? You chicken, or what?' he said eventually.

The next day, alone for the first time in many weeks, I wandered around Pershore aimlessly until I finished up in the Abbey which dates from the seventh century when Ethelred, King of the Mercians, donated land to establish a monastery on the site. It's one helluva building, part of a much larger religious foundation of mainly Norman design which over the years had survived fire, gales and flood until the Reformation finally did for it and Henry VIII's commissioners pulled most of it down. They would have razed the rest too except that to their eternal credit the people of Pershore clubbed together to buy them off for £400 so they could use what survived as their parish church. The bit they bought was the Monk's Choir, a great vaulted space which is itself the size of other cathedrals, and is worth an hour or two of anyone's life. The roof is spectacular, soaring above you in a breathtaking 'ploughshare' design.

The Monk's Choir, in case you were wondering, got its name because... well, because the monks used to sing there. And the vaulted 'ploughshare' design is so-called because the vaults resemble... erm, how about the blades of ploughshares? A funny coincidence, all this, but it does demonstrate how easy it is to get your head around the bullshit of medieval architecture if only you don't panic.

I couldn't concentrate on it, though. I kept thinking about the conversation I'd had with Jay the night before. I kept thinking about Bristol and the Severn Estuary. I kept thinking about the bizarre implications of getting to a place I'd intended going by a route I didn't know existed. Most of all, I kept thinking about some article I'd read in a waterways magazine years before which I vaguely remembered was about cruising the Severn Estuary. I seemed to recall that it said it was possible to hire professional pilots for the trip, making it – if not exactly risk-free – then at least far from foolhardy.

So that night, and with some trepidation, I telephoned Em to run the idea past her. She had some holiday still owing, and she'd been planning to join me again later in the summer. Her response surprised me. I found it – to say the least – a little chastening.

'Right!' she said straight off, without even thinking about it. 'Why not? I'll come with you. Sounds a lot of fun. It could be a great adventure.'

'But aren't you worried about the currents? The tide fall? The weather? It can be dangerous, you know.'

The line went silent. When she spoke again I don't think I was mistaken in detecting a slight hint of disdain in her voice.

'So? You chicken, or what?'

I set off the next day down the river. It was one of those mornings when the barometer which hangs in the boat was set for fair when outside it quite clearly *wasn't* fair, and when you didn't need a degree in meteorology to see that it wasn't going to be that way, or anything like it. So unusual was this disparity between technology and reality that it was mentioned on the weather forecast on Radio 4's *Today* programme, and so it was no surprise whatsoever that after about half an hour of cruising, the sky darkened and it began to pour down with an unusual intensity – the rain warm and heavy, plummeting to earth like so many tiny explosive charges which burst in crystal shards on top of the boat and pitted the surface of the river into a thousand craters.

Considering how much rain we have in England, and how rich is our language, it's surprising we don't have more terms for it. There are only about half a dozen alternatives and one of them is 'precipitation' which sounds more like a coy sexual sweat than the good rutting downpour I endured that day. At first the deluge seemed to be hitting me head-on in a frontal attack, not so much stinging my face as bruising it with the remorseless force of the torrent. But then great peals of thunder broke out, and nature seemed to mount an additional attack on my flanks with raindrops the size of saucers playing an exuberantly percussive fortissimo up the sleeves of my coat. Soon I was raked by a bitterly cold wind and the dark sky was seared with lightning; and the heavens which had opened long before now seemed as if they must now be available for immediate occupation, if not general and wide-scale colonisation.

This wasn't rain as we know it: this was a combination of war and Wagnerian opera. This was the *Ride of the Valkyries* as perceived by Francis Ford Coppola. This *was* the apocalypse, and it was very much happening now.

Then all of a sudden the whole show stopped. One moment it was detonating with the metaphoric equivalent of a 60-piece orchestra and a percussion section to match, and the next all was totally calm. Like a celestial millpond. No wind. No rain. No nothing, except for the first glintings of sun reflecting off the water as the river arched around in the gentle series of wide, gracious sweeps which take it towards Nafford Lock. Needless to say I was soaked to the skin, though it didn't seem to matter at this point. In fact, nothing seemed of much consequence. It was as if the storm had acted as a reminder of the raw force of nature, and thrown life into perspective; and as if not just me, but the countryside itself, counted itself fortunate to have come through the whole thing unscathed.

Just at that moment, as if to mark this return to normality, I was regaled by the cacophony of what seemed like a dozen flocks of birds noisily celebrating this part of the morning with the same sort of ebullience they normally welcome the dawn.

Nafford Lock is a fearsome creation for a boat the size of a bus coming downstream when the river's a bit lively. For a start, it's difficult to work out where you're supposed to be going, since at first the river seems totally blocked by a set of massive iron gates. Once you've worked out that these are part of some mechanism of water management, you've so little time to react that it's easy to miss the sharp right turn needed to avoid them and get you back on course. Immediately afterwards, just as you've started to think you've got over the worst and can relax, you have to swing a sharp left to get you into the channel for the lock itself. This is so short it hardly gives you the opportunity to decelerate from the speed you've been travelling.

As if to remind me that I was supposed to be a seasoned boater, accomplished enough to be considering navigating the Severn Estuary to Bristol, fate dealt me an added challenge as I approached the lock. A hire boat happened to be emerging at the same time, and as he saw me bearing down on him he lost his head completely, panicked, and went careering across my path. To avoid what could have been a very nasty collision, I swung into the only clear water available to me which turned out to be the channel of Nafford's somewhat ferocious weir, where only the expedient of running myself up the bank and virtually hitting a fisherman in the process prevented me going over the top and making a somewhat quicker descent to the lower river than would have been either wise or safe.

I went through the lock and pressed on, though matters seemed to get little better. The intricacies of Nafford were at least marked on my map, even if – like the barometer earlier in the day – they seemed at odds with reality. But at least some sort of detail *was* evident. Which is more than could be said for the finer points of topography necessary to navigate *after* Nafford where the river transforms completely. Not that you'd have noticed any change from the map, though. This still showed the route as a gentle blue line elegantly curving across the page.

But the real thing wasn't like this at all. The wide, graceful sweeps that had characterised the river to this point had gone, replaced at first by a series of arching swans' necks, and afterwards by a progression of meanderings similar to the summit of the Oxford Canal. Except that instead of the Oxford's radio mast to confound me, I now had the pinnacle of Bredon Hill looming above me on the horizon. At first it seemed to be to my right, and then to my left, and finally behind me, so that I finished up so utterly confused that for the second time that day I ran up a reed bank from which it took me half an hour to extricate myself.

The irrational wanderings of any waterway can leave you disoriented but it's much worse on a river. For a start the bank of one river is much like the bank of any other, which is to say – since you can't see over any of them – that they consist of just the edge of fields and incessant lines of willow trees. Take my word for it, even for an anorak like me there is a limit to the enthusiasm you can muster for a willow tree. There aren't many bridges on rivers either, and so unlike canals where you're lucky to go more than ten minutes without passing under one, there's nothing on a river against which you can really gauge your progress. Travelling along one becomes hypnotising, particularly when you're on your own as I was, and especially when the river starts to straighten out as the Avon finally does as it moves towards the Severn.

I completely lost track of where I was, and was constantly arriving at places hours before I thought I'd reached them, or sometimes – when impatience set in – hours after I thought I should have passed them.

I vaguely recall going under Eckington Bridge, a fiery-red sandstone structure etched with the ancient patterns of two hundred winters or more. Then there were one or two railway bridges which I can just about remember, and then the M5 motorway, until finally – eventually – there were no bridges at all any more, and I seemed to be drifting in the insensate lacuna between earth and sky where nothing but the gentle feathering of the water from my bow provided any connection with the moment.

The river got wider, and wider yet. It got straighter and flatter and windier until I could been have been cruising the Fens, or maybe the level wastes of the Low Countries where the land has been clawed from the sea. In truth my mind was so abstracted from the present I could have been anywhere or nowhere, until the appearance of a flotilla of sailboats and a line of plastic coastal cruisers three-storeys high signalled that at last I had arrived somewhere.

It was Tewkesbury.

Nineteen

IT WAS TOM ROLT'S IDEA.

In the 1930s, long before he'd written *Narrow Boat* and years before he was involved in getting the Inland Waterways Association off the ground, he'd gone through a tough period in which he'd been kicking his heels, picking up work here and there as best he could after finishing his apprenticeship. These were the Depression years, and any sort of job was hard to come by. Eventually he'd borrowed money from his father and gone into partnership with a friend running a garage in the small village of Hartley Wintney in Hampshire. This was a natural move for him since he'd always been interested in cars – old cars especially – and he'd had a succession of them himself, including a rare example of a 12/50 Alvis two-seater which he'd bought in the early 1920s and which he was to own for most of his life.

Next door to the garage was a pub called The Phoenix, and fortuitously its landlord was another motor enthusiast; so it wasn't long before the two of them cooked up the idea of a club for classic sports cars – an idea from which they both benefited, since the pub became its unofficial headquarters, and the garage picked up trade from members. The Vintage Sports Car Club still exists today; and though Rolt's old garage has become a self-service petrol station indistinguishable from so many thousands of others across the country, The Phoenix remains relatively unchanged, and car buffs still meet there with their vehicles on the first Thursday of every month for a chat and a pint as they've done now for decades.

The club's grown a bit over the years, though: today it's got more than 7,000 members worldwide and it employs a full-time staff of seven, most of them involved in organising a calendar of thirty or so events which the club holds every year. One of the biggest of these is an annual hill climb in Prescott in Gloucestershire which Rolt created. It's a sort of an uphill time trial which has been running since 1938 and which today attracts many thousands of spectators over the August weekend on which it's held. It's a must-see for anyone who's a sports car enthusiast; in fact, nowadays it attracts so many aficionados from across the world that the races have become a bit of a side show to the car park, which is better than many motor museums.

For a long time the club used to organise rallies for its members, awarding prizes not just for place positions, but under different exhibition categories such as the best turned-out vehicle, or the best maintained engine. In 1949 Tom Rolt suggested a similar idea to Robert Aickman as an event for the IWA.

Aickman must have jumped at the proposal. The concept was just up his street: flamboyant enough to be exciting, yet fundamentally sound enough to be practical. He could see immediately that an assembly of boats at some central location could be more than just a focus for members – it could also be a method of raising the public profile of the waterways in a unique way. Aickman was twenty years ahead of his time in recognising the value of publicity to a campaigning organisation, and he would have known instinctively that if you could get boats travelling to a single point from all over the country, then it would be possible to tie individual issues of local closures into a national debate about the future of the whole waterways network. With this end in mind, the plan for a rally was an inspiration and a perfect demonstration of how, when they worked together amicably, Rolt and Aickman were world-beaters.

Unfortunately, at other times, the two of them could tear themselves to pieces. Notionally they might be working towards the same end, but their perspectives could be totally different; and even when they were thinking along the same lines they could actually be going up the track in opposite directions. Rolt was a diffident man, serious-minded and determined, and he'd been drawn to the canals by the opportunities they offered to escape from the contemporary world. Essentially he was a very private person; it just wasn't in his nature to be gregarious, and on those rare occasions where Aickman wanted to use him for campaigning or wanted to push *Cressy* into the limelight for publicity purposes, Rolt only agreed to cooperate reluctantly after having his arm twisted.

Tom Rolt would have seen the rally as he had those early get-togethers of the Vintage Sports Car Club at Prescott; simply as an opportunity for a few like-minded people to socialise. As a way of demonstrating how people cared about the things they were interested in. Just a bit of fun really.

For Robert Aickman, though, it was an entirely different proposition: it offered a platform on which he could show off his organisational abilities and indulge his wider artistic and cultural obsessions – a stage on which he knew he could engineer events to finish up the leading actor. And so he immediately hijacked the idea. The rally now became not just a boat festival, but a Festival of Boats and Arts, growing in Aickman's grandiose imagination until the little town of Market Harborough in Leicestershire, which had been chosen as the venue for the event, became in his mind a sort of test bed for the Festival of Britain planned for London's South Bank the following year. OK, so Aickman wasn't exactly strong on self-awareness, and it's easy enough to laugh at his affectations. But there are a lot of people like him around – strong personalities who are so caught up in their own lives that they lose touch with reality and distort events in the process of persuading the rest of us of their vision.

So now, there would be a waterways exhibition associated with the rally. And there would be an art show too, with a display of paintings by Peter Scott, and a film festival, and – the *pièce de résistance* – a play produced specially for the occasion. There would be fireworks. There would be a fun fair. And boat trips. You wonder who this was all for? Members of the IWA? The public who Aickman was confident would come flocking to the event? Actually, you don't need to wonder – it was all for Robert Aickman.

And, of course, being the man he was, he didn't harbour the least doubt that what he was doing was the right thing. Indeed, he was always ferociously proud of the inspiration that he'd brought to bear on the whole venture, and many years afterwards he boasted with some justification that one of the reasons it developed in the way it did was just because he personally 'wanted to run a Festival'.

Pompous or what?

The relationship between Aickman and Rolt had never been the same since Jane Howard's arrival on the scene, but their clash over Market Harborough was to represent a new nadir between them. At the beginning, at least, Tom Rolt attempted to keep a level head about matters. He was far from convinced that Aickman's plans for a strong arts element in the festival was going to achieve much for the waterways, but he suggested reasonably enough that if they *had* to have a play as part of the programme, then maybe they ought to get some professional outfit like the Bristol Young Vic to produce it. The suggestion only had the effect of sending Aickman scurrying away to cost the idea and, on discovering unsurprisingly that it was far too expensive, suggesting that – well, who needs the Young Vic? – he'd do it himself.

It was the same when Rolt pointed out the obvious problem that the Market Harborough assembly rooms where the plays were going to be performed lacked a proscenium arch and wasn't really a suitable venue. Not a problem, said Aickman. There were two association members who would build a stage…

At last the whole thing became too much for Rolt: it wasn't just that working with someone so intractable was getting him down, but that the commitments of his waterways interests were having a profound effect on the rest of his life. Tom Rolt was a professional writer and the IWA was taking up more and more of his energy – energy that he could have used more profitably on his own projects. But it was more than this: it was the growing feeling he had that he wasn't his own man any more, that his time was being taken up by a series of honorary positions which he somehow kept accumulating and which were curtailing the freedom he'd worked so hard to achieve.

It was bad enough that Aickman had drafted him onto the festival organising committee without consulting him, but the final straw was an officious letter summoning him at short notice from where he was moored on *Cressy* in Northamptonshire to a planning meeting on the other side of the country in Newbury, Berkshire. At first he refused to go: it was his birthday and he'd arranged to take his mother to the theatre at Stratford. But Aickman, as was his way, insisted; and eventually Rolt succumbed to the pressure. It was the last time he ever would, though, and of all the rivers he negotiated in his life, crossing this Rubicon was probably the most significant.

Of course no one would deny that there weren't weighty matters of IWA policy dividing the two men. Should the organisation agitate for the restoration of all waterways or just a selected few? Should it prioritise the future of commercial traffic, or should its first concern be the fabric of the waterways themselves? Should it campaign from within the establishment, or confront the waterways authorities from the outside?

But with people who are personally sympathetic, and who basically respect the integrity of each other's position, weighty issues of this tenor can usually be resolved before they become major disagreements. Beliefs which are honestly held can be argued and negotiated; but it's the trivial things that always prove the sticking point; the host of small and apparently insignificant details that actually aren't small and insignificant at all but which betray what people really think about each other.

Like that mysterious 9/4d (48p) that Rolt owed or didn't owe Aickman, but which – incredibly – Aickman was still banging on about in his autobiography forty years later. Like the argument that also gets mentioned in the book which seems to have come about after Aickman, acting as Rolt's agent, sold a collection of ghost stories to the publishers Constables. Nothing more is mentioned about it, though – cause or outcome – and this leads me to suspect in a very uncharitable way that given Aickman's self-serving view of the world, it was somehow tied up with his own as yet unfulfilled ambition to write himself. Perhaps with the benefit of hindsight he realised this too and censored himself before his life story went into print, so saving himself the condemnation of posterity.

It obviously couldn't go on like this. As Tom Rolt wrote, 'The brutal truth was now becoming only too clear, [the IWA] was becoming a band-wagon, as good causes, often started with the best of intentions, are apt to do... We, who had originally sought refuge on the canals to escape from all we disliked in the modern world, deeply resented what we felt to be our exploitation for such purposes by others.' So in January of 1950 – perhaps as a New Year's resolution? – Rolt invited Aickman to visit him on *Cressy*. Aickman stayed the night and there, frozen in by ice so thick you could walk on it, Rolt told him he was going to resign as IWA secretary.

And at this stage it would have been the best thing for everyone if he'd been allowed to go cleanly, just walking away from the organisation completely, and totally severing his ties. But this wasn't Aickman's way. For Robert Aickman, Rolt quitting the way he did represented a personal betrayal, and though he didn't really want anyone of such disloyalty to be around him, he didn't want them to move outside of his influence either.

This left him in a bit of a *Catch-22* situation.

It meant that things would get a good deal messier yet between them.

River towns are at their most inert from the water, and coming into a new one on a boat – even a large city – it always seems as if they're locked into a different age. The exception to this is

Tewkesbury. As soon as you catch sight of Tewkesbury from the Avon, you just know that this isn't a place that *seems* of a different century, this is a place that *is* of a different century.

And what you see from the river is what you get, so that if you walk up the main street, even on a Saturday afternoon when it's at its busiest, you can squint your eyes and almost believe you're trapped in some time warp. Perhaps the place livens up in leap years. Or maybe when there's an eclipse of the sun. On the other hand, like so many English towns, maybe its attraction is that it never rises above the soporific. Wandering about, it seemed to me most people in the place were of pensionable age, and those that weren't were visitors like me.

As for Tewkesbury's younger generation... well, just outside the town I'd seen a small cruiser moored on the river with the improbable name of – wait for it! – *Flashes from the Archives of Oblivion*. Not, as boat names go, one that exactly trips off the tongue. But it gives you a pretty good clue to what the Tewkesbury under-25s get up to in their spare time. And a pretty good idea of the quality of the stuff they use to do it too.

Of course, all this could be prejudice, and maybe *Flashes* etc. is owned by some middle-aged Church of England cleric with a soft spot for hippy rock music and a fascination with transcendentalism. After all, people are more complex than we give them credit for, and they name their boats for a thousand different reasons. Much of the time, of course, what they choose just reflects their idealised view of the waterways and the role they expect their boat to play in their life; so that I've lost count of the number of *Narrow Escape*s and *Slow Motion*s that I've seen over the years. Sometimes names are more twee like *Not for Sail* or – quite clever this for a small version of a narrowboat – *Along Shortly*. Other times people just use them to make a joke, though like most jokes they pale a bit with familiarity. Like the Grand Union boat *Union Bargee*. Or *Nervous Wreck*. Or the second boat owned by a family called the Nunns, christened predictably but amusingly enough, *Second to Nunn*. One boat cruising around the system has the beautiful Italian-sounding name *Tiami*, which you think must translate as some passionate declaration of love except that it's got more to do with the practicalities of marine finance since it's an acronym for 'This is a Major Investment'.

This happens even at higher levels too, and I'm told that one of the yachts in the Sydney–Hobart boat race the other year was called *The Office*, which I suppose provided a ready-made excuse for those embarrassing telephone calls to which mobile phone technology has made us all susceptible. Far and away my favourite, though, is on a vessel I've never actually seen myself but which I've been told about so often that I'm beginning to wonder if maybe its existence is apocryphal.

One way or another, *Sir Osis of the River* gets my vote as the ultimate in boat names, making reference as it does to a pastime which for so many people is the essential attraction of contemporary cruising.

Though quiet, Tewkesbury's actually rather a pleasant place in the summer, even a bad summer, for there's a bank-holiday atmosphere about it which in part emanates from the colourful pennants the size of tablecloths which hang from every available window around the centre and give it a festive air. It makes the town feel like Siena before the horse race that's held annually around the main piazza. In the *Palio* as it's called, the flags are those of the various neighbourhoods which compete against each other for prizes; in Tewkesbury, more darkly, they represent the standards of the main baronial factions who fought in 1471 at the Battle of Tewkesbury, virtually the last Yorkist victory of the Wars of the Roses, and the town's main claim to historical fame.

Not that everyone in Tewkesbury values its past. Only a few years ago the local council gave the go-ahead for a development on the actual battlefield site. It was to have been one of those awful postmodern executive housing estates you see littered all over the country; but mercifully, the decision was later overruled by Whitehall after an almighty row during which one councillor admitted he couldn't understand why there was all this fuss about an event which he described as just 'a couple of blokes having a slap'.

I wandered around the town in the weak afternoon sunshine. It was a place I really didn't know much about except that the novelist Barbara Cartland had once lived here, and that it was here the comedian Eric Morecambe had literally died on stage, keeling over one night with a heart attack. Eventually I finished up outside the John Moore Countryside Museum where in the front window was a charming display of miniature models of Romany vardos – or caravans – which no doubt in some mythical time long since past used to travel the highways and byways of Merrie England. They were skilfully fashioned by a local craftsman; and were brightly painted, lovingly decorated and meticulously worked. One, I remember, had a series of tiny copper cooking pots hanging from a rear door. On another there was a diminutive cage filled with ferrets done in such detail you could see the strands of their fur.

John Moore was apparently a local writer on rural affairs, and I reckon he must have been a fun sort of a guy since the staff of his museum have obviously inherited his sense of humour. Well, I take it that they have, since I can't believe that the timing of this exhibition was anything other than a droll joke, given the national obsession that summer with asylum seekers – many of them Romanies – to which I've already had cause to refer. Indeed, earlier that very week there'd been an incident in some one-horse town on the South Coast where a couple of families from Slovakia who'd got fed up with persecution at home had made a break for the bright lights of Albion. Regrettably they'd landed up in a derelict flat on a run-down estate where the only bright light as far as I could see was the one remaining street lamp that hadn't yet been vandalised.

Sad really, because in the past in this country anyone suffering bad luck on this scale could have at least counted on our sympathy, if only because more than any other nation we have a naturally sardonic sense of humour and know what a bastard life and fate can sometimes be. Now it became the signal for a riot in which the locals complained of how foreigners were stealing their homes from them and how – barring the erection of a 20-foot-high barbed-wire fence around the entire coastline – the country was about to be overrun by swarthy hordes who would completely swamp their culture, being entirely untutored in Middle English and totally incapable of singing a madrigal.

I stood for a long while completely entranced by the John Moore vardos, but it wasn't just me who was attracted by them; and before long a small but animated crowd gathered on the pavement, pressing their noses to the museum window with fascination. Which you might think a little contradictory under the circumstances until you remember two things about the English: the first that as a race we mistrust anyone who's different to us – or at least until they're dead and have receded far enough into the past that they no longer represent a threat, and so can be safely sentimentalised.

So I'd bet serious money that no one standing on the street with me that day in Tewkesbury made the slightest connection in their mind between the models of the Romany caravans they were looking at and the Romanies currently finding themselves hassled from their homeland in Slovakia. Any more, for instance, than they'd make a connection between contemporary Germans and our own royal family descended from the Hanovarians. Contemporary Germans, like contemporary Romanies, are far too threatening. They are hell-bent on world domination and want to steal the pound from our pockets. Royal Germans on the other hand – Germans from the past – are like traditional Gypsy travellers: they have been historically appropriated as our own and made safe, like torture implements of a bygone age which we might hang as decoration from the walls of our homes.

The second thing you need to remember about us English is that we just love anything tiny. There's something about miniatures that melts our hearts.

How else can we explain the plethora of advertisements in the colour supplements for minuscule teapots, or Lilliputian toby jugs or teensy-weensy reproductions of country cottages? It's extraordinary! There are so many factories churning out this stuff that it's become a major industry in some parts of the country. I was in Bath only recently and there is a shop totally dedicated to it, filled with row upon row of figurines, none bigger than your thumbnail: fairies, soldiers, historical characters. And tiny little gardens too, with tiny sets of garden furniture and tiny garden plants. And if all this weren't enough – something I hadn't seen before – tiny kitchens with plate after plate of tiny miniaturised food: joints of ham, bacon and egg breakfasts, and platters of poached salmon.

So can someone please tell me what all this is about since I'm damned if I know? I have a funny feeling that miniaturising like this is the only way we English can come to terms with the terrifying realities of a world the same size as we are. Indeed, I have a sneaking suspicion that if Hitler had invaded in 1940 he might well have prepared us for it beforehand by flooding the country with diminutive platoons of model SS Panzer divisions and dwarf wind-up gramophones playing *pianissimo* versions of 'Deutschland, Deutschland Über Alles'.

I left the crowd outside the museum stewing in its own paradoxes and walked round the corner to Tewkesbury Abbey, a great barn of a building which originally dates from the twelfth century. It has a cavernous nave with a vaulted ceiling supported by a couple of rows of huge Norman pillars so that just being in the place seems to generate an almost palpable sense of the past. All the same, the abbey seemed to me a lot more in tune with the Zeitgeist of the new millennium than a lot of other places I could mention which – like the Countryside Museum – persist in presenting history as some sort of picturesque soap opera, totally without contemporary context.

There was a display of the work the Abbey was doing combating poverty in Africa through Christian Aid projects, for instance – impressive work by anyone's standards. And there was a notice board on which people had posted anonymous requests for prayer which made a deep impression on me. One was from a woman who was in depression after having lost her husband not long after their golden wedding anniversary; another was from a young couple whose 12-week-old baby had suddenly died. There was a barely legible appeal from an eight-year-old who was being bullied at school; and another from a man who admitted to writing the note in tears, desperately frustrated at his recalcitrant teenage daughter who he loved deeply, but with whom he was totally unable to communicate any more.

Take it from me, anyone reading appeals of this sort for long begins to count their blessings.

But there were other things about Tewkesbury Abbey which made me realise that recognising the importance of the past didn't necessarily mean you had to be locked out of the present. There was, for instance, a wonderful sculpture of an owl representing wisdom, fashioned out of domestic household items salvaged from a junkyard. It brought a genuine smile to my face. And brought me up short as well when the penny dropped and it eventually struck me what the artist was saying about today's world. There was a splendid contemporary altar too in one of the chapels, made out of what I took to be rosewood, and carved in an extraordinary style of lettering. Tewkesbury's regard for the craftsmanship of our modern age even extends to a functional but rather beautifully made set of storage cupboards tucked away on a back wall in the church where if they'd wanted they could have got away with stacking a pile of crates.

Except that doing that wouldn't have reflected the tenor of what this place was trying to do, and how much people cared about it.

And people *do* care about places like this in contemporary England. Twenty years ago there was a bitter row in Tewkesbury about where to move the abbey organ – a dispute which eventually had to go to the church courts for resolution. And if you think that's archaic and twee and not the sort of thing that could ever happen today, let me tell you that that is precisely what *was* happening as I passed through Pershore where an equally bitter row had been rumbling on for more than two years about the replacement of some pews removed from the church during building work. That too had to go to the church courts for resolution. In fact, I don't think it was resolved, even after that. Actually, I doubt it ever will be resolved.

For that's another thing about us English, you see: our concern for the detail of our lives can lead us, as it led Rolt and Aickman, to get worked up about the smallest things.

And God knows, we can bring a powerful stubbornness to bear on them once our blood's up.

Twenty

A SET OF INSTRUCTIONS from the authorities for navigating the Severn Estuary had arrived. They read like rules for rounding Cape Horn, filled with all sorts of dire warnings about the dangers that we faced doing the trip. Everything on a narrowboat, it seemed, represented a potential hazard; the whole shebang so badly designed there was nothing that wasn't a risk. The main problem seemed to be that our hull was the wrong shape; it was flat-bottomed and too low in the water. Among other things, this meant the drainage holes on the deck which were designed to let water *out* on calm canals were too susceptible to letting it *in* on what was effectively a sea journey. Mind you, this was just the start of it – according to the authorities everything from our ventilators to our air intakes were too close to the water for a trip like this.

Even our diesel tank was inadequate. Our diesel tank! I doubt I'd ever thought about the diesel tank on *Justice* once in the ten years we'd had her, except to notice when the diesel in it was running low. But no, apparently our tank, like the tanks of other narrowboats, was prone to fill with sludge, which could get churned about in the swell and sucked into the engine – which would then immediately break down, leaving us drifting powerless as the massive ebbing tides flushed us into the Bristol Channel and certain death...

Well, something like that.

So we were advised to 'purge' the tank. I had visions of strapping it to a chair under a bright light and interrogating it for questionable political beliefs. Or perhaps feeding it a plateful of rhubarb and a cup of stewed senna pods. But then I realised they meant purge as in the sense of 'clean', or 'remove impurities'. But that wasn't much help. What was I supposed to do? Open it up with a can-opener and give it a wipe down with Flash?

We were instructed to block up the drainage holes too. And it was recommended we sheet over the deck. We were cautioned to do everything except buy ourselves a new boat better equipped to do the trip – which was clearly what the authorities would have preferred us to do, since every line of their advice carried the unstated subtext that we were lunatics to even think about doing this journey in a boat like ours which was fitted for nothing more sophisticated than crawling along country ditches.

Mind you, I confess this was a view with which I was beginning to find myself increasingly in sympathy. After all, I'd never really been *that* keen on doing the passage. It had really been my brother's idea – well, his idea and Em's enthusiasm. I felt that I'd had my arm twisted into biting off more than I could chew, if you see what I'm getting at. What brought the enormity of it home to me was discovering that once on the estuary my 'movements' (the official word) were not now governed by the simple expedient of adjusting the tiller from one side to the other, but instead by the grandiose-sounding *International Regulations for Preventing Collisions at Sea*, a copy of which I was instructed must be an essential part of my equipment. This informed me that 'a vessel of less than 20 meters' (i.e. me) should not impede the passage of 'a vessel which can only navigate within a narrow channel or fairway'. Since, in effect, the whole of the Severn Estuary comes under that definition, the message to a minnow of my sort was unmistakable: I was bottom of the food chain. Either I kept out of the way of the big stuff or I risked getting reduced to industrial scrap.

This was not reassuring.

Neither was the other equipment I was advised to carry with me, like life-buoys with smoke and light signals attached, and distress flares, two red and two orange – the colours no doubt carefully chosen so that as I was drowning I could coordinate to match my outfit. Other essential kit I was instructed to take with me included tide timetables and Admiralty charts, both of which I dutifully obtained, only to discover that they were both so incomprehensible, a book of Arabic grammar would have been more use getting me to Bristol. Tide tables? They reminded me of those books of school logarithms we used before calculators were invented. And it was the same with the charts. They looked a lot like Ordnance Survey maps except that anything familiar that might have made them intelligible seemed to have been purposely omitted.

I was terrified about ringing the pilots to arrange the trip. I imagined them breaking down in hysterical laughter just listening to me. 'Take you where? In *that* heap of junk? With *your* level of expertise? I think I'd rather not if it's all the same to you...'

In the event I needn't have worried. I spoke to a pilot who sounded as excited about the job as he might have done getting on a 36 bus to Peckham.

'I'll tape up all the doors and cover the deck with polythene,' I attempted to reassure him the first opportunity I got.

'All right – fine – if you want to...'

'And I was planning on maybe blocking up the drainage holes – cutting out wedges of wood and jamming them in...'

'OK. If it makes you feel happier,' he said. 'When do you want to go anyhow? Next Wednesday evening OK? On the second tide?'

All this was a bit sudden. And a bit too real as well. Up until now this crazy idea of navigating the estuary had been a bit of a faraway fantasy. Now here was a pilot who seemed totally unconcerned about the fact that he was committing himself and me to a boat that would almost certainly sink on us. One who was seriously asking me if I wanted to 'go' next Wednesday on the second tide. Go? Where? To hell? And on the second tide? Until he'd mentioned it, I hadn't even been aware there was a first tide.

'Next Wednesday?' I repeated mechanically, my body feeling

somewhat numb at the prospect. 'Next Wednesday,' I mumbled again.

And before I knew where I was, it was all sorted.

At least now there was a purpose to my travels. Before, I hadn't even had a destination. Now I'd got a destination *and* a deadline. It was therefore with a certain urgency that I cast off from Tewkesbury the following morning, passing through the lock and the small cutting that takes you from the Avon onto the River Severn for the 30-mile journey down to Sharpness and the sea.

Suddenly I was in a totally different environment, for if a canal differs in character from a river, then so too does a big river differ from a small one. The lower reaches of the Avon had been inhospitable enough – wider than I was used to, and windier, and the water much choppier; but now as I began accelerating towards the sea on the Severn at what seemed an alarming speed, I seriously began to doubt if this pleasure-cruising lark was everything it was cracked up to be. For a start, the river banks seemed not so much distant as attached to an entirely different waterway to the one on which I was travelling. Certainly too far away for me to swim to if ever – God forbid! – the need arose. Additionally, what little of the water's edge I could make out in any detail as it rushed by seemed entirely unlike anything I'd become familiar with on the Avon, being in the main composed of ugly hawthorn bushes not made any more attractive by the host of plastic supermarket bags that were left littering their branches as a result of flooding in the past.

Of more immediate concern was that I suddenly found myself in the eye of the second storm I'd faced inside a week. It blew up without any warning from nowhere, and it seemed to single me out for attention – or maybe it just seemed that way since as far as I could make out, I was the only boat foolish enough to be on the water at that time. One way or another, it came at me from two sides, hitting me with the force of a gale on both my bow and stern, but in separate directions, so that the boat began to roll about alarmingly. This had such peculiar ramifications on my stomach that it was all I could do to keep down breakfast.

The squall brought rain with it too, and this was blowing almost horizontally, pushing up some pretty impressive waves for a stretch of river which was, for all its tumult, nevertheless technically described as 'still' water. Soon it became a struggle just to keep *Justice* on course, for now she began to pitch as well, her bow towering up out of the water before plunging down again in a welter of crashing spray. All this was accompanied by some rather troubling sounds from below deck, which from where I was standing – clinging on to the tiller for dear life – sounded remarkably like plates and glasses smashing to the floor.

At this stage the dangers of the estuary were the last thing on my mind, for in truth I'd begun to wonder whether I was ever going to get that far. If it had been possible I'd have stopped as soon as I could and waited for conditions to improve, but what is true of the Avon is even more the case on the Severn: there simply aren't the places to moor; and those few which were available I was passing at such a rate of knots that no sooner had I clocked them than they had flashed by, a quarter of a mile behind me and receding with every moment that passed.

It was obvious that the level of the river was rising – and rising at a spectacular rate; and although I didn't know it at the time, this was to be the pattern for the rest of the year. So much rain had fallen onto already sodden countryside that it simply couldn't absorb any more. The fields were entirely waterlogged and as quickly as it was falling, the rain was running off the surface of the land into streams and brooks – and finally into rivers like this which had already got to the stage where they couldn't take much more. Before the autumn not just the Severn, but the Trent, the Soar, the Ouse and a host of other rivers across the country would flood, causing immense damage and widespread distress to many thousands of people.

Near Apperley, where the B4123 crosses Haw Bridge, there

are a couple of pubs, and I was confident I'd be able to manoeuvre myself in there somehow. Except that by the time I'd navigated the single arch of the bridge through which you are advised to pass, I'd been flushed so far downstream I seriously doubted I'd have enough engine power to make it back against the flow. Yet I knew that sooner or later this was exactly what I was going to have to do, for you can't take a boat directly into a mooring when there's this much water running behind you. You wouldn't have any control and would be dashed against the bank by the momentum. So you have to go past the spot you're aiming for and turn against the current so that you can come in with at least a vestige of confidence.

Eventually I decided that come what may I had to risk it, regardless of the consequences; and a mile or so further on, at the small hamlet of Ashleworth where I knew there was a landing stage, I turned against the full force of flow and revved up the engine as high as it would go.

Believe me, my heart was in my mouth.

Justice lurched uncharacteristically as the water hit her broadside, but as I wrenched the tiller around she straightened up against the current – and there was a long listless moment where she did no more than hold her own against the spate. It was as if she was making up her mind whether she was capable of moving; and then deciding whether she could be bothered to… Eventually, after what seemed an eternity, she began to edge forward with a reluctant sluggishness, and with some relief I found I could just about guide her to safety.

Once I'd tied up – which wasn't exactly easy since the jetty was awash with water – I glanced at my watch. I'd left Tewkesbury at about ten o'clock and travelled about eight miles, a journey I'd estimate under normal conditions might take me a couple of hours, perhaps a bit less.

I'd actually done it in half that time.

Ashleworth is a little gem of a place, like so many tucked away in the backwoods of rural England close to the waterways. Tom Rolt wrote about some of them in *Narrow Boat*, and though the march of progress has obliterated a few of the ones he identified which even then were remnants of another age, most still survive, surprisingly unspoiled; and many others which didn't figure in the book – like Ashleworth – remain all but undiscovered even today, known only to local people or visitors from the river. The village is actually larger than it first seems, but that part of it close to the water is just a hamlet separated from the rest and really hardly a part of it, for The Boat pub on whose jetty I'd landed lies at the end of a lane where there are only about three or four other buildings.

One of them is a small fifteenth-century manor house standing adjacent to an unpretentious but rather exquisite parish church. Next to this is a farm and a massive barn which is actually the most interesting structure in the place, for in the past it was used to store the produce from local farms paid over to the ecclesiastical authorities as tithes. It's still used for storage today, though it's now owned by the National Trust, which presumably allows it to be occasionally used as a village hall too, since on the day I visited it was clear that it had only recently been the venue for a local theatrical revue. Scripts of sketches lay scattered over the floor, and on bales of hay that had lately served as the stage were draped various costumes and props. There was still a sweet smell of stage make-up in the air.

It was bizarre finding the place in this state, for on such a stormy day with the rain hammering down relentlessly, this part of Ashleworth seemed totally uninhabited, the roads deserted, the manor house quiet and desolate. Despite the fact that it was lunchtime, even the pub was empty too – though I'd have expected it to be packed to the rafters with trade from Gloucester, which is only a short journey away by car. This all added to my strange sense that the village had somehow been abandoned, as if at the outbreak of a plague or the onslaught of some advancing army. The detritus littering the barn was eerie; as if people had been in the middle of clearing up but then had been abruptly interrupted in their work and had hurried away, leaving behind them a silent presence and the peculiar aura I could sense. It spoke not just of contemporary times, but of worlds inhabited by countless generations before who had worked the land in these parts and used the barn for their own different purposes.

There were marks in the stonework that compounded this overwhelming impression I had of having just stepped into another age. They were similar to ones I'd seen in Tewkesbury Abbey only recently: fastidiously fashioned initials in a scholarly classic style, every last serif etched with meticulous care. It was graffiti, but not graffiti as we know it today, produced instantly from a spray can by kids who have been made to feel so alienated from the culture in which they live that they don't feel they have a place in it any more, and who live in a world where change is fêted for its own sake so they don't expect permanence from anything. These carvings were produced by people who may have been constrained by principles we would frown on today to know their place in society, but who were at least secure in the knowledge that they actually *had* a place; so that what they were looking for wasn't to advertise themselves to their own age but to trumpet themselves to posterity. Which I suppose, in their own way, was what they finally succeeded in doing.

And that's not bad for a bunch of vandals, eh?

I wandered into the church which was having work done to it, though activity here – like in the barn – seemed to have been halted abruptly as well. There were dust sheets hanging from scaffolding, and bricks and bags of cement stacked next to piles of hymnals, and copies of the parish magazine, the *West of Severn News*. I picked one up and took it back to the boat, and later in the day I looked at it again with no real intention of doing more than idly flicking through it. Except that I began to find it totally compulsive, and eventually – sad case that I am – I finished up scrutinising it from cover to cover, even poring over the advertisements at the end.

It made me breathless, filled as it was with so many references to charity walks and jumble sales and bingo evenings and home furnishing classes and the other thousand and one activities that I know from my own experience engage a rural community. What I found extraordinary about it, though, was not how different to the urban world was the one it described, but how curiously alike they both were. Metaphorically I could have squinted my eyes and been back on the London local paper where I first started work as a journalist years ago.

There was a report of the parish council meeting which I found particularly engaging since except for the scale of it all, it might have been an account of the proceedings of any London borough with almost exactly the same concerns expressed over planning proposals, road safety and dog shit. Dog shit! Is there a community tucked away anywhere on this island of ours that isn't obsessed to some degree with dog shit? Dog shit surely must have replaced royalty now as our favourite national preoccupation.

Crime and vandalism too were problems for Ashleworth, and there were reports of seven cases of theft and attempted theft in the district in the previous month – a period that had seen the church targeted by vandals twice in a fortnight.

Now, I'm no great advocate of consensual politics; in fact, one of the things that most frustrates me about us English is our reluctance to accept and argue honestly held differences between us on things like politics, religion and the defensive vulnerability of Manchester United down the right flank. OK, so maybe this emanates from our somewhat intemperate past when it was generally thought that the way to a greater understanding of the complex issues dividing you from your fellow man was to rip out his guts before decapitating him.

It made us think twice about opening our mouths too much – understandable under the circumstances, it's only fair to say.

Even so, I can't for the life of me see why we've thought it necessary recently to declare a sort of civil war between town and country. It's as if now we don't get so steamed up about our traditional class divisions, we feel the need to establish a whole set of new ones predicated on how comfortable we feel around animals. If we are very comfortable around them – relaxed enough to start sticking our arms up their backsides if they're ill – than we qualify as fully fledged country folk whose reward is to be able to dress up like a pillar box in order to kill foxes. On the other hand, if we don't feel at all comfortable, and certainly not enough to consider putting dead ones in our mouths and swallowing them, then this marks us out as die-hard townies who shall be forever stigmatised by the mark of the green welly whenever we set foot outside the suburbs.

It occurred to me that people who live in places like Ashleworth and who are rooted in the land must have a particular perspective on these things, so one evening long after my trip had ended I rang up the editor of the *West of Severn News* to get her take on all this. It was not, I have to confess, the most sensitive time for someone in London to ring someone in the shires seeking guidance about rural matters, seeing as how half the countryside had been under water most of the winter following floods, and the other half had been under siege conditions following an outbreak of foot-and-mouth disease in the spring. So why had I called? In truth, it was really just prying metropolitan inquisitiveness. And she'd have been perfectly within her rights to tell me where to stuff it.

In the event her reaction couldn't have been politer, though. She'd only just finished making dinner, which was bubbling away on the stove, with the TV purring reassuringly in the background; and we had a delightful chat about life in Gloucestershire. It was clear, though, that the rural-urban divide wasn't exactly causing her to lose a lot of sleep. Mind you, why should it? It turned out by an odd coincidence that she'd spent part of her life in suburban Bexleyheath just a few miles from where I live, and so her view of city people was at least based on experience, not prejudice. At least she didn't think city people were all devils incarnate, hell-bent on destroying the fabric of rural life by rape, pillage and leaving farm gates open all over the place.

'But I think in reverse that's how some people in towns see *us*,' she said. 'As sort of clichés, really – yokels with straw in our mouths living the life of Riley on taxpayers' subsidies. But things have changed, you know; they've changed for us all. And really, this country is just too small for us to be constantly squabbling with each other all the time.'

Things have certainly changed around Ashleworth, or at least they have around The Boat where up until a few years back when the landing stage was built you couldn't moor with anything like the ease you can today. It was too shallow, you see. In the past it was a matter of finding a place with enough depth for you to be able to nudge your bow into the bank and moor to a tree; or if you couldn't do that, then getting in as far as you could and dropping anchor and paddling the rest of the way. This was OK in the blazing heat of an August afternoon when the water was flowing clear and you'd be walking on clean and solid shingle. It lost its attraction at other times when the rain was running down your neck and when the river bed seemed to have turned into a subaqueous quicksand determined to suck you under. At times like this when you were cruising it was a temptation not to go on or turn back the way you'd come, where there were other pubs with less character but more easily accessible beer.

So you can't blame the pub for installing a landing stage. All the same, somehow I just can't help but see it as yet another example of the way the waterways are being changed into a linear suburb where everything is homogenised to the lowest common denominator, and where local idiosyncrasies get ironed out and individuality eradicated.

But isn't this just the situation with the whole country too? And isn't this part of the reason that we're all at each other's throats so much, since we're all holding everyone else responsible for the loss of what is actually being eroded by things we're all to blame for?

I'm as bad myself – worse in a way – for didn't I bang on evangelically about the waterways when everyone thought I was mad spending every spare moment God sent crawling through derelict bits of cities along rat-infested ditches? And didn't I get incensed, banging on the table and telling them that no, canals weren't like that at all, that mostly they were like picturesque lanes winding through the fields and anyhow the bits in towns could be a wonderful facility too if only people would be radical and wake up to their potential and spend some money on them?

Until one day they did, and things began to change. Not gradually, with the gentle passage of the seasons; but suddenly, time flying like an arrow, straight and abruptly, so that no sooner had I gone off to bed one night than I'd woken the following morning to a new world in which everything I wanted to happen had come about in the way I had desired it.

So tell me, why did I feel the need to keep belly-aching? Why do I still feel that need now?

I drank too much that night in The Boat; got into conversation with an old guy who I chatted to most of the evening until it dawned on me that despite my first impressions, he was actually younger than me. A shock like that was what I needed to snap out of whatever mood it was that Ashleworth had put me in.

After all, I was going to Bristol. I'd got an estuary to deal with.

Twenty-One

I SET THE ALARM to wake early the next day with the intention of getting through Gloucester as quickly as I could. I know the place well, and despite its cathedral and its impressive complex of docks, which among other things houses the National Waterways Museum, I wasn't much attracted by the idea of a big city. In fact, even though I'd been returning to London regularly throughout the summer to deal with the percolations plaguing the Crumbling Pile, the idea of staying somewhere as large slightly unnerved me after so long in the countryside. After all, Gloucester was the biggest place I'd passed through since Oxford.

But sometimes when you're on a boat events conspire to thwart you. As they did me that day as soon as I'd struggled out of bed, bleary-eyed, hung-over and desperate for a hit of caffeine to jolt my sluggish brain into first gear. As is normal for me in the mornings, especially after a night like I'd just had at The Boat, it took me a while to locate my place in the universe, so finding the kettle was a bit of a struggle. After that I set my mind to looking for the tap which was no easier a task – especially since after I'd tracked it down, it struck me there wasn't much in the way of water coming from it. In fact, there wasn't *any* water coming from it; none at all.

This was a bit perplexing.

It's bad enough at any time of day when the world fails to conform to predictable patterns, but it's far worse after a night on the tiles when you're not up to intellectual challenges like… well, like thinking, for a start. I rubbed my eyes, fully expecting to find myself still in bed and this some strange dream from which I'd not yet woken. But no, for all intents and purposes, a world where water didn't now come from taps appeared to be one I was condemned to live in.

I checked the tap to reassure myself that it actually *was* the tap, and not the boat engine, the Forth Bridge or even the Cheddar Gorge. Then I scrutinised it again. Finally, when I'd satisfied myself that it was indeed what I believed it to be, I attempted to turn it on once more since I couldn't be certain so early in the day that I hadn't done something stupid on my first attempt. Like pulling it instead. Or pushing it. Or even scratching my armpits when in fact I'd been asleep and actually hadn't touched the tap at all.

But no, try as I might, there was no water going to come from this tap. This led me to one inescapable conclusion: I had run out of water.

I sat for a moment or two considering the implications of this news. I even flirted with the idea of going back to bed – a move I knew wouldn't exactly solve the problem, but which would at least make it a somewhat less pressing one. However, the more I thought about it, the more I had to admit to myself that this difficulty I was having wasn't as much of a surprise to me as it should have been. As consciousness dawned, I gradually began to remember that there are various factors on a boat that govern the supply of water.

Like the fact that you can't connect to the mains, for instance. Which means you have fill up a tank at regular intervals. I did have some vague recollection of doing something watery with a hose pipe at one point in some small village the far side of somewhere or another… but that was a long time before; and the only thing I could remember with any certainty filling up recently was myself with beer the previous night.

As if all this wasn't bad enough, when I attempted to fry myself an egg in place of the boiled one I sometimes have in the mornings, I discovered I'd run out of gas too. And not just my main bottle was empty, but my reserve bottle as well. The one which – when I thought about it – I remembered I'd been promising myself to replace for the last month or so. There was no cereal on the boat either. Indeed, there wasn't much else that was edible, so I was reduced to having a glass of milk for breakfast – and, if I'm honest, even that tasted a bit offish.

To cap it all, when I retired to the bathroom for my morning constitutional, it was only to discover that the holding tank on the lavatory was full and that what I was attempting to put in had an insistent tendency to want to come out…

There was nothing for it – regardless of whether I *wanted* to stop in Gloucester, I had no choice. I *had* to stop there. I needed to get my life together.

Travelling on a boat, you know you're getting close to a town when the graffiti under railway bridges is less about the performance of local football teams than about the accomplishments of local girls. Don't ask me why this is. I put it down to the more advanced sexual maturity of your average urban oik; though despite all their braggadocio, I don't think it's backed by much in the way of what I suppose you'd have to call hands-on experience. Or not at least judging by some of the depictions of the female form I saw as I got closer to Gloucester which made it apparent the lads in these parts have got a thing or two yet to learn about female anatomy.

Mind you, I suppose you can't expect much better from a generation brought up on the pneumatic improbabilities of Lara Croft.

Later that morning I attempted to tie up next to the chichi bistros in Llanthony Basin which is close to the Waterways Museum, and far and away the most pleasant visitor mooring in the city. Except – wouldn't you know it the day I was having? – every space was occupied. After searching around, the only place I could find to pull up was a floating pontoon a little further on, beyond a swing bridge that crosses the water at this point. This is opposite a derelict warehouse where, as if laid on for my delectation, a group of homeless punks covered in tattoos were sitting around a bonfire toasting sausages on sticks and listening to loud music through a ghetto-blaster. They could have been acting out a tableau entitled 'Urban Badlands'.

Now this sort of thing isn't unusual in towns in the Midlands or the North, but it *is* in Gloucester. Not because there isn't as much poverty and privation in the city as anywhere else, but because what there is, is normally kept well concealed; so as a casual visitor you can wander around for days thinking that Gloucester's just another English cathedral town frozen in the 1950s with very little function except as a location for classic TV detective stories.

But appearances are deceptive.

These derelict docks I was moored opposite were once the source of the city's wealth, and in the nineteenth century great ships of a thousand tons and more would sail up from the estuary laden with cargoes of timber and grain to feed the country and supply its industries. As that industry declined, so did Gloucester docks and Gloucester itself, leaving the place with a catalogue of the sort of problems that plague so many English cities today. Away from the small area of poncey waterside redevelopment and the cathedral precincts over the other side of town, there are some rough areas in Gloucester. There's a big drugs problem too. And a lot of raw violence seething angrily under the surface.

And as for the city as a setting for whodunnits – well, believe me, nothing could be further from the truth. I made a documentary about a real murder in Gloucester once. Take it from me, the police in that case acted nothing like Inspector Morse. Mind you, they didn't act much like the police either. The killing had happened as a result of a stabbing and the flat where it had taken place had been left virtually untouched, so that when I visited the walls were still smeared with the crusted black stains of what had once been blood. I don't know if seeing this contributed significantly to the quality of the documentary, but it certainly gave me another perspective on the legacy of our old medieval towns.

Actually, working on this film I missed a much better story by far. We were looking for someone you see, and my researchers set off on house-to-house enquiries to get information. One of them knocked on a door in a place called Cromwell Street.

It was number 25, where the Wests lived.

Since I'd left Stratford and begun cruising on rivers I was travelling too great a distance each day to make it feasible to pick up the Debsmobile regularly; and it had been left languishing, sadly if safely, at a farm belonging to some friends of mine who live in a village not far out of town. But now I was moving back on a canal, and once again it was feasible to have it with me. At Gloucester the River Severn becomes tidal, and so treacherous with sandbanks and rapids that it's unnavigable for a boat of any size; and so in the late eighteenth century, in order to ensure a more reliable route to the sea which avoided the unpredictability of a natural waterway, the Gloucester and Sharpness Canal was dug the remaining sixteen or so miles to the estuary.

So that day, once I'd done everything I'd set myself to do, I hopped on a train to collect the car; and that same afternoon, I drove back to Gloucester by a route I'd devised to keep me away from main roads.

Unusual weather had been a characteristic of my whole journey, and it was still odd and constantly unsettled: a period of violent storms and heavy rain would be followed by a day or so when the sky became a luminous blue and when it was suddenly so warm that you could almost believe you were in the Mediterranean. It was like this the afternoon I picked up the Debsmobile from Stratford, the sun high in the sky and hardly a cloud on the horizon. It was uncomfortably hot, but on occasions it was unusually fresh as well, and intimidating winds would abruptly blow up from nowhere, lapping around the treetops until they subsided apologetically, as if incapable of carrying out whatever it was they were threatening.

I folded back the roof of the car and though I was open to the air I still couldn't get away from that delicious mustiness that characterises all old vehicles. Even so, I was still acutely aware of the extravagant smells of the season that were assailing me on all sides: the sweetness of hayfields or the occasional vehement blast of honeysuckle from a hedge. From time to time I would become aware of the cloying odour of warm tarmac, and occasionally as I passed under a dark canopy of trees I'd be almost overcome by the succulence of their cool leaves.

The Herald has a very low carriage so that you sit close to the ground, which exaggerates its speed and makes you feel – much more than modern cars do – that you're in physical contact with the road. It makes driving feel more intimate, and this sense of communion, man with machine, is intensified by its suspension which even on a straight course on a smooth road has a good deal of tremulous movement in it so that you feel like you're handling a slightly nervous stallion.

If I love being on the tiller of a narrowboat because of its relentlessly ponderous movement – the sense that you don't so much steer it, as request it to make a movement with which it might then consider complying – then I love being at the wheel of the Herald for exactly the opposite reason: its immediate hair-trigger responsiveness which keeps you on your toes and makes you think – perhaps unjustly – that the slightest lapse of concentration on your side and you'll finish up in the nearest ditch.

Most people seem to know the Herald for its steering. Or at least they know it for its remarkable steering lock, which is tighter than a London taxi and means that you can swing the car around in a perfect circle, like a second hand on a clock sweeping around the dial. You have to have good clutch control to do it, though, since you get 'scrub' which is the technical term for when your front wheels are pointing in one direction so acutely that the rest of the car isn't following them and instead is moving forward against the tread of the tyres – a manoeuvre which has been known to strip the wheel of a Herald totally bare.

During the development of the car its road handling was always something of a problem, and its tendency to be over-sensitive caused so much concern to Standard Triumph engineers during early tests that eventually the whole set-up had to be damped down to make it safer. Coincidentally, a lot of the analysis which led to this and other modifications took place in the area through which I was now driving, since in these early days of motor manufacture, before there were the technological facilities to do everything in a workshop or on private tracks, the only way cars could be evaluated was by putting them through their paces on public roads under ordinary driving conditions.

One of the company's favoured routes for this was a 200-mile circuit from company headquarters in Coventry around a great loop through the Cotswolds by way of Birdlip Hill, close to Gloucester. These outings generally took place at night which you'd think with today's concern for industrial espionage was probably for security reasons – except that so many Midlands carmakers used Birdlip Hill for their 'secret' prototypes that it was said they were in danger of running into each other. Actually, the more prosaic reason the drives were done in the dark was so that the cars could be back at the factory the next morning when the designers would spend the day working on modifications before sending them out for another spin. Motor engineers were always running to a tight deadline, and there was constant pressure to get mileage on the cars – the Zobo no less than any other design on which so much was riding.

The second Michelotti prototype was treated more furtively, and it was delivered directly from Turin to Spain for more extensive tests in the spring of 1958. This model was given the registration number VRW 589, and there's a photograph of it on that trip filling up with petrol at one of those small old-fashioned continental garages built like a hacienda, with great overhanging eves and chunky biscuit-clay roof tiles. There's something about the picture that seems to epitomise Spain in those pre-EU years under General Franco when it seemed like a Third World country and not part of Europe at all. Perhaps it's the typically Mediterranean white brickwork of the building, a bare vine trained across the wall ready to burst into bud. Or maybe it's just that the weather's not really what we think of as Spanish at all, for despite the sunshine casting sharp shadows across the scene, it's obviously quite chilly since everyone in the picture is wearing a heavy topcoat.

It's a compelling photograph, a snapshot of a single moment that at the same time seems redolent of an entire age. And what is extraordinary about it is that apart from a marginally different radiator grille and an alternative paint job to replace Michelotti's original idea of a two-tone finish, the car looks almost exactly the same as the model that would go on sale just a year later.

But before that finally happened, the Herald was to be put through its most testing ordeal yet – a 10,000-mile slog the length of Africa, from Cape Town in the south up to what is now Zaire and Chad, through Nigeria and into Morocco in the north. It was a journey that would test the car to its extremes, pitting it against jungles and deserts, in tropical rains and remorseless heat. Quite how such an ambitious itinerary came about in the first place is uncertain, except that whoever came up with the idea had so little grasp of what it actually involved that initially a journey twice as long was planned. But an expedition on this scale was a declaration of confidence, not just in the car, but in the fragile stability of this part of world which was at that time in the death throes of colonisation, with the very names of the countries – places like the Belgian Congo, French West Africa and Rhodesia – a testament to the subservience of the continent to one European conqueror or another.

Certainly nowadays no company would consider such an odyssey, if only because the political situation would make it too risky. In late 1958, though, it was only after nearly three months on the road, and in the final two weeks of their journey, that the Standard Triumph team encountered any problems of this sort whatsoever; and they had to call for military protection as they passed through Algeria where a civil war had not long started. Of course, they couldn't have known it then, but these were the early stirrings of a liberation movement that would eventually sweep the French from the country – the first of a series of such offensives which, fanned by the winds of change, would eventually spread across Africa like wildfire.

Mechanically, the Herald took the safari in its stride, and, apart from some problems with *that* suspension, the main difficulty facing the company as it prepared to unveil the car publicly to the world was the old one of what it was going to be called. Up until Africa, it had still been known to everyone involved in the project as the Zobo, but in the summer before it went on sale Alick Dick called a board meeting at which the directors studiously considered a series of options before deciding in the absence of any better suggestion that it should be christened the 'Triumph Torch'.

There wasn't a lot of enthusiasm for the name, though, and partly because Dick had 'a relaxed and open management style', discussion on the subject went on beyond the point where efficiency might have dictated it should have ended. Eventually one board member suggested that what was needed was 'a name heralding Triumph's positive emergence from the greyness of motor vehicle similarity'.

'Herald's blew funny trumpets,' someone else observed. 'We can't call the bloody thing a Triumph Trumpet,' another frustrated director retorted.

Eventually they all bowed to the inevitable and went home happy. But the wonder was not that they finally arrived at the name they did, but that it took them so long to choose it when it was all but staring them in the face.

The board meeting was held on a boat belonging to Alick Dick, you see. It was called *The Herald*.

Of course, even if we hadn't got access to the details, we could all probably guess how the story ended after this: how the car was finally launched to a fanfare of enthusiasm by the motoring press who welcomed it as 'Britain's outstanding new car', singling it out as 'one of the most exciting specifications to come from any of the large manufacturers for a long time'; how it was put on the market at an unprecedented speed so that the entire project went from prototype to production in just 19 months, a rate we couldn't compete with today despite our new technology; how the orders came in by the thousand and the car soon became the company's bestseller. Yes, we could almost fill in the background for ourselves, but somehow this wouldn't express it all, for the Herald somehow transcended the statistics of its own history and became something more, redefining what people thought cars were, and what they could be. It became a paradigm not just for the industry, but for its age, and in some way it touched people emotionally and won a place in their hearts as well.

Just as well it did really, because as a nation we weren't winning much else at the time. It was the period just after the Suez fiasco, and though we didn't totally realise the implications of what was happening, we were finally losing our Empire.

It was one spawned by an industrial revolution fed by canals. Funny how it should end in a wrangle over one.

Like the Suez Canal, the canal between Gloucester and Sharpness was built for ocean-going ships not boats; and unusually for ventures like this which were almost exclusively funded by private capital, it was financed by government money. It opened in 1827, ten years before Queen Victoria came to the throne in the early years of the imperial period which it reflects in the confidence of its design; for it's wide and straight and deep and has a certain indisputable grandeur about it which speaks of an age proud of its great civic projects. You see this most at the bridges which had to accommodate the towering superstructures of large commercial vessels and so were built as swing bridges, each operated by bridge-keepers who were housed in cottages built for the purpose alongside.

These places might be small, but they have a certain bijou

style, for they were built to a classic design, each on its own pediment and each with a set of fluted Doric columns so that they look like little temples transported from the Peloponnese – a conceit with which some of the current occupants have conspired by putting bay trees in plant pots outside their front doors.

Even today the bridges are operated automatically by men employed for that sole reason and – as far as I can make out – for absolutely no other. Posh, or what? To have men sitting in the control boxes of bridges waiting for you to come along just so as to be able to press a button and open them for you? This is a quality of service we're not used to today – a bit like going to the Ritz and having a man in a morning suit open the door for you. And in just the same way that at the Ritz you could just as easily open the door for yourself, so on *Justice* – and most other narrow-boats for that matter – you're so low to the water you could probably go underneath most of the bridges with room to spare and without anyone having to go to the trouble of opening anything.

But who'd want to do that and risk making the bridge-keepers redundant? They must have the best job in the world. With an average traffic in the high season of what – a dozen boats a day? two dozen? – this is hardly a profession likely to engender much in the way of stress, especially since a major part of the work is actually looking out for the boats in the first place – and that's done to a large extent by closed circuit TV cameras.

To be fair to them, though, their job isn't *just* a matter of pressing a button. No, they have to drop barriers across the road to stop the road traffic too, and that means leaving their boxes sometimes. This must be a swine in the winter when it's a bit parky. Actually, it must be a bit irritating at any time of year because, believe me, I've seen inside those places and they're like little palaces with their easy chairs, TVs and microwaves. They're so cosy you could live in them. In fact, I think the bridge-keepers probably have to, seeing as how the cottages built for them were sold off as private houses years ago.

I spent a disturbed night next to the punks in Gloucester, the only thing to be said for it being that I learned everything there is to know about punk music. This can be summarised succinctly under three headings:

Take two clashing chords and play them very loudly over a strong drumbeat.

Play them again.

Erm... that's it.

The next morning I couldn't get away fast enough, and I cruised the ten miles or so down to Frampton on Severn in divine silence, arriving in time for an early lunch of sausage and mash in a pub overlooking the huge village green there. This green is supposed to be the biggest in the country, and I've no reason to believe otherwise. OK, it may not be as big as some of the gardens you get in stockbroker Surrey, but it's certainly bigger than most French farms. In fact, if it were a French farm it would qualify for a generous EU grant. Mind you, it probably does anyway, and thinking about it, most Surrey stockbrokers are probably claiming set-aside on their gardens too.

The pub specialises in sausages and is famous locally for the range it serves. I would have enjoyed lunch more except that it struck me soon after sitting down that there are as many ways to eat a sausage as there are types of sausages to eat. And not all of them pleasant, I have to say.

I could just about put up with the bloke at the next table slurping noisily over his Leek and Garlic, but the woman opposite who was eating with her boyfriend was an altogether more difficult prospect since some of the things she was doing with her Traditional Pork and Sage verged on the obscene. But it was the guy in the corner of the room who I found the most difficult to stomach. He was drooling so much over his Rough Chopped Spanish Chorizo that I swear you could have used him as a spirit level by putting him in the centre of the room and seeing which side he dribbled from most.

Believe me, I didn't tarry long over coffee.

That afternoon I went for a walk around Saul Junction where the Stroudwater Canal cuts across the Gloucester and Sharpness in an unusual crossroads junction, more like a road than a canal. The Stroudwater is derelict now, though like most abandoned canals of any substance it's under renovation, and once it's finished it will be a critical link in the system, connecting to the River Thames at Lechlade above Oxford which is for all intents and purposes the limit of current navigation.

The junction's one of those messy and intriguing spots which is a magnet to a canal enthusiast like me. There's a boatyard there nestling among a group of higgledy-piggledy buildings, with bits of propeller lying around and odd engines waiting for attention. And there's a massive dry dock too, with enough idiosyncratic boats about to make you lose all sense of time as you wander about examining them.

The shadows were already beginning to lengthen when I set off back to *Justice*, and on the other side of the wide estuary, the sun had already thrown the hills of the Forest of Dean into shadow so it looked like a great cloud on the horizon. Even so, the canal itself was still illuminated like an airport runway, a dazzling mirror reflecting the flaming sun which became more burnished as it moved ever lower in the sky. Because it was such a fine evening there were a lot of fishermen around doing the sort of things that fisherman do. Normally this wouldn't interest me very much at all.

You know what they say about fishermen: give a man a fish and you feed him for a day; teach him how to fish and you give him an excuse to sit around endlessly playing with maggots.

But this is zander territory, a fish that is supposed to be one of the tastiest and most delicate to be had in British waters – and one I'd never eaten. I was hoping that with a bit of luck and a smile, I might be able to blag one or two out of a keep net. The fact that these fish are foreign predators – Germans to boot – doesn't exactly endear them to the country's coarse fishermen. Neither does it help that they prey on our indigenous fish, and have been so successful in colonising us over the last few years that in some places they've taken over completely and fishermen are encouraged to kill them on sight to give the local species more of a chance of survival.

But fishermen and women – for increasingly the sport is attracting both genders – are canny people. They spend a lot of time in their own company, pondering the nature of the universe and their place in it. None of them are mugs, especially not in this part of the world where they know the worth of a fish like a zander which can fetch £10–15 a portion in a London restaurant – assuming you're lucky enough to find a restaurant which serves it at all.

I was put in mind of that story about the guy who was browsing in a tatty second-hand bookshop in a back street in the middle of nowhere a few years back when he came across an original Gutenburg Bible, one of the most valuable books ever produced. He could scarcely contain his excitement, and it was as much as he could do to marshal himself as he nonchalantly sidled over to the owner of the shop.

'So how much do you want for that old Bible over there, then?' he asked.

'Oh, the Gutenburg? Give me a couple of million quid, mate, and it's yours.'

Not true of course – but it *was* like that with the fisherman on the Gloucester and Sharpness that night.

'So what are you going to do with those nasty beady-eyed bastards with teeth like razor blades?'

'Oh those zander? I sell them for a tenner each. There's a bloke I know who'll take as many as I can catch.'

Actually it's a shame fishermen don't catch more of them, for they've become a big problem recently, and a lot of money has been spent unsuccessfully trying to keep them under control. These 'freshwater sharks' as they've been christened were introduced into the country by the Duke of Bedford in 1878. He shipped 24 of them over from Schleswig-Holstein where –

as in most of Europe – they were classed as a game fish and much valued for their flavour which, like their appearance, is a cross between pike and perch. Indeed, one of them proved too much of an early temptation for the Duke and immediately finished up on the dinner table at Woburn Abbey where at least it caused no damage to anything – with the possible exception of His Grace's aristocratic digestion.

The rest were released into the estate lakes where a century later, thanks to some inane bureaucrat at the Great Ouse River Authority, a few of them were set free into the Fens on the pretext of providing more interesting sport for fishermen. This is a bit like loosing a virulent disease on Essex in order give doctors more interesting work. The doctors, you'd guess, wouldn't be too keen on this idea, and – no surprise, this – neither were the fishermen who complained at the time about the zander and have been complaining ever since.

Its success is mainly down to the unique quality of its eyes, which allow it to see in the most impenetrable murky gloom by reflecting light back onto its retina. It leaves it at a bit of an advantage over indigenous species like roach which need more than a trip to Vision Express to compete at this level.

The rise and rise of the zander has been inexorable, and there are now great swathes of the country infested to such an extent that British Waterways have been reduced to culling them by (honestly!) a mass programme of electrocution. Except they realised a while back that despite the cost, it simply wasn't working. And anyhow, why spend money, because along with their other questionable charms, zander are cannibals. Leave them alone for long enough and they regulate themselves.

But like buses, you can never get a zander when you want one.

Eventually I went back to *Justice* empty-handed so that my recipe for zander poached in wheat beer, or baked with a mustard crust, will have to wait for another day. Instead, here's one for a more commonly available freshwater fish – trout. It's based on a

Jane Grigson recipe from the north of France where, in season in places like the Val de Loire, there are so many of them waiting to be caught they've introduced a queuing system at the hooks.

We're not quite so lucky on English waterways, but these days you never seem to be far from a commercial trout lake where you can sometimes pick up a couple cheap if you've got the gall to ask. They can taste a bit muddy, though, and they benefit from a night soaking in fresh water with a good squeeze of lemon juice to freshen them up.

The Final Recipe

This dish is very quick to prepare, so ensure that if you're going to eat it with potatoes they are almost cooked before you start, and your oven or back-cabin stove is up to heat. This way everything will be ready at the same time.

Finely chop a medium onion and a carrot, along with two or three of the pale green inside leaves of a stick of celery if you happen to have them to hand. Scatter them across the bottom of a generously buttered ovenproof dish with some parsley, a bay leaf, salt and a generous pinch of coarsely ground black pepper. Put the trout on the top and dribble some more melted butter over it. Then pop it in the top of the oven at about 200 °C for about 15 minutes or until the skin begins to burn and you're getting the odd black spot appearing. Take it out very quickly and douse it with a glass of white wine. Then pour a small carton of double cream over it along with a good squeeze of lemon juice. Put it back in the oven for another couple of minutes until the cream has heated.

To serve, extract the fish carefully to avoid breaking it. Give what's left in the dish a good stir before arranging it tastefully around the edge. Don't under any circumstances be tempted to ladle the sauce over the top of the fish which is guaranteed to make the whole thing look a complete mess. If you have to put something on the top, make it a couple of lemon slices or a single sprig of fresh parsley.

This goes very well with a green salad served with a sharp dressing to counteract the cream.

Twenty-Two

YOU CAN NEVER PLAN anything on the waterways; there's too much that can go wrong. The uncertainty is about the only thing you can rely on.

We were hoping to make the estuary crossing on the Wednesday. Em had taken time off from work for it, and was actually getting quite excited at the prospect; and even I'd finally got my head around the idea that since I had to die sometime, this was a rather valiant way of shuffling off the old mortal coil. I had visions of us hitting an unexpectedly violent storm. I imagined *Justice* beginning to take on water until we had to abandon ship. I could see myself kissing Em lightly on the cheek as we said our goodbyes, me tossing the hair from my eyes before peeling off my sweater to lay it across her shoulders comfortingly. Finally, I saw us stepping off the stern deck hand in hand as the boat succumbed to the battering waves, my last words to her a reassurance that we'd see each other in a better world…

But on the Friday night after I'd got back from Saul Junction it began raining – which, I have to admit, wasn't exactly an unusual occurrence on this trip when it always seemed to be chucking it down. What *was* unparalleled, though, was its intensity. And the fact that it didn't stop. It was still raining on Saturday morning when I collected Em from the station. And still raining on Sunday too. In fact, it didn't let up for one moment the whole weekend, great raindrops the size of dinner plates battering down on the roof with the force of sledgehammers.

On Monday I rang up the pilot again as we'd arranged. 'Everything OK for later in the week?' I asked.

I could almost hear him sniggering. I could almost see him

covering the receiver with his hand, shouting over to one of his mates: ''Ere – listen to this one Fred – there's a bloke on a narrowboat thinks he going down the estuary Wednesday. After all this rain. What a wally, eh?'

Instead, he said: 'Well, it's up two feet already and there's a Force Nine coming over from the Azores and the current's running to 15 with a 20 cross wind and several gumbos coming up from the rear and strawberries and cream expected in the next post…'

Or at least that's what it sounded like to me…

Anyway, I got the message clearly enough: we didn't stand a snowball in hell's chance of getting across the estuary on Wednesday. I should ring him the following week, maybe things would be better then. Conditions might have improved. I should be prepared to be patient and wait.

There is a temptation with every narrative to want to make it seamless, as if life itself were seamless and moved smoothly from one event to the next towards some inexorable conclusion. But this just isn't the way it happens. The fact is that most of life is disjointed in its own random way, without any of the structure we later endow it with. The truth is very few things in this world run at all effortlessly.

Certainly the estuary crossing didn't.

With no immediate hope of cruising, Em left later in the week; and after she'd gone I moved a mile or so up the canal to Patch Bridge, close to Peter Scott's Slimbridge Wildlife and Wetlands Centre where there was a boatyard and a pub with a car park convenient for the Debsmobile sited virtually on the water's edge. To be honest, I thought I'd only be there for a couple of days – a week at most. As it turned out I was there for so long I could probably have got on the electoral register if I'd filled in the right forms. I was there so long I became a landmark and locals taking their dogs for a walk would ask after my family.

The rain, you see, just wouldn't let up.

Days became weeks, and the weeks became a month; and still it continued to pour down incessantly. It rained every day without cease, every hour that God sent – day after relentless day, and night after remorseless night, so that the towpath became a quagmire and the river and estuary a raging torrent so swollen that not only could I not get to Bristol, but I couldn't even have gone back to Gloucester. Like it or not, my only option was to sit it out and wait.

I spent a lot of time at the Slimbridge Centre where, with the wetlands being wetter than usual and visitors being thin on the ground, the birds were having a fine old time of it, and a sort of riotous party mood prevailed. There was one goose called a *cereopsis* which particularly fascinated me, an unprepossessing creature which lived in a wired compound down by one of the ponds and which was so pugnacious it would have had your hand off given half a chance. On one occasion, my curiosity about the creature got the better of me, and before I was forced back in a flurry of flying feathers, I managed to get close enough to its cage to read a sign that had been put there about it. It said 'Beware – Aggressive Species', which at the time I confess I didn't find entirely helpful.

Every couple of days, by way of a distraction, I'd ring the pilot for a weather update and a chat. Eventually, I reckon he used to look forward to my calls: there was that special something between us.

Or then again, maybe not. Maybe I was just a pain in the neck.

Hassling him didn't help much, though. 'You'll have to wait a little bit longer. It's really not safe at the moment,' he'd always say.

'But it's nearly the end of the summer,' I'd protest. 'If I don't get away soon I'll be stuck here until next year.'

'Yes, I know, but what am I supposed to do, let you drown? You'll just have to wait. Conditions just aren't safe at the moment.'

Eventually I was there so long I couldn't bear to be there any longer, and I left and drove back to London where in my absence the Crumbling Pile had developed two or three more inexplicable oozing ingresses somewhere skyside of the back bedroom window. This could have kept me happily up to my neck in damp proofing and wood shavings for weeks on end – except that during one of my forays up a ladder in the name of home maintenance my mobile rang in my back pocket.

I could see from the number that it was the pilot. Ringing me! I was in so much of a fluster I almost fell off the roof with the excitement of it.

'It could happen this week,' he said conspiratorially, as if we were arranging the illicit exchange of some military secret or other.

'This week? But it's still raining here,' I said. 'I can testify to this. Indeed, even as I talk to you, evidence of this is running down my neck…'

'It's raining here too,' he said. 'But that's not the point. The point is that soon it will stop raining. And then the estuary will drain, and soon after that conditions will become…' – he lowered his voice – '… perfect.'

'Perfect?' I repeated.

'Perfect,' he said again, such an unmistakable note of anticipation in his voice that I could almost picture him tapping his nose with his forefinger. 'I would advise you to be ready.'

The next day I went back to Patch Bridge and as always on the waterways, when you leave a place you've been for any length of time – even somewhere you've been compelled to stay – you become sentimental about your departure. That night as the rain finally began to abate, I took a walk up the towpath in the soft light of a gentle moon which for the first time in ages wasn't obscured by clouds.

It was along this part of the towpath that Peter Scott walked one summer night in July 1946 towards the end of his marriage with Elizabeth Jane Howard. Afterwards, by way of an attempt at reconciliation, he wrote her a love letter in which he described to her, not the cliché of the stars in the sky, but the ones twinkling in the grass – glow worms lit by their own halos. It's a remarkably beautiful and touching piece of writing, one that could only have been produced by a naturalist, and then only by one whose heart was fixated so resolutely on another. 'I am afraid it will not please you if I tell you how much I love you,' he wrote. *'Embarras de richesse* – everyone loves you and why wouldn't they – poor things.'

The letter, of course, was never sent.

It was along this part of the towpath that Scott kept his narrowboat *Beatrice* which was used as accommodation for visitors to Slimbridge, but which in the summer of 1950 he took to Leicestershire to become the official headquarters of Aickman's Festival of Boats and Arts. By this time Scott and Howard had begun divorce proceedings, and her affair with Robert Aickman was more or less out in the open. However, the process wasn't complete, the separation hadn't become absolute so that, strictly speaking, they were still married. It meant things could have been awkward between Scott and Aickman – except that by now they'd become close friends in their own right.

Perhaps it's natural that two men attracted to the same woman should find they have things in common that draws them together. But maybe what Aickman and Scott felt was more specific than this. Perhaps something connected to the intensity of emotion that Jane Howard was capable of inflaming, the heat of which could weld people together.

Earlier that year the two of them had taken *Beatrice* on a 450-mile trip around the waterways which Scott had used to promote the concept of his bird sanctuary at Slimbridge in a series of public lectures. It may have been a *quid pro quo* that afterwards Scott reciprocated by throwing himself behind Aickman's ideas for the Market Harborough festival, especially the controversial plays which Aickman was still stubbornly determined to mount. By now it had been decided to put on two solid middlebrow productions: Alfred Sutro's *A Marriage has been Arranged*, and Benn Levy's farce *Springtime for Henry*; and Scott guaranteed to underwrite their costs. He even took a role in the Levy play himself, despite the fact that all the other actors performing were professionals and he'd never set foot on a stage before. In fact, with Aickman asking Jane to produce the Sutro piece, the theatrical part of the festival became something of a nepotistic affair – which can't have done much to assuage Tom Rolt's opposition to the whole idea.

Indeed, it seems to have exacerbated his antagonism and he remained implacably opposed to the plays. 'I felt it was their job to organise a rally rather than spend time on a venture which I thought was of no conceivable use or relevance as far as the waterways were concerned,' he said with an outspokenness that irritated Aickman, who didn't respond well to this sort of criticism. In fact, he wasn't a man who responded well to *any* sort of criticism, being so totally incapable of conceiving that other people might have views at odds with his own that he thought anyone disagreeing with him was attacking him, and so guilty of grave disloyalty.

Other men might have been totally indifferent to someone taking an opposing line on such a relatively minor matter, but the plays were just the climax of a series of disagreements with Rolt; they had begun to represent so much more between them – something that struck at the very core of what was left of their relationship and would eventually destroy it finally and irrevocably.

For Aickman, no one could be allowed to oppose the plays. Least of all Tom Rolt.

What was it? Jealousy at Rolt's success as a writer? Envy at his ability to forge for himself a lifestyle that Aickman himself wanted? Or was it more, something vaguely sinister perhaps? The single-mindedness of an autocrat? Or something more fundamental? Something that Aickman saw as impugning his manhood, challenging his status as an alpha male?

Perhaps it was simply the petulance of a spoilt child who'd determined on a course of action and wasn't to be thwarted.

Whatever it was, an angry Aickman, stung by Rolt's opposition, eventually decided to confront him, and he tabled a motion to the festival committee demanding that Rolt resign. Since Rolt hadn't exactly been overjoyed at being conscripted as a member in the first place, it can't have been an entirely unwelcome development. He was anyhow in the process of relinquishing his official waterways responsibilities, and despite initially being dissuaded from it by Aickman, he'd only just managed to offload his role as honorary secretary of the Inland Waterways Association. This seems to have goaded Aickman even further, and in a move that smacks of vindictiveness, he attempted to stop the Rolts going to the festival at all by banning them, a move which provoked an angry row among the organisers and a further resignation.

It didn't work anyhow. In fact, it had the opposite effect, for until they received the letter telling them of the decision, Tom and Angela were in two minds about going to Market Harborough at all. Now they were both livid. And determined to attend.

'As the IWA has grown in both stature and prestige so you have grown equally arrogant and intolerant of the views of others when they failed to coincide with yours,' Rolt wrote to Aickman in a long and bitter three-page letter. 'That you should dare to request me not to come astonishes me, accustomed though I am by long experience to your ways.'

The situation wasn't helped by the fact that Rolt's latest book *Inland Waterways of England* was scheduled for publication in the same week as the festival. Though it could have been useful to the general aim of promoting the canals – which was, after all, the principal purpose of the event – Rolt's publisher Philip Unwin had been specifically instructed by the organising committee not to use the Leicestershire gathering to advertise it. The clash of the publication had anyhow been total coincidence, but the threat this decision posed to his livelihood outraged Tom Rolt, and for a while he even considered taking the matter to court. Eventually common sense prevailed and he decided against it, but from now on it was – as he put it himself – 'hell or Market Harborough'. From Lechlade on the Thames where he and Angela were moored, he immediately set off northwards in *Cressy*, pressing on at such a pace that unusually they didn't even stop to look up friends as they passed through Banbury.

Despite the unpleasantness that preceded it, the festival ultimately proved to be a huge success. Initially some twenty or thirty boats were expected to attend, but at the end of the day 120 turned up from all parts of the country, and the weather remained perfect for them throughout. An astonishing 50,000 people attended – a single crowd of 20,000 turning out just for a fireworks display on the penultimate night. This was one of a series of public attractions laid on, many of them the sort of activities which you'd have found at any country carnival or gala at that time, and which in many ways seem typical of the era, encapsulating something of the quintessential nature of England in the hiatus of those grey but somehow reassuring post-war years between the defeat of Hitler and the release of the Beatles first LP.

Apart from the controversial arts events, there were dancing displays and a police band; there was model car racing and a fancy dress dance for children; the election of a Festival Queen, and – inevitably – a cricket match. Every night there was alfresco dancing to the Rogues of Rhythm Dance Band. The Rogues of Rhythm? A dance band? The term itself is redolent of a lost age before the Cavern Club and the Mersey Sound changed the world.

Even Tom Rolt had to admit that he enjoyed the occasion, though on a personal level the atmosphere of the event was poisonous. The row between him and Aickman had so festered that now it divided the whole of the IWA, and the two factions they represented could hardly bring themselves to speak to each other the whole week, despite a brave attempt at reconciliation by the President of the IWA, Sir Alan Herbert. The truth was that a climate of such suspicion and mistrust had grown up between the parties that even the most innocent fraternisation was liable to be seen as provocative.

So the two camps epitomised by *Cressy* and *Beatrice* stood apart, eyeing each other suspiciously like the flagships of two indomitable fleets facing each other at anchor.

This sort of unpleasantness wasn't what Rolt had come onto the canals for; this wasn't part of his 'design for living'. In any case, his days on the canal were drawing to a close now. But they'd been numbered even before Market Harborough: the relationship with Angela, never easy, had been deteriorating; and *Cressy* itself – the physical manifestation of their marriage – had been diagnosed with serious rot in her hull which would eventually prove to be terminal. The festival and the bitterness engendered by Aickman may not have been the cause of him leaving the canals, but it was the straw that broke the camel's back.

For Rolt the waterways had anyhow always been an untenable fantasy – a hopeless way of escaping that painful paradox in which he was trapped that meant he had to live in a modern world he largely resented. But the nature of paradox, like life, is that it's irresolvable – and the nature of Rolt's dream of the canals was that it was essentially a delusion. Canals might be a respite from modern life, but they're no escape from it. Narrowboats, after all, aren't time machines.

Eventually, even on the waterways, things change. It was another contradiction of Tom Rolt's life – one for which me and thousands of others are constantly grateful: for in struggling with such futile enthusiasm to retain the things of the past, he created the shape of the future. Angela and he became like the Adam and Eve of every pleasure boater on the canals today, and *Cressy* the model for every boat that's afloat. Oh, how he would have hated it. And hated us too, I suspect.

All he wanted to do was preserve the canals as he knew them, but in doing that, he had to change them. It ensured that as far as this part of his life was concerned he could only ever fail in what he did.

Funny that, really, isn't it?

To see your goal so clearly, and to work for it with such resolution, only to have everything bent out of shape?

Banana-shaped, I suppose you could say.

My long wait at Patch Bridge ended a couple of days later when the pilot's predictions proved spot on and the weather changed completely. Some pressure centre somewhere had shifted and it suddenly became stiflingly hot without even a breath of air to cool things down. More importantly, the sky became perfectly clear with not so much as a wisp of cloud to threaten further rain. The idea now was to move off on the Friday evening tide once my crew (i.e. Em) had managed to get up from London. To that end, and on the pilot's advice, I'd alerted the harbour-master at Sharpness who was made aware that yet another crazy flat-bottomed bastard in the form of NB *Justice* was going to play at real boats by trying for a passage to Bristol. The harbour-master in turn had alerted the local British Waterways office who manage the sea lock and the approach to it where there's a low-level railway bridge that has to be swung to allow access.

Of course, something was bound to go wrong. It's sod's law, isn't it? It's like I say – you can never plan anything on the waterways.

I slipped moorings late afternoon for what was intended to be a pleasant potter in the sunshine to Sharpness where I'd already earmarked one of the spectacular moorings adjacent to the estuary wall which look out across the reedbeds and the sandbanks to the river and the sea. But no sooner had I turned the gentle bend which takes you out of sight of Patch Bridge than 27HP of pulsating engineering was brought to an abrupt and humiliating halt by what – after I'd spent a couple of hours fishing around in the water extracting it from the propeller – turned out to be a length of slimy water-sodden, triple-plaited ship rope 12 strands thick.

Mmmmm… nice, eh?

Not too good for the estuary schedule, though, since by this time the bloke who looks after the two swing bridges which remained to be navigated before I got to Sharpness had packed up and gone off home for the day. Mind you, who'd blame him? It was the weekend, after all.

So a new communiqué had to go out to the pilot, the harbour-master at Sharpness, and British Waterways – all of whom by now had gone home too, and all of whom no doubt eventually concluded when they received the message I left on their respective answerphones that the crazy flat-bottomed bastard had had an attack of common sense and decided to abort the whole lunatic plan. And I probably would have done if I'd have been aware of what other pitfalls lay in wait for me before I completed the trip.

Instead, I moored the boat, cycled back to the Debsmobile and took the more conventional road route to Bristol where I picked up Em from where I'd arranged to meet her at Temple Meads Station. She was incredulous.

'You mean, after more than a month hanging about waiting for the right moment, you've got the pilot, the harbour-master and British Waterways all expecting us out on the midnight tide tonight?'

I nodded.

'Except that we're not going to be on the midnight tide tonight,' she went on. 'Because the tide is on one side of the swing bridge and we are on the other?'

I nodded again, somewhat sheepishly this time. 'That's about the sum of it, yes. I've left them a message, though,' I added brightly.

'That'll be useful when they get it. Probably on Monday morning, I'd guess.'

'Well, they'll definitely know we're not going tonight when we don't turn up.'

'And that'll be great for our reputation for reliability,' she said. 'Not to mention our bank balance, since I presume that if the pilot turns out at that time of night he's going to want paying, come what may.'

'Good point,' I said. 'I suppose I better get on the phone again.'

Eventually I did manage to track everyone down, and the crossing was aborted and rearranged for the following afternoon. Unfortunately, this meant that since you can't make Bristol on a single tide, it would be dark when we arrived at the mouth of the River Avon and we'd have to moor the night among the six-storey high leviathans which ply the water there bringing in most of the country's car imports.

It was like taking a pedal car into a busy HGV lorry park and it confirmed my gut feeling that we weren't going to get out of this one alive.

Em, though, was altogether more upbeat. 'Don't be such a wimp,' she said. 'Let's have a drink and you'll feel better. Your round, isn't it?'

Twenty-Three

THE NEXT DAY IT DAWNED bright again, and as soon as the bridge-keeper had arrived and let us through, we cruised the short distance to Sharpness where I tucked *Justice* into one of those moorings I'd had in mind for the previous day. Afterwards Em and I sat outside on the towpath in the warm morning sunshine, munching on a mound of bacon sandwiches as we looked out towards the wide mouth of the river where it meets the estuary.

I was still apprehensive about the day, but at least the food settled my fluttering stomach. Not that I had a lot to worry about, for conditions really couldn't have been any better. It was perhaps chillier than was ideal, with summer all but over now, and autumn in the air; but it was so completely still and windless that across the black reed-covered mudflats and the derelict sunken barges that lie there, you'd have thought the water was glass except that from time to time you could just about make out a gentle shimmering on the surface which was the movement of the river sliding towards the sea. Away in the far distance where the land rises towards Wales someone had lit a fire in a lonely house on the hillside and a thin plume of smoke rose almost vertically to the sky. Above us a small flock of seagulls glided in the placid air, occasionally breaking the silence with their shrill cries.

Before finally committing myself to the trip I'd cycled from Patch Bridge to Sharpness to reconnoitre the lock. The worst fears are usually in your mind, and more often than not they can be assuaged by confronting them. I thought it would help to see what I was letting myself in for.

It didn't.

It had been filthy that day, rain-lashed and gusty with the wind kicking up and the estuary showing white horses to the horizon. I made my way gingerly to the lock and walked across the top gates facing the sea where the force was so strong I had to lean into the gale to keep my balance. Frankly, if the idea of all this was to make me feel better about things, then it was soon clear I'd got things badly wrong. This was Sharpness and the estuary at its very worst. Eventually I plucked up courage to peek over the edge where waves were crashing relentlessly at some vertiginous distance below. The tides in these parts, remember, are some of the highest in the world, and the gates have to be tall enough to resist them. They were certainly tall enough to turn my stomach.

I kept asking myself how I'd got into this position and why I was even considering making the trip. It's not as if I've any inclination towards canal adventuring as some people have; I was just a guy in a narrowboat who wanted to be in Bristol, and who, if he could have clicked his fingers and magically been there, would have done it without hesitation.

But now, as Em and I surveyed the very same scene, it was completely different. It was as if it wasn't Sharpness at all, but another place entirely, though one in its own way equally as impressive and equally dismaying, since for anyone used to the restrictive spaces of inland waterways, always bounded by banks and towpaths, there is something inherently daunting about a flat expanse of water like the one at which we were gazing, stretching out endlessly on all sides to the faraway skyline.

We were scheduled to go into the lock at 4.30 p.m. when the low-level railway bridge blocking our way was to be swung open to allow us access, so we spent the day pottering around in the sunshine, relaxing and taking it easy. In fact, we took it so easy that – doesn't this always happen? – it was suddenly four o'clock and we were running late. Getting away on time now became a panic, and I suppose I was rushing a bit when I finally engaged gear and cast off, swinging the tiller to pull us out into the centre of the canal.

Even so, this didn't entirely explain the peculiar thing that happened next. Without warning the tiller rose out of its housing an inch or so, leaking a couple of pints of water over the stern deck; and then it dropped back in what seemed to be the same position – but clearly wasn't because when I pulled on it, it resolutely refused to move except by jolting abruptly, locking at another equally unmoveable angle. At the first sign of trouble I'd instinctively gone into neutral gear, but this left me without control; and with our initial impetus still driving us forward, we powered straight across the canal and hit a wall on the other side with a sickening crunch of metal and a cloud of brick dust.

It was then I noticed two men in British Waterways uniforms. They were clearly part of the team who'd come to open the bridge for us, and they'd been watching all this attentively. One of them smiled in that quietly censorious way that British Waterways men do when they've caught you making a balls-up of a manoeuvre. I giggled back self-consciously: the balls-up wasn't my fault, but I realised that no one in a month of Sundays would ever believe me.

I yanked the tiller back to something resembling a straight line, and we limped into the lock where we had an hour's wait for our pilot to join us, and where serious amounts of tugging and jerking and hauling did nothing to solve the problem – though it almost succeeded in putting my arms out of joint.

I guessed that I'd moored above a dislodged coping stone or something of that sort, and that when I'd engaged gear and my stern had dropped in the water I'd trapped the bottom of the tiller, causing it to rise from its housing and dislodge itself when it fell back. But who knows for certain? Maybe it was something entirely different? Maybe the previous night's cussed ship rope had something to do with it all?

The question now, though, was simple enough: were we going to abort the trip or continue with it? Eventually we decided that the safest thing was to let the pilot survey the situation and allow him to make the decision. Except that by the time he arrived the harbour authorities were already emptying the lock and we were dropping fast to sea level, and he was shouting to us from the top to meet him at the jetty on the other side where he jumped on board at the first opportunity. Suddenly there seemed to be rather too much of an expanse of water ahead of us to start carping about details like how we were going to make the boat go the way we wanted it to.

Besides, the estuary's a couple of miles wide at Sharpness, broadening to – what, four miles at Avonmouth? Five? It doesn't exactly call for precision steering, does it? Just as well really, since in practice the awful truth was that we didn't really have any steering. Or at least not in the sense that you'd normally understand the concept. OK, so it was actually still possible to make the boat go roughly in the direction you wanted by treating the tiller much as you might do a jammed door or a recalcitrant garden gate. That is to say that if you used both hands, leaned against it and pushed it with all your strength until your eyes popped. But that was about as far as it went, and our pilot Jim, who took over steering duties the moment he was on board, nearly ruptured himself as soon as he attempted it.

'Bloody hell! It's a bit stiff, isn't it?' he grumbled. He was slightly miffed, I think, that *Justice* had not taken him immediately to its heart.

I shrugged my shoulders noncommittally. Jim had told me he'd been something in the Merchant Navy. In my view he should have been used to this sort of thing. Anyhow, I couldn't see the use of worrying him unduly – especially when it seemed to me that a tiller locked in a single direction could actually make his life a good deal easier. After all, he hardly seemed to need to steer the boat at all, since from the moment we'd left the lock we'd been moving down the estuary on a course that was so straight it wouldn't have shamed a flying crow. It seemed to me at this rate we could have left the boat to its own devices and it would have got to Bristol itself.

It was like this for about an hour until Jim mentioned in the sort of casual, offhand way you might point out a plane in the sky, that we were passing a couple of nuclear power stations – one of which he'd heard that very morning on the news was on red alert and in danger of exploding.

At first I didn't register what he was saying. 'Red alert? Exploding? Are you serious?' I stuttered disbelievingly.

'Absolutely serious,' Jim said.

I felt my breath leave my body, and for a moment my legs went weak. I grabbed at the handrail of the boat.

Jim suddenly threw back his head. 'Only joking!' he screamed, suddenly convulsing in a throaty paroxysm of laughter. 'Hold on tight!' he shouted, before turning a sharp right angle to swing the boat over the other side of the estuary and begin the long approach that leads under the older, more elegant, of the two motorway bridges that carry the M5 across the water.

I have to confess, I didn't find this at all funny. In fact, I have to confess I found it distinctly *un*funny. Crossing the estuary in a narrowboat was bad enough, but worse was crossing it in the company of a superannuated comic whose sense of humour had been honed in the company of similar crusty matelots fighting Force Ten gales off Finisterre.

Unfortunately, though, this wasn't to be the last example of Jim's droll wit, and not long afterwards as we passed under the motorway *Justice* suddenly and inexplicably began shuddering violently in a way that made me think she was in imminent danger of breaking apart. Jim gave me a look of such pure, unadulterated terror that I'd have had to be made of stone not to have reacted to it in some way or another.

But before I could say anything I was treated to another of the strangled outbursts of choking which he called laughter. Eventually he explained to me that the shaking was being caused by the interaction of the current and the ebbing tide over the shallows hereabouts. It was perfectly normal and nothing to worry about at all.

'I was just pulling your leg,' Jim explained, as if by now I hadn't worked this one out for myself. Then he nudged me in the ribs so hard it was a wonder I didn't go flying over the side.

By now I'd had enough of him and went off to join Em who'd been sitting quietly in the bow of the boat keeping an eye on things up that end. For people like us, used to the sense of enclosure of the canal system, cruising in these expansive waters was a strange and unsettling experience. Offshore – at the distance of a mile and more – even nuclear power stations have a certain mystical grandeur to them; and on such a calm afternoon with absolutely nothing else on the move and a thin mist beginning to rise from the estuary, it was as if we were gliding through a fantasy world where I half expected a unicorn to rear up out of the vapour.

Gradually the afternoon became evening and soon darkness began to fall and the gloom of the far-off shores became speckled with a myriad of lights in orange, white, red and green; some were static, some blinking nervously, others winking lethargically.

This was the point at which I think I appreciated Jim the most, despite his terrible line in comedy, for without his experience it would have been all too easy to become hopelessly confused by this nautical Piccadilly Circus. Conditions were totally unfamiliar to ditch crawlers like us, and we were even moving in a way different to any I'd ever experienced before too: the shifting waters drawing us along with them, compelling us to follow. If you concentrated on the clear surface of the water at the point where the wash of our bow wave broke it into ripples, you could actually see the murky flow of the tide sucking underneath. It was at its fastest now, and we seemed to be totally at its mercy, being carried along at the sort of pace that felt as if it would get us a speeding ticket on land.

It was clear that this part of the trip was trickier than any other so far, and when I glanced at Jim on the back of the boat he was locked in concentration, the veins beginning to stand out on his brow as he was called upon to wrestle increasingly with the tiller, sometimes effecting quite spectacular changes of direction which even in these apparently calm conditions sent *Justice* skewing about, bobbing up and down like a cork.

I have to confess to being addicted to night-time boating of any sort. In summer it's a particular delight, since even when it's overcast, the sky illuminates the water and you rarely need to use headlights to see your way ahead. In the dog days of June, under a harvest moon, the canal becomes a floodlit trail to the stars; and when it's balmy and the scent of new-mown hay is thick in the air, it's as if you become part of the countryside, quietly slipping through the night like some strange creature of the dark. Mind you, we did have a shock some years back when something out of *The War of the Worlds* with two great headlamps for eyes started lurching down a meadow towards us at about two in the morning.

It turned out to be a local farmer with a combine harvester making the most of the good weather.

Winter, of course, is an entirely different matter, and I don't think that anyone in their right mind actually plans to be slogging up the Grand Union on a bleak December day with the wind so fierce it's throwing a spray across your bow deck that freezes in minutes. But if you cruise at all in winter when you've only a few hours of light a day, you're bound to experience this at some time, delayed by a cussed lock gate, or pressing on that extra mile to get to a favourite pub where you know there'll be a fire blazing in the hearth.

At moments like this it's best to accept that boating can be a tough business sometimes, and just knuckle down to the job in hand; though even in the very worst conditions England has the potential for beauty as no other country in the world. I remember one afternoon a decade or so back, coming into Leighton Buzzard one frosty night against one of the most vivid scarlet moons I'd ever seen. The countryside was spectacularly burnished and the icy black boughs of the trees reflecting the colour looked strangely like those diagrams of the blood system you sometimes see in children's books.

The lights of Avonmouth suddenly appeared out of the gloom, and I took Jim a cup of tea and a sandwich. A sharp wind had blown up but we were basically on a straight course again. He stood eating, the engine on *Justice* throbbing away so softly that you could hear the water lapping against her hull. Eventually Jim finished his snack and brushed away the crumbs from his coat, reaching at length for a VHF telephone which he'd earlier tossed into the back cabin. There was a lot of crackling and a technical conversation I couldn't have understood even if I'd been able to hear it through the distortion.

Afterwards he said, 'We'll head for that light over there.' He pointed it out. 'We should arrive in about twenty minutes, perhaps a bit less. You can take over the tiller then, and I'll tell you where to bring her in. You can leave me on the landing stage…'

For a moment I looked at him with a sort of resigned smile on my face, half expecting him to throw back his head in one of those cackling outbursts of his that accompanied his attempts to be funny. Because, of course, he was being funny, wasn't he? It was another of his jokes. Of course it was. It had to be. After all, we were going to Bristol, weren't we? This wasn't Bristol. This was Avonmouth, wasn't it? Or at least it *looked* like Avonmouth, judging by the shadowy outline of rows of massive oil containers and derricks which I could just about make out along the shoreline, not to mention the preponderance of enormous and somewhat threatening boats of one sort or another that were dotted about like ominous apparitions from hell.

Yes, I knew that leaving at the time we did meant that we'd have to moor overnight until we could go up to Bristol on a second tide. But I can't say I was entirely aware the pilot would be leaving us to it on our own.

'Well, you don't have to stay here if you're not comfortable,' Jim said. 'You could always go up river and moor somewhere midstream until the water's high enough to get you into Bristol lock.

'Mind you, you'd still be on your own,' he added. 'But you do at least have a choice.'

Since this so-called 'choice' of Jim's would have involved another couple of hours of night-time cruising, only this time on our own; and since it would have meant navigating *Justice* around the lip of the estuary and up the mouth of this river neither of us knew; and since it would also have required us to drop anchor in the middle of nowhere and stay up half the night to ensure we didn't drift off, or someone didn't hit us; then I don't think that strictly speaking the alternative he presented counted as a 'choice' at all. Or if it did, it was a 'choice' akin to being able to select which of your two arms you'd prefer to have chopped off. Or which eye put out.

Eventually – reassured by Jim that the rest of the journey would be a doddle in daylight – we decided to stay put, and so it wasn't until the morning that the full import of our predicament fully hit us. In the previous night's darkness Jim had guided us towards one light among a thousand speckled along the shoreline, and though I was vaguely aware that under his instruction we'd come into some haven and moored against another larger boat that was itself moored to a sort of jetty, I'd no real idea what sort of haven, or what sort of boat, or what sort of jetty.

The next morning, though, everything became awesomely clear. I woke early, disturbed by the agonising sound of our mooring ropes groaning in the swell like a soul moaning in Hades. I slipped on a dressing gown and stuck my head out of the front door. Em was still asleep – but not for long.

'My God! This you have just got to see,' I said, shaking her. 'You have *got* to see this *now*.'

We were moored against a battered old dredger which was, I suppose, about five times our size. But this was nothing, for the dredger was itself moored to a block of flats. Or at least to something that looked like a block of flats. On closer inspection what it actually turned out to be was an immense wharf towering above us. It was constructed of steel and must have been a quarter of a mile long, curving around us like a protective arm.

Despite Jim's stricture that we weren't to get off the boat until high tide when we were ready to leave, we got dressed and took the opportunity of exploring. That's when we found out how high this colossal quay was because to get to the top of it we had to climb flight after flight of salt-rusted steps, like an endless fire-escape to the sky. On the top the view was spectacular for it was another perfect day, the sun already brilliantly hot and the light so crystal clear that on one side in the far distance you could make out the two motorway bridges we'd come under the previous night, and on the other you could see the thin furrow of the faraway shoreline as it curved off towards Cardiff.

At first the whole panorama was virtually empty of boats, except for an odd yacht or two lazily tacking in the gentle breeze; but the closer we got to high tide at midday, the busier it became until eventually it was positively hectic, swarming with vessels of different sorts including those immense cumbersome vehicle transporters which ply this stretch of water and which seem less like boats than moving car parks. They'd clearly been waiting for their moment, and as two or three of them began to lumber in towards land, the waters around became active with flotillas of tugs buzzing around like horse flies on cattle.

We decided to be patient, though it wasn't as if there was any alternative. If we'd been foolish enough to get in the way of these leviathans, they'd have ploughed over us like a car running over a Coke can. And worse, they wouldn't even have been aware that they'd done it. At length things began to calm down, and at last we saw a gap in the traffic and made our move. In what was a manoeuvre of no more than twenty minutes or so, we rounded the low spit of a mudbank and darted into the sanctuary of the river where we were soon heading upstream towards Bristol in the wake of a couple of other boats who'd seen the same opportunity and gone for it with similar apprehension. Though God knows why they were worried. They were all ocean-going yachts or small ships. They could move a good deal faster than us.

The tenor of the Avon changes almost immediately you leave the estuary. No sooner are you clear of Avonmouth than the industry which is so predominant suddenly vanishes, and what one moment was a workplace suddenly becomes a park. At first the banks are like those of any other tidal river, lined with great expanses of cracked grey mud; but they gradually get higher and higher until almost without you noticing they've mutated into a series of thickly wooded cliff faces, with paths at the top and bottom. On the sort of fine Sunday that this had turned out to be, it seemed like the whole city had decided to come here for an afternoon walk. There were families out strolling with the kids, groups of people on bikes, lovers walking hand in hand, and so many dogs being exercised I couldn't help remembering how the canine contribution to the state of the towpath in Oxford so many months before had prompted my decision to abandon going to Bristol at all and made me decide to head north until I'd discovered I could get there by this roundabout route.

And now here I was, coming into Bristol by the back door, as it were, a passage made by – what, a dozen or so narrowboats a year out of the thirty thousand on the system. It was strange because even though I had the impression I was creeping into the city up some back alley, at the same time the streams of people along the banks – so many of them waving as I passed – made it seem as if I'd come to the conclusion of an exhausting marathon and they were welcoming me home. The long shadow of Isambard Kingdom Brunel's famous suspension bridge at Clifton crossing the roof became a sort of finishing tape as I navigated under it.

Of course, this journey hadn't been a race or anything like it – though it was difficult to see what it *had* been, especially since it started so negatively and with such apparent purposelessness. But I guess that's the way a lot of things in life are.

At least this trip had developed its own justification, however haphazardly. Admittedly, I hadn't travelled far – the sort of distance you could probably cover in a couple of days in a modern car if you put your mind to it. But with the Debsmobile I'd travelled along routes a vehicle like that would never normally take, and with *Justice* I'd followed an itinerary it never could. It had taken me through some of the prettiest parts of the country, and led me to some of its most hidden places. The journey had given me the opportunity to cogitate a bit too. About myself. About the country. About some of the people who'd contributed to the present in a tiny way – their achievements modest, but even so, far greater than anything most of us will ever accomplish.

And if nothing else, I'd had the chance of cooking and eating some decent food, and drinking some good beer. And having a laugh from time to time.

Can you expect any more from any journey?

Even life itself?

Now it was time to get back to London for good; time to find *Justice* a mooring of longer duration for the winter that was fast approaching. The graceful suspension bridge receded behind us in the distance, and we prepared ourselves for the very last manoeuvre of our time on the river: the passage through the river lock into the safe waters of the Floating Harbour, that triumph of Victorian architecture which laid the foundation for Bristol as one of the greatest trading centres of its age.

A number of other boats were already in the lock when we got there, most of them highly expensive sailing vessels with vulnerable hulls made of thin fibreglass not much thicker than a yogurt carton. After the trip we'd just completed we felt fairly relaxed about the operation.

Too relaxed, in fact.

You see, coming across the estuary, the pilot had throttled up *Justice* to its maximum, winding up the speed wheel which controls the engine. I'd done the same thing as we'd come up the river that morning, pushing the engine to get as much power as I could to punch the flow.

But in screwing the wheel up so tightly, I'd loosened the nuts that hold it in place. And coming into the lock, with the best part of a quarter of a million quid's worth of luxury ocean-going yacht directly ahead of me, didn't it just come off in my hand…?

Twenty-Four

AT LEAST WITH A JOURNEY, when it comes to an end it's over, and that's that.

Stories are altogether more complicated: they don't exist in isolation, they're just part of other stories. They're like strands of a rope which are woven into other strands, which themselves are woven into bigger strands yet until one fragment becomes so much a part of the whole that you can't say where any single one ends any more than you can say where it begins.

Tom and Angela Rolt went back home to Banbury after the Market Harborough festival. It was a grim voyage for both of them: the death of love is always a painful affair, and their marriage was on its last legs. Tom reflected later that the problems between them sprang from the psychological burden Angela had to carry after being cut off by her parents for marrying him. But, if you ask me, that puts too much of the blame on her weaknesses. Angela herself probably got closer to the truth years later, not long before she died, when she hinted that a major reason for their break up was the clash that ensued from her desire to travel and his deep commitment to England and the English way of life.

They'd already cruised the Irish waterways, providing Tom with material for a book called *Green and Silver*. Now she wanted them to explore further afield. 'I said, "Why don't we buy another boat? Let's go and get a bigger one and go and explore the French canals." But this didn't appeal to him. You see he hadn't even enjoyed our cruise across Ireland... simply because it wasn't England. He refused to live anywhere else and during that winter he didn't seem to want to budge out of *Cressy*. He just sat there chain smoking at his little desk, deeply hurt by the unpleasantness at the IWA.'

'I didn't relish the… prospect of continental travel, even by canal,' he admitted later. 'With all their faults it was the British Isles that had prior claim on my affections.'

Tom would later describe this winter and the following spring as the most unhappy period of his life. The nadir was when Angela left him. She bought herself an old banger for £10, but – being the woman she was – even that had to have a certain style about it, and she chose a two-seater Morris Oxford coupé. Tom did it up for her. He watched her from the deck of *Cressy* as she drove over the wooden lift bridge at the end of Factory Street. Afterwards he went inside the boat which 'suddenly seemed to have become very silent'.

It was 20 years before they met again.

Angela joined Billy Smart's Circus where she took up with the ringmaster and sometime clown, a man called Joe Isaac who she travelled with for many years until she finally came into family money and settled in the Dordogne where she lived until her death.

Left on his own, Tom attempted to sell *Cressy*, but to no avail: with a mixture of wet and dry rot plaguing her hull no one would buy her at any price in the state she was in. For a couple of years she lay in a boatyard in Staffordshire before she was eventually broken up and burnt. It was an ignominious end for a vessel which had become an icon of the waterways movement, and yet as one commentator has observed, *Cressy*'s destruction by fire was 'in the best tradition of long and narrowboats through history'.

Tom used to dream about her anxiously for years afterwards. Generally there'd be some dire emergency threatening and he'd be drifting powerlessly towards a dangerous weir, or something like that. He explained it to himself as the physiological price he had to pay for the hazards he'd managed to escape during his boating years, though I think a modern psychiatrist might view that interpretation with some derision. After all, he conceived an existence on the canals as a source of joy and hope, but ultimately it brought him nothing but anguish and disappointment, so that he lost control of his own happiness.

And in his heart of hearts he must have known this.

All this was far from being the end of his life, though, or even the end of his connections with the canals, for later he was persuaded to sit on an official government committee on the waterways; and despite his reluctance, he finally did go cruising in France which he made the subject of his last canal book. But after the separation from Angela and the destruction of *Cressy*, his priorities changed. He still wrote, of course – it was his job. And he still found time for campaigning, spearheading the fight to save the famous Tallryn narrow-gauge railway in Wales which became the model for every railway preservation society that followed and the basis of the Ealing comedy film *The Titfield Thunderbolt*. But domestic life now became the main focus of his energies, and he moved back to the family home, remarried and raised a family of two sons.

He was 64 when he died in 1974.

Robert Aickman resigned from the council of the Inland Waterways Association in 1964 after yet another explosive internal row of the sort that was so regularly associated with his tenure that if you didn't know it already, you'd begin to suspect that all these arguments had more to do with his character than they did with the problems facing the organisation. Afterwards, in the remaining 17 years of his life, he set about building the literary career he'd always coveted. Originally he'd seen himself as a novelist, but it was as a writer of idiosyncratic 'strange tales' as he called them that he finally made his mark, publishing seven books of them before 1981, as well as editing eight collections of ghost stories for Fontana. He also published the first part of his autobiography.

The second part, *The River Runs Uphill*, which covers the IWA years, was published posthumously in 1986 after his own publishers had turned the book down during his lifetime. It's not difficult to see why, since it's written with all the flamboyance of a set of committee minutes, and with a pomposity that is sometimes breathtaking in its conceit. Aickman put the cap on it at the last moment by censoring nearly anything of any personal note that might have made it interesting: so there's nothing about his wife Ray and their break-up; very little about his affair with Elizabeth Jane Howard; and virtually nothing except the barest outline of his differences with Tom Rolt.

Two chapters of the book – virtually an eighth of it – are devoted to just five days of his life: the period of the Market Harborough festival which he describes as his 'happiest week', and a 'climax of my life up to that point'.

After the first night of the plays he'd fought so bitterly to mount, one of the lead actresses came off the stage and 'fell' into his arms. 'I am not sure I can recall any single moment in my life that excels that one,' he writes in a tone of such naive, boyish enthusiasm that you can't help but conclude that there was something very shallow at the core of this man.

A shame, really, for he achieved so much which had genuine and solid worth that you'd have thought he might have valued it more himself and been content not to have gone raking over old enmities.

And yet the only point where the autobiography becomes animated is in its terse and somewhat bitter final chapter, the single purpose of which is to put on record the separate authorship of the stories he and Jane Howard had written in their co-authored book *We Are for the Dark*. It's a strange way to end any autobiography, and you wonder why Aickman felt the need to do it. Except, of course, that knowing the sort of man he was, you could have predicted that sooner or later Jane Howard would fall foul of him – as Tom Rolt had done before her, and as anyone close to him always did whenever they were presumptuous enough to assert their own autonomy against his.

His wife Ray, on whom he'd always been strangely dependent despite his unfaithfulness, eventually lost patience with him and walked out – to become an Anglican nun in a convent in Oxfordshire, of all things. She took the name Sister Benedicta. After she'd gone, Aickman was furious and broke off all contact with her. 'She was the sort of person made to be devoted to someone,' Jane Howard said of her, 'and it was bad luck that she was devoted to him because she deserved somebody who was more rewarding. In the end she wanted someone to be devoted to, and God seemed the best bet.'

Jane Howard's own estrangement from Aickman came after she gave up her own work for the IWA. 'I became *persona non grata*,' she said. 'Robert decided I was out of the IWA altogether and he didn't want me to have any contact with any of his friends.' Actually, it was worse than this: he wouldn't – literally – even have her name mentioned in his presence; though oddly, Jane struck up a clandestine relationship with Ray and seems to have known that she was leaving Aickman even before Aickman himself did.

The final chapter in the autobiography seems in some way to be settling old scores with Jane, and Aickman comes out of it very badly because his attempts to mitigate his bitterness towards her by making reference to her 'beauty and persuasiveness' actually compound the problem. His tone strikes a modern-day reader as insufferably patronising, and he emerges as someone petty and resentful. The best that can be said for *The River Runs Uphill* is that it's written by someone who never really learnt much in his life. Not about the things that matter, anyhow.

But we could have worked that out ourselves without an autobiography, couldn't we?

Even so, when it was published the IWA were so sensitive to the running sores that still existed in the organisation that they wouldn't even accept a paid advertisement for it in their magazine without prior sight of the manuscript.

You'd wonder then how Aickman could be so successful

creatively. He writes in a curiously stilted, formal style, heavy with commas, so that it gives his writing a distanced feel, as if he's stammering, and is just writing as he thinks, adding one idea onto the next, until he reaches some sort of halting conclusion that adds to his uncertain edginess. His stories are full of characters with unsettling, unreal names like Wedley Roper, Nera Condamine and Perry Jesperson; and they all take place in a world where ultimately the normal rules don't apply, a world where central relationships between men and women are characterised by a perverse and corrupted sexuality, and where there's always a moral vacuum at the heart of things.

A very modern world, in fact.

'She realised that to display moral qualities demands practice, just as much as intellectual and manual qualities,' says one of his characters who you almost feel could be Aickman writing about himself. 'She had never really attended when, down the years, such truths had been hammered into her.'

Some of the stories have been adapted for radio, and it was after I'd missed one and was trying to get a tape from the BBC that I got a telephone call from someone involved in the project, curious to learn who else in this world could be as fascinated with Robert Aickman as he was. It turned out to be Jeremy Dyson, one of the *League of Gentlemen* whose eccentric TV comedy show was scooping just about every industry award there was to win at that time. We arranged to meet one night in a pub, and I wasn't surprised to find that Aickman had been a major influence on his writing, for you can see Aickman's vision stamped all over the characters in Royston Vaisey – the grotesque and freakish Pennine village which is the setting for the programme.

Robert Aickman saw himself as a bit of a highbrow, and I don't know if he'd have been altogether flattered to have been at the heart of popular culture in this way, though I know he would have relished the fame that's accrued to him over the years – a fame which he never enjoyed in his lifetime. For he's become a cult writer now. Tap his name into any Internet search engine and you'll get scores of references to him, many of them special sites run by people who testify to the way he's changed their lives. Jeremy could hardly believe Aickman's popularity in cyberspace. He could hardly believe that Aickman was the sort of person he was either.

'I still think I'd have liked him, though – despite everything,' Jeremy said at one stage after he'd listened to me banging on about Aickman's faults.

And I know what he means. Strangely, I feel the same way. I even went to the Robert Aickman Lock near Stratford-upon-Avon to commemorate the twentieth anniversary of his death. The lock is his only memorial, and there's a bronze relief of him in profile set into an adjoining wall commemorating his work for the waterways. I'd publicised the anniversary as widely as I could, and the IWA certainly knew about it.

Even so, only two other people turned up with me.

Elizabeth Jane Howard became a writer too, of course, though many think she never fulfilled the early promise she showed in her first book which she dedicated to Aickman and which won her the prestigious John Llewellyn Rhys Memorial Prize. Eventually she married the novelist Kingsley Amis, and regrettably – for she's one of the most interesting women writers of her generation – she's become known since then more for her personal life, and a list of former lovers which includes Arthur Koestler, Laurie Lee, the Poet Laureate C. Day-Lewis, and God knows who else too.

In fact, as the *Daily Telegraph* once said of her, 'There was a time in London when it was fashionable for a man to say he had been to bed with Elizabeth Jane Howard.' Or as her erstwhile stepson Martin Amis once put it, 'Jane has been around – and at a high level…'

As she is one of the very few people involved in this narrative who is still alive, I naturally wrote to her hoping that we might be able to meet, and she was kind enough to reply personally with a polite note. Polite, but very defensive. Mind you, you can understand it really. Jane Howard's been exploited by a lot of men in her life and it's hardly surprising if she's cautious about new ones appearing out of the woodwork claiming to be writing crazy books about cooking and canal journeys – especially when they involve Robert Aickman about whom, as she admits, she still feels uncomfortable. Out of fairness to Jane, though, this isn't because she's antagonistic to Aickman. They were reconciled during the final illness which led to his death, and she gave a reading at his memorial service.

'It's just that she's writing an autobiography and she's under contract not to talk about her life,' her agent explained, a little unconvincingly.

'Well, couldn't I just sort of… well, you know, just meet her then?' I said, 'As a… a fan?'

I was told that she hadn't got any time for that sort of nonsense, though I noticed a few months afterwards when some of her novels were serialised on the BBC that she struck up a friendship with the executive producer, Joanna Lumley, with whom she seemed to be forever having cosy get-togethers.

Mind you, you can understand that too. Me? Joanna Lumley? No contest really, is there?

I managed to avoid a collision with the posh yacht in the lock coming into Bristol. I somehow succeeded in stretching forward far enough to catch the connecting rod to the engine throttle before it fell off completely, so that at least I avoided a complete catastrophe.

I eventually succeeded in getting to the Dome too before it closed. I went on the day thieves attempted to steal one of the exhibits, a diamond valued at more than £1 million.

It was, as they advertised it, one amazing day.

But still not quite as amazing as canals, which to this day obsess me in the way they always have.

— END —

THE WORST JOURNEY
IN THE MIDLANDS

ONE MAN, HIS BOAT AND THE WEATHER

SAM LLEWELLYN

summersdale *travel*